# Opening Doors Wider

*Edited by Sylvia Bashevkin*

# Opening Doors Wider
## Women's Political Engagement in Canada

**UBC**Press · Vancouver · Toronto

20 19 18 17 16 15 14 13 12 11 10 09 5 4 3 2

Printed in Canada on ancient-forest-free paper (100% post-consumer recycled) that is processed chlorine- and acid-free, with vegetable-based inks.

**Library and Archives Canada Cataloguing in Publication**

Opening doors wider: women's political engagement in Canada / edited by Sylvia Bashevkin.

Includes bibliographical references and index.
ISBN 978-0-7748-1563-5 (bound); ISBN 978-0-7748-1564-2 (pbk.);
ISBN 978-0-7748-1565-9 (e-book)

1. Women in public life – Canada. 2. Women in politics – Canada. 3. Women legislators – Canada. I. Bashevkin, Sylvia B.

HQ1236.5.C2O64 2009 320.082'0971 C2008-907824-1

Canada

UBC Press gratefully acknowledges the financial support for our publishing program of the Government of Canada through the Book Publishing Industry Development Program (BPIDP), and of the Canada Council for the Arts, and the British Columbia Arts Council.

This book has been published with the help of a grant from the Canadian Federation for the Humanities and Social Sciences, through the Aid to Scholarly Publications Programme, using funds provided by the Social Sciences and Humanities Research Council of Canada.

UBC Press
The University of British Columbia
2029 West Mall
Vancouver, BC V6T 1Z2
604-822-5959 / Fax: 604-822-6083
**www.ubcpress.ca**

# Contents

# Figures and Tables

## Figures



## Tables

# Abbreviations

| | |
|---|---|
| ADQ | Action démocratique du Québec |
| BQ | Bloc Québécois |
| CAWI/IVTF | City for All Women Initiative/ Initiative: Une ville pour toutes les femmes |
| CES | Canadian Election Study |
| CEW | Committee for the Equality of Women |
| CMA | census metropolitan area |
| DGÉQ | Directeur général des élections du Québec |
| FPTP | first past the post |
| GBLT | gay, bisexual, lesbian, or transgendered |
| IULA | International Union of Local Authorities |
| MNA | member of the National Assembly |
| MPP | member of provincial parliament |
| NAC | National Action Committee on the Status of Women |
| NDP | New Democratic Party |
| NOIVMW | National Organization of Immigrant and Visible Minority Women |
| NZES | New Zealand Election Study |
| OWD | Ontario Women's Directorate |
| PC | Progressive Conservative |
| PLQ | Parti libéral du Québec |
| PQ | Parti Québécois |
| PR | proportional representation |
| RCSW | Royal Commission on the Status of Women |
| SMP | single-member plurality |
| VMIW | Visible Minority and Immigrant Women committee |

# Opening Doors Wider

# 1
# Introduction

*Sylvia Bashevkin*

From the days of the fur trade through the contemporary period, women have played important roles in the public life of Canada (Bashevkin 1993, ch. 1; Van Kirk 1980). Until approximately the 1970s, however, these contributions to civic engagement, including to local voluntary associations and formal political institutions such as parties, were generally overlooked, despite their significance to the growth of democratic values and practices.

After more than three decades of scholarship and activism designed to raise the profile of women's involvement, we fortunately have an opportunity to pose two crucial sets of questions. *First, are the doors to participation presently open wider than they were in the past?* What obstacles as well as possibilities face specific groups of female citizens, including immigrant women in Canada's major cities and rural residents living far from metropolitan centres of settlement? Have patterns of media coverage shifted to such a degree that women as a group, and individual female citizens, can expect to engage in community groups and party organizations on something approaching an even playing field?

*Second, how can these passageways be widened, both in terms of real-world participation and our scholarly understanding of public engagement?* What remedies have been proposed? Which ones have served to enhance women's involvement, and which have been less effective? What research directions need to be pursued in order to shed more light on barriers to participation and opportunities for meaningful involvement?

In setting forth these two main questions, we are guided by the literatures in history, political science, and women's studies that have thus far shaped the field. The emergence of second-wave women's movements during the late 1960s and the decades that followed directly influenced historical research, and feminist scholars in particular grew increasingly interested in women as public actors (Bacchi 1983; Kealey 1998; Kealey and Sangster 1989; Strong-Boag 1972). They posed important questions that had not been widely pursued by earlier generations of academics, most notably: Who were the first-wave pioneers who pressed for the rights to vote and hold public office and to introduce major social policy reforms in the post-suffrage era? What ideas propelled their claims for each of these changes, and what blind spots characterized their outlooks on public engagement?

The literature that evolved in this area during the past thirty years has demonstrated the impact of progressivism on early feminism from the late nineteenth century onward, and it has shown how suffragist arguments were often closely intertwined with temperance, trade union, and anti-immigration streams in the same period. Historians who sought to uncover or recover the early interventions of women in Canadian public debates thus revealed the chances activists took to stake out their arguments, as well as the challenges many faced when they tried to reconcile their claims as white women who hailed from religious majority and colonial power backgrounds with the interests of other (notably immigrant and Aboriginal) women who lived in the country or were seeking to enter it. Historical research, in short, did far more than simply celebrate the efforts of first-wave feminism: at its best, this scholarly stream raised tough questions about the limits and blind spots of early activists.

In the discipline of political science, researchers began, in the early 1980s, to document the obstacles and openings available to women in mainstream institutions. Focusing for the most part on parties and legislatures, scholars interested in the intersections of gender and politics examined the relatively low numerical representation of women, especially in the upper echelons of these structures (Bashevkin 1985; Brodie 1985). One observation, made in 1985 and summarized in the phrase "the higher, the fewer," continues to resonate because it identified the increasingly limited presence of women as one looked up the ladders of political parties, legislatures, cabinets, and public bureaucracies (Bashevkin 1985, ch. 3).

During the two subsequent decades, studies in this area charted the contours of female participation in mainstream political institutions, examined the causes of under-representation at different levels, and considered various formal and informal efforts to increase women's engagement (Anderson 1991; Arscott and Trimble 1997; Newman and White 2006; Tremblay and Trimble 2003; Tremblay and Andrew 1998; Trimble and Arscott 2003). Not surprisingly, this literature paid particular attention to barriers to legislative involvement. It emphasized limited financial resources to pay for expensive nomination battles, discriminatory attitudes among party recruiters, socialization experiences that robbed women of necessary confidence and ambition, and distorted media treatment of women who entered public life as critical obstacles to enhanced participation. The remedies that were suggested included increased public funding of election costs, changes to Canada's electoral system, and party quotas for women candidates – all of which had the goal of moving women beyond the roughly 20 percent plateau of legislative representation that characterized the federal House of Commons and a number of provincial legislatures during this period.

This literature seems dated in many respects. On one level, it has generally ignored public engagement beyond the party and legislative environments, thus overlooking a wide array of important civic venues in which women participate. These include local community groups, feminist organizations, and other streams of activity outside official political organizations. On another level, this scholarship has also failed to probe the links between organized women's movement activism, broader demographic shifts in the country, and changes in mainstream political institutions (for one important exception, see Young 2000). It has not extensively probed, for example, how the decline of second-wave mobilization would likely shape legislative engagement or media portrayals. If feminism has waned as a social movement, then what has happened to feminist challenges to political institutions? Can women in top positions, including those holding cabinet office, operate as carriers of the movement's claims when the movements themselves appear dormant? How has the growing demographic diversity of Canada's cities, in particular, reverberated in terms of women's political engagement? Finally, few studies have systematically assessed the effectiveness of proposed remedies to female under-representation, including quotas for parliamentary candidates.

From the perspective of fundamental institutional change in Canada, the women and politics literature has also been relatively silent on questions of centralization, decentralization, and policy change within the federation. Created in 1867 as a quasi-federal system that bridged significant religious and regional differences, Canada has evolved over time in an increasingly differentiated and devolved direction. Particularly since the introduction of major structural reforms to federal social policy during the early 1990s, organized interests seeking to shape government decision making have faced a multiplication of access points and relevant actors – which creates an especially challenging scenario for groups with limited resources (see Bashevkin 2002).

The fact that provinces have enjoyed widened opportunities for policy experimentation, and that federal governments have systematically constrained their own abilities to limit this innovation, means that many of the Canada-wide solutions proposed by English Canadian feminism since the early 1970s may no longer be workable. In particular, the traditional preferences of many English Canadian women's groups for a strong federal state that would establish and enforce national standards across a variety of policy domains seems distinctly at odds with the reality of a highly devolved federation. Conversely, the focus since the 1970s of Quebec-based women's groups on a strong provincial or, in some cases, sovereign regime based in Quebec City appears to have offered far greater leverage for feminist interests in that environment. In short, as more and more windows of opportunity opened at the sub-national level across Canada, it seemed that activists in Quebc were best placed to push them ajar.

Women's studies scholars have long been interested in the dynamics of second-wave feminist mobilization in Canada (Adamson, Briskin, and McPhail 1988; Carty 1993; Vickers, Rankin, and Appelle 1993; Wine and Ristock 1991). Yet, their contributions reflect a strong emphasis on societal rather than state-focused research questions. Just as the political science literature has tended to gloss over what is considered "non-political" engagement in community and social movement groups, women's studies research has often neglected more formal dimensions of participation, notably in parties and legislatures.

Among the most promising contributions to our understanding of the links between formal political and informal social movement engagement can be found in the work of Nadia Urbinati. A political theorist based at Columbia University, Urbinati views participation in state structures (including the electoral system, parties, bureaucracies, and legislatures) as being closely related to engagement in non-state venues such as women's organizations. She posits that citizens relate to democratic governments and government elites along a spectrum, or continuum, of sites that bridge what has traditionally been seen as a silo-like dichotomy between institutional participation, on one side, and social movement advocacy, on the other (Urbinati 2000, 2006). This conception permits us to see women's engagement with politics in Canada as being spread across multiple venues – from local, community-based, grassroots organizations to legislatures and cabinet tables.

Across these various sites, the dynamics of opening doors and of ensuring that both women and men pass through them may vary considerably. In some contexts, notably in the realm of contemporary electoral and party politics, *demand* for women candidates may eclipse the *supply* of willing participants. As Pippa Norris and Joni Lovenduski demonstrate with respect to British politics, voters may be well disposed to vote for women who run, and party recruiters may actively seek female nominees in promising seats, but these demand-side patterns will exert little real-world effect if few women choose to join parties, agree to stand as candidates, and contest elections (Norris and Lovenduski 1995, ch. 6).

In turn, supply-and-demand trends are closely related to the values, traditions, and practices of particular institutions. Within a single political system, some parties may be more welcoming than others towards women, Aboriginal people, or immigrants. In addition, local and community organizations may seem more porous to individuals from these backgrounds than do provincial- or federal-level parties. These types of institutional openings and limitations have been theorized by scholars under the rubric of political opportunity structures, an approach that initially gained prominence with the publication, in 1989, of Joyce Gelb's comparative study of women's movements in the United States, Great Britain, and Sweden (Gelb 1989).

Since the 1980s, the rise of conservative political leaders in Canada and elsewhere has focused attention on how citizens can make successful political claims in any venue – given larger global shifts towards international trading regimes that highly privilege markets and devalue states. Many aspects of the rise of what is known as neoliberalism lead us to question long-held assumptions about political engagement. For example, should women as a group seek policy leverage via bureaucratic channels (and, specifically, the use of women-centred or femocrat strategies) if public servants hold little influence over decision making (see Bashevkin 2006; Chappell 2002; Lovenduski 2005; Malloy 2003)? As states retrench and reconfigure their budgetary commitments, how likely is it that critical advocacy organizations will obtain public financing? Will those groups be drawn towards service-provider roles for the state as resources for advocacy work come under threat (Bashevkin 1998, 2002)?

Although they address this bureaucratic dimension only indirectly, the chapters that follow take up the challenge to probe engagement across venues, and over time, in order to assess both the opportunities and challenges facing women's involvement, broadly defined.

## Why Engagement Matters

Why does women's participation matter to contemporary democracy? Scholars in this field often build on the work of political theorist Hanna Pitkin. Writing in the late 1960s, Pitkin (1967, 11) highlighted the distinction between what she termed descriptive or "standing for" representation – a demographic similarity between mass and elite – and substantive or "acting for" representation, which required a policy-based linkage between citizens and political leaders.

From the perspective of descriptive representation, women's presence as public actors confirms, while their absence disconfirms, the legitimacy of democratic practices. Institutions in which the percentages of female participants resemble those in the general public appear more politically credible than others in which proportions of women fall far short of those in the general population. Descriptive representation is also relevant at the level of political symbolism, since seeing significant numbers of women in public life suggests to observers, including small children, that females can contribute to society as engaged political actors. Women politicians, for example, can inspire young girls to consider legislative careers, shape cultural perceptions in such a way as to undermine stereotypes that promote the idea that women do not belong in responsible positions, and erode traditional associations of men with public roles and women with private ones. Moreover, political organizations could benefit from even symbolic efforts to enhance the number of female participants, since such efforts would widen their recruitment base by drawing in diverse sources of new talent.

Pitkin's discussion foreshadowed a significant body of empirical research on the issue priorities of female politicians. This work, conducted primarily in North America and western Europe, reported that elected women were on average more liberal, and more committed to the policy claims of second-wave feminism, than their male counterparts. Studies of the substantive interventions of women legislators, for example, tended to support Pitkin's view of an important "acting for" dimension in political representation (Dodson 2006; Sawer, Tremblay, and Trimble 2006, pt. 2).

In Canada, efforts to elect more women were often defended as a way to ensure greater substantive representation for women as an interest. Early research in this field offered empirical support for that position. Accounts of federal and provincial politics between the mid-1970s and early 1990s showed that, as more women legislators were elected and more women cabinet ministers were appointed, more pro-feminist policies were enacted at both levels. One of the highest percentages of women in a government caucus and cabinet was achieved in Ontario between 1990 and 1995. Premier Bob Rae's New Democratic Party (NDP) caucus included about twenty women (out of seventy-four members, or more than one-quarter), at least half of whom were active in second-wave feminist organizations (Burt and Lorenzin 1997, 209). As Lesley Byrne's study in this volume explores in greater detail, eleven NDP women were appointed to the Ontario provincial cabinet (out of twenty-six members, or 42.3 percent). The Rae government extended child care provision, increased funding for shelters for battered women, raised the minimum wage, strengthened pay equity laws, and legalized midwifery. Even though leading women's groups wanted more policy action of this type, the numbers-to-policy record in the Ontario NDP remained clear. No Ontario government before or after had as many women in caucus and cabinet positions, and no other government was as responsive to feminist groups on the policy side.

At the federal level, electing women to the House of Commons in the period before 1993 generally meant electing more NDP, Liberal, and Progressive Conservative (PC) women, most of whom were sympathetic towards the issue positions of second-wave feminism. As in other political systems, women's movement ideas generally overlapped with left (as opposed to right) political attitudes and with progressive (as opposed to conservative) party positions. As in other political systems, the beliefs of the women's movement were closely associated with left/right attitudes and with party identification, such that, not surprisingly, female NDP legislators tended to be more pro-feminist in their views than females in the Liberal and PC parties. That being said, research consistently demonstrated that, before 1993, NDP, Liberal, and Progressive Conservative women MPs worked closely together on such issues as promoting the constitutional rights of women, ensuring open access to abortion services, preventing violence against women, and strengthening gun control legislation (Young 2000).

The ability to build all-party consensus among women, however, declined in 1993, following the arrival in the House of Commons of a right-wing, regionalist Reform Party caucus that rejected the view that women were a politically relevant interest. Right-of-centre organizations that eclipsed the Progressive Conservative party in 1993 and following included the Reform Party, the Canadian Alliance, and the merged Conservative organizations. Each of these successor parties consistently maintained that territory was the overarching, politically salient cleavage in Canada. After 1993, many MPs from these parties vigorously pressed an anti-government intervention, anti-debt and deficit, anti-Charter of Rights and Freedoms, anti-reproductive choice, and anti-gay rights agenda that merged economic laissez-faire ideas with the "family values" norms of social conservatism.

Given the contrast between these ideas and second-wave feminist beliefs, it is not surprising that relatively few women ran as Reform, Alliance, or merged Conservative Party candidates or won seats as MPs for those parties (Newman and White 2006, 116-17; Young 1997, 84). Moreover, right-wing formations hold a tenuous electoral base among women voters in Canada, even in their target regions (on the background to this gender gap, see Bashevkin 1993, ch. 2). Yet, the presence of this political stream in Parliament since 1993, particularly since the election of a Conservative minority government in 2006, complicated the assumption that increased numbers of women MPs and cabinet ministers would translate into pro-feminist policy influence.

Dovetailing with Pitkin's thesis, two additional sets of arguments have been advanced in response to the question of why women matter. One set follows from research on the tenor of debate in political groups and institutions, claiming that a meaningful presence of women in these bodies is associated with lower levels of political conflict, greater emphasis on collective consensus, and higher standards of interpersonal respect. Although considerable debate has focused on how to define a meaningful presence or "critical mass" of women in politics, this procedural perspective suggests that the number of women can matter for the climate and conduct, as well as the content, of group debate. Scholars who study many different political environments observe that the tenor of debate in political spaces where women hold a significant proportion of seats is more reasonable and collegial and less adversarial and conflictual than in spaces dominanted by men (Sawer, Tremblay, and Trimble 2006, 18-20).

Finally, from the perspective of political justice, women matter because their presence or absence serves as a barometer of basic fairness in democratic systems. Looking back to Aristotle and others in the classical political theory tradition, we can trace the long-standing role of citizen voice and citizen representation in grounding a common-sense understanding of democracy. From this vantage point, women's under-representation places in stark relief a lack of voice in legislatures, for example, and reminds us of barriers to access that potential political participants face. Representative democracy seems impaired, partial, and unjust when women as a majority of citizens fail to see themselves reflected in the leadership of their polis and when men as a minority of citizens control most levers of power. Justice arguments thus focus attention on women's right to participate in public decision making and their right not to face discrimination in civic life.

Given patterns of urban immigration since the 1970s, Canada's cities attracted increasingly diverse residents from all corners of the world. As the people of Toronto, Montreal, Vancouver, and other large centres looked less and less like Canadians of earlier generations, issues of ethno-cultural and racial representation in civic and political groups were raised widely. How would local community groups, women's organizations, and political parties respond to the challenge of representing diverse identities within their ranks? Could media outlets be pressed to present women actors from non-traditional backgrounds, including lesbian politicians, in a fair and balanced way? The chapters that follow begin to take up these and other questions about the contemporary dynamics of public engagement.

## Research Contributions

Overall, this volume demonstrates the variety of opportunities as well as the obstacles that women participants in community and feminist organizations, as well as in parties, legislatures, and public life generally, continue to face. The challenges represented by ethno-cultural, geographical, sexual, and other differences among women, alongside a more general waning of feminist activism, cast a critical light on the view that progress in women's participation forms part of an automatic or inevitable march of democratic progress (on intersectionality as a tool for political science analysis, see Hancock 2007; Weldon 2006). Moreover, the reluctance of many women to engage with electoral and, especially, party politics means the supply of willing candidates is not necessarily growing over time.

Part 1 of this volume considers community and women's group engagement, focusing on openings as well as limitations to involvement at that level. Caroline Andrew's discussion opens with a review of Canadian and comparative arguments that non-partisan neighbourhood, ethno-cultural, and other local groups are more open to women's participation than parties and legislatures and thus provide a valuable springboard to mainstream politics. Using one civic engagement initiative in Ottawa as her focal point, Andrew assesses efforts to draw diverse groups of women – including those from Aboriginal and immigrant backgrounds – into municipal politics. She concludes that although femocrat strategies were useful at this level, participation in local groups in Ottawa did not directly transfer to the realm of municipal politics. Andrew speculates that female activists were more likely to be changed by their community group experiences in public life than they were to actively change local politics.

Parallel with Andrew's study of community group engagement, Mary-Jo Nadeau's chapter grapples with the challenge to civic participation that followed from an increasingly diverse population in the 1970s and in subsequent years, questioning how diversity among women challenges their civic participation. "Rebuilding the House of Canadian Feminism" probes the internal dynamics of the National Action Committee on the Status of Women (NAC), a leading feminist umbrella group established in 1972, during a period when tensions over racial difference tended to eclipse more established organizational cleavages along the lines of region, language, or sexual identity. Nadeau situates NAC's internal challenges in the broader context of struggles over the ability of feminist organizations to claim to represent women as a group in Canada. She shows how efforts to construct an anti-racist women's movement at the federal level unfolded at the same time as major external threats jeopardized overall movement legitimacy. The rise of neoliberalism coupled with the declining relevance of the federal government to social policy in Canada meant that progressive social movements were squeezed between, on the one side, an over-arching attack on the core relevance of the state and, on the other side, a proliferation of sub-national and supra-national actors that few outside Quebec had the resources or expertise to access. Nadeau's chapter reveals the extent to which women-only organizations faced multiple internal and external obstacles that made participants turn more of their attention inward, towards each other, rather than outward, towards the formal political realm.

Taken together, these contributions demonstrate the extent to which doors to women's participation remain only partly open in community and feminist groups. While Andrew's account of the City for All Women Initiative (CAWI), which involves municipal decision makers as well as immigrant women in Ottawa, documents how efforts were made in some localities to create new spaces for engagement, this same study shows that transitions from community groups to mainstream political involvement were neither smooth nor automatic. Similarly, Nadeau's account of anti-racist politics in NAC during the 1980s and after underlines tense relations between minority and white women in Canada's largest feminist umbrella organization, which, in turn, undermined the group's political legitimacy and credibility as a voice of women.

Part 2 of this volume tackles questions of legislative participation, notably opportunities and obstacles relevant to winning parliamentary seats. Existing research in this area identifies a number of structural barriers to female engagement and frequently concludes that women are advantaged by proportional representation and disadvantaged by single-member plurality arrangements (Anderson 1991). In her chapter, Manon Tremblay evaluates this argument in light of the relatively high numbers of women who won seats in Quebec's National Assembly. She reports that, during the period from 1972 to 2002, nationalist politics in Quebec mobilized women into both major provincial political parties. In fact, many female candidates in Quebec obtained nominations and contested seats in constituencies in which their party was likely to win. The two parties competing for provincial power in this period, the Liberals and the Parti Québécois (PQ), built reasonably close links with organized feminism. Tremblay speculates on the ties between these contextual factors and the ability to win legislative office, asking whether a first-past-the-post system is necessarily unfavourable to women. She notes that, although women had held roughly one-third of National Assembly seats and prominent cabinet and opposition portfolios for some time, it was not until 2007 that a woman (Pauline Marois in the PQ) became a major party leader in Quebec.

In her chapter on federal-level engagement, Louise Carbert asks whether cities are more congenial to women's involvement than less densely populated areas. Research on Westminster systems suggests female participation is enhanced by electoral system reform, by high rates of seat turnover that offer women a chance to win open seats, and by internal party rules and initiatives – usually in centrist and progressive parties – that actively seek out female candidates. Carbert highlights a significant rural versus urban dimension of the story that has been neglected to this point: female MPs in Canada are overwhelmingly drawn from urban and suburban constituencies, notably in the Toronto and Montreal areas, and federal and many provincial electoral systems tend to under-represent those urban populations. Her contribution probes the origins of the former pattern, including relations between organized feminism and parties in different parts of the ideological spectrum, as well as challenges facing rural and urban women's mobilization in Canada. Carbert concludes that the rural deficit provides a durable, stable, and robust explanation for the stagnant number of women MPs in the House of Commons.

By interrogating many powerful assumptions in this field of scholarship, the contributions to Part 2 shed critical light on our understanding of doorways to participation. More specifically, Tremblay's assessment presses hard against claims that single-member plurality electoral rules have constituted, by themselves, an obstacle to women's involvement. Her discussion raises the possibility that effective feminist mobilization in Quebec, combined with the presence of nationalist sentiment elevating the significance of the government in Quebec City and the long-term dominance of relatively centrist political parties in that environment did more to advance opportunities for legislative engagement than the absence of proportionality did to limit those chances. In a parallel way, Carbert's analysis casts considerable doubt on across-the-board (as opposed to targeted or selective) efforts to encourage parties to nominate more women in winnable constituencies. Her rural-urban comparisons reveal that federal parties on the centre-left and centre were already reasonably effective in recruiting female candidates – but they did so in cities rather than less densely populated areas, where seats were often held by conservative formations.

Part 3 of this volume explores the complex interplay of opportunities and obstacles with respect to cabinet and party leadership. Lesley Byrne's account of Ontario provincial politics probes the policy consequences of representation at this level, exploring what happened in the 1990s when a centre-left party nominated women candidates, voters elected them, and leaders appointed many to cabinet positions. At first glance, such circumstances appeared tailor-made for realizing Pitkin's concept of standing-for representation. Byrne argues, however, that, despite the feminist backgrounds of many NDP women, organized women's movements were far from satisfied with the policy changes emanating from the Ontario government of the day. Her account suggests that even as major gains occurred in elite-level numbers, views differed as to the substantive impact of more women participants in cabinet.

Sylvia Bashevkin's chapter distinguishes between systemic or stage limits, on one side, and individual or actor obstacles, on the other, as they affected women's campaigns for federal party leadership between 1975 and 2006. Stage factors include a party's ideological environment, its relations with organized feminism, and the level of political competitiveness. Actor-level variations include the personal confidence, occupational background, and financial assets of individual candidates. Bashevkin's study shows that women contenders did better on the stages of uncompetitive parties, particularly those of the left and centre-right, than on the platform of competitive parties or hard-right organizations. At least one well-resourced, confident female candidate with a business background – Belinda Stronach in the 2004 Conservative race – was unable to overcome stage-level obstacles in order to win party leadership. Bashevkin's account finds little empirical support for assumptions that individual attributes can trump or overcome structural barriers to elite-level engagement in Canada and elsewhere.

Since Agnes Macphail first entered the Canadian House of Commons in 1921, news accounts have often considered women politicians to be deviants from the stereotypic profile of a heterosexual, married man with children. By also training attention on the personal style (including hair and clothing) of women in public life, media stories have tended to treat these individuals as lightweight "fluff" rather than political actors with ideas, beliefs, and policy positions. What happens when journalists confront a party leadership candidate who deviates from the norm along the lines of gender and sexuality? Joanna Everitt and Michael Camp examine the treatment of Allison Brewer who, in September 2005, became leader of the New Brunswick NDP and the first openly lesbian leader of a mainstream party in Canadian history. They compare coverage of Brewer with media accounts of gay men in Canadian public life and with portrayals of heterosexual women in politics. Everitt and Camp explore how Brewer was labelled a pro-choice "activist" early in her partisan career and seemed unable, despite repeated attempts, to deflect that label. Consistent with Bashevkin's findings, Brewer led an uncompetitive party; after trying unsuccessfully to improve the fortunes of the New Brunswick NDP, she resigned as leader in November 2006.

Considered as a group, the research findings in Part 3 reveal the various shadows and blockages that surround doors to elite-level participation. Byrne's study unearths the complex and often fraught conversion in Ontario, from numbers of women in cabinet during the 1990s to substantive policy changes expected by feminist interests. Bashevkin's chapter shows that even as individual women made their way through party networks to become leadership candidates, their ability to win top positions was constrained by institutional factors, including the competitiveness of those same political organizations. Everitt and Camp confirm this pattern, demonstrating how Canada's first openly lesbian party leader was marginalized not only by her gender and sexuality but also by the weak political circumstances of her party. Brewer's media image in New Brunswick newspapers tended to reinforce this pattern, in the sense that the opening of space for a lesbian politician to present her policy platform was compromised by a narrow media focus on Brewer's activist background in the pro-choice movement.

Part 4 of this book follows directly from Everitt and Camp's study. Elizabeth Goodyear-Grant asks in Chapter 9 whether, given patterns of media stereotyping, female MPs can create and maintain favourable public images. In particular, do Canadian legislators confront the same obstacles to balanced coverage as do their counterparts in other Westminster systems? Using data drawn from interviews with women and men MPs, Goodyear-Grant examines how politicians perceived their coverage and tried to craft alternate images, and she shows how female MPs were often unable to divert journalists' attention away from their family status, clothes, and speaking style. Her chapter concludes with a comparative account of media coverage challenges facing women MPs in Canada and elsewhere.

In Chapter 10, Elisabeth Gidengil, Joanna Everitt, and Susan Banducci use evidence from Canada and New Zealand to assess voter stereotyping of women candidates. Existing research shows that members of the general public evaluate the personal characteristics and competencies of female political leaders differently than those of males, but this research has relied on experimental designs rather than surveys that ask voters about actual leaders. Gidengil, Everitt, and Banducci saw an opportunity to shift the focus from hypothetical to real politicians in the 1993 Canadian and 1999 New Zealand elections, when women led multiple parties in both countries. Their analysis finds little evidence that voters engaged in gender stereotyping, but it does show that they engaged in party stereotyping.

Both chapters in Part 4 uncover a mixture of participatory constraints and opportunities. In terms of limits, Goodyear-Grant shows that female MPs understood they were constructed and presented to the public differently than their male counterparts. On the level of openings, her chapter reveals a sense among women parliamentarians that they could proactively shape media accounts. Possibly the most hopeful finding in this volume follows from Gidengil, Everitt, and Banducci's data on the tendency of voters in Canada and New Zealand to stereotype women leaders on the basis of party rather than gender. This pattern challenges claims that citizens not only find it difficult to conceive women and power in the same frame but also to dissociate female politicians from substantive political ideas (including party platforms).

Part 5 explores remedies and prescriptions and asks, what can be done to push forward women's participation, including at the level of scholarly contributions? In Chapter 11, Sylvia Bashevkin uses the studies in this volume as a guide to propose a brief agenda for future research and lay out some related avenues of political action. What assumptions in previous research have been unsettled by the analyses presented here, and what directions appear most promising for scholarship in the field? Can academic studies provide useful lessons for political activism, particularly for Canadians who want to heighten and improve women's public participation? In short, how might research in this area help to open doorways further?

**References**

Adamson, Nancy, Linda Briskin, and Margaret McPhail. 1988. *Feminist Organizing for Change.* Toronto: Oxford University Press.

Anderson, Doris. 1991. *The Unfinished Revolution: The Status of Women in Twelve Countries.* Toronto: Doubleday.

Arscott, Jane, and Linda Trimble, eds. 1997. *In the Presence of Women: Representation in Canadian Governments.* Toronto: Harcourt Brace.

Bacchi, Carol Lee. 1983. *Liberation Deferred? The Ideas of the English-Canadian Suffragists, 1877-1918.* Toronto: University of Toronto Press.

Bashevkin, Sylvia B. 1985. *Toeing the Lines: Women and Party Politics in English Canada.* Toronto: University of Toronto Press.

–. 1998. *Women on the Defensive: Living through Conservative Times.* Toronto: University of Toronto Press.

–. 2002. *Welfare Hot Buttons: Women, Work, and Social Policy Reform.* Toronto: University of Toronto Press.

–. 2006. *Tales of Two Cities: Women and Municipal Restructuring in London and Toronto*. Vancouver: UBC Press.
Brodie, Janine. 1985. *Women and Politics in Canada*. Toronto: McGraw-Hill Ryerson.
Burt, Sandra, and Elizabeth Lorenzin. 1997. "Taking the Women's Movement to Queen's Park: Women's Interests and the New Democratic Government of Ontario." In *In the Presence of Women*, ed. Jane Arscott and Linda Trimble, 202-27. Toronto: Harcourt Brace.
Carty, Linda, ed. 1993. *And Still We Rise: Feminist Political Mobilizing in Contemporary Canada*. Toronto: Women's Press.
Chappell, Louise A. 2002. *Gendering Government: Feminist Engagement with the State in Australia and Canada*. Vancouver: UBC Press.
Dodson, Debra L. 2006. *The Impact of Women in Congress*. Oxford: Oxford University Press.
Gelb, Joyce. 1989. *Feminism and Politics: A Comparative Perspective*. Berkeley: University of California Press.
Hancock, Ange-Marie. 2007. "When Multiplication Doesn't Equal Quick Addition: Examining Intersectionality as a Research Paradigm." *Perspectives on Politics* 5, 1 (March): 63-80.
Kealey, Linda. 1998. *Enlisting Women for the Cause: Women, Labour, and the Left in Canada, 1890-1920*. Toronto: University of Toronto Press.
Kealey, Linda, and Joan Sangster, eds. 1989. *Beyond the Vote: Canadian Women and Politics*. Toronto: University of Toronto Press.
Lovenduski, Joni, ed. 2005. *State Feminism and Political Representation*. Cambridge: Cambridge University Press.
Malloy, Jonathan. 2003. *Between Colliding Worlds: The Ambiguous Existence of Government Agencies for Aboriginal and Women's Policy*. Toronto: University of Toronto Press.
Newman, Jacquetta, and Linda A. White. 2006. *Women, Politics, and Public Policy: The Political Struggles of Canadian Women*. Don Mills: Oxford University Press.
Norris, Pippa, and Joni Lovenduski. 1995. *Political Recruitment: Gender, Race and Class in the British Parliament*. Cambridge: Cambridge University Press.
Pitkin, Hanna Fenichel. 1967. *The Concept of Representation*. Berkeley: University of California Press.
Sawer, Marian, Manon Tremblay, and Linda Trimble. 2006. "Introduction: Patterns and Practice in the Parliamentary Representation of Women." In *Representing Women in Parliament: A Comparative Study*, ed. Marian Sawer, Manon Tremblay, and Linda Trimble, 1-23. London: Routledge.
Strong-Boag, Veronica. 1972. Introduction to *In Times Like These*, by Nellie L. McClung, vii-xxii. Toronto: University of Toronto Press.
Tremblay, Manon, and Caroline Andrew, eds. 1998. *Women and Political Representation in Canada*. Ottawa: University of Ottawa Press.
Tremblay, Manon, and Linda Trimble, eds. 2003. *Women and Electoral Politics in Canada*. Don Mills: Oxford University Press.
Trimble, Linda, and Jane Arscott. 2003. *Still Counting: Women in Politics across Canada*. Peterborough: Broadview Press.
Urbinati, Nadia. 2000. "Representation as Advocacy: A Study of Democratic Deliberation." *Political Theory* 28, 6 (December): 758-86.
–. 2006. *Representative Democracy: Principles and Genealogy*. Chicago: University of Chicago Press.
Vickers, Jill, Pauline Rankin, and Christine Appelle. 1993. *Politics as if Women Mattered: A Political Analysis of the National Action Committee on the Status of Women*. Toronto: University of Toronto Press.
Weldon, S. Laurel. 2006. "The Structure of Intersectionality: A Comparative Politics of Gender." *Politics and Gender* 2, 1 (June): 235-48.
Wine, Jeri Dawn, and Janice L. Ristock, eds. 1991. *Women and Social Change: Feminist Activism in Canada*. Toronto: James Lorimer and Company.
Young, Lisa. 1997. "Fulfilling the Mandate of Difference: Women in the Canadian House of Commons." In *In the Presence of Women*, ed. Jane Arscott and Linda Trimble, 82-103. Toronto: Harcourt Brace.
–. 2000. *Feminists and Party Politics*. Vancouver: UBC Press.

# Part 1
# Community and Women's Group Participation

# 2
# Women and Community Leadership: Changing Politics or Changed by Politics?

*Caroline Andrew*

The objective of this chapter is to advance our understanding of the ways in which women exercise political leadership. I want to bring to this subject reflections based on a very specific project and then use these observations to reflect on more general questions about women and leadership. The subtitle of the chapter situates its major theme: changing politics or being changed by politics? This is one of the fundamental questions in the research literature on women and politics – to what extent do women transform politics, or, rather, does politics transform women?

This chapter looks at this question through a very particular lens: the work done by women in positions of community leadership. What happens to these same women when they begin to act in the formal political system? What kinds of leadership did they demonstrate in the community context? Is their local leadership style eliminated, transformed, or enhanced when transferred into the arena of formal politics? Do they then understand that the community work they were doing was political?

Before examining the specific case evaluated in this study, it is important to point out that local government in Canada is not a constitutionally recognized level of government on a par with federal and provincial regimes. Cities in Canada are very much the creatures of provincial governments but, for the most part, do not have political parties that replicate in an exact way the parties operating in their respective provinces.

## Case Study

The specific case considered in this chapter is the City for All Women Initiative or Initiative: Une ville pour toutes les femmes (CAWI–IVTF) in Ottawa.[1] I am a participant-observer in this project; conseqently, the discussion that follows reveals an intimate knowledge of process but less of an analytical perspective than would otherwise be the case. The project had two interrelated dimensions: first, providing civic engagement training for women from community-based organizations – including new immigrant, Aboriginal, and disabled groups – and from backgrounds in which they were marginalized by poverty and the experience of violence; and second, integrating a gender and diversity equality guide into both municipal decision making and public policy in the City of Ottawa. The project seeks to integrate politically the full diversity of women in Ottawa. The chapter thus deals with the same political issues as those addressed by Mary-Jo Nadeau in Chapter 3, in which she examines the anti-racist politics of NAC. Chapters 2 and 3 are, therefore, not simply about the political engagement of women; they also expand that subject to focus on the particular challenges faced by marginalized groups of women in the exercise of political leadership.

The transition described in this chapter extends from leadership in community-based organizations to leadership in municipal policy advocacy. It may seem relatively minor when compared to the leap from local to national or international political leadership, but the transition illustrates many of the same questions. Do women practice an identifiable type of leadership? Are women's leadership styles at the community level compatible with participation in mainstream political institutions? Are leadership styles in formal, mainstream politics by definition masculine or simply characteristic of formal politics? These questions are not meant to suggest biologically based explanations of public leadership; they are intended to highlight the social conditions of leadership. The transition I want to reflect on is the movement from community politics to formal politics and what this means for women's exercise of leadership.

The case study is quite specific since community politics in Ottawa is not the same as community politics in Toronto, Montreal, or Vancouver. Size has a lot to do with this, but so too does the socioeconomic profile, extent of ethno-cultural diversity, and history of immigration in each city.[2] Ottawa is a big small town, dominated principally by the federal government and, to a lesser degree, the technology sector. Ethno-racial diversity remains a relatively new phenomenon in Ottawa, despite the long history of relations between francophone and anglophone communities. Simplifying the story considerably, one can say that community activity in Ottawa is polite and muted compared with that of Toronto or Montreal, but is considerably more assertive and diversity-focused than that of the small towns and rural areas discussed by Carbert in Chapter 5 of this volume. The former generalization relates both to the more middle-class socioeconomic profile of Ottawa and to the reality that larger cities tend to bring forth a more diversified and more polarized politics (Community Foundation of Ottawa 2006).

Reflecting on the specific character of community politics in Ottawa also sharpened my reflections on methodology and the value of case studies, as outlined by Bent Flyvbjerg in *Making Social Science Matter* (2001). Flyvbjerg argues for the merits of what he calls "information-oriented selection," where "cases are selected on the basis of expectations about their information content" (79). The CAWI was chosen in order to be able to examine in detail the interactions between this particular group of community actors and the municipal political system. The level of detail was possible because of my participant-observer position and necessary because the subject being studied, the translation of the community leadership of women into formal political leadership, required an analysis of specific interactions.

The following discussion is divided into four parts that situate the analysis of the community leadership of women, describe the CAWI, analyze the ways in which models of leadership were and were not transformed and, finally, attempt to theorize our findings about women's political leadership, respectively.

## Women's Community Leadership

Given the vast literature on community development work, this chapter cannot examine the entire field. Rather, my intention is to understand how women's roles have been understood and, particularly, to probe the specific characteristics of women's community-based leadership.[3] One very helpful analysis is Kristina Smock's book (2004) on community organizing and urban change. Smock describes five models of community organizing: power-based, community building, civic, women-centered, and transformative. They vary according to what is identified as causing inequality and, therefore, as resolving inequality. Proponents of the power-based model see a lack of group power as the problem and prescribe confronting those who have power (so as to gain respect through recognition) as a resolution. The community-building model focuses on the lack of internal group or neighbourhood capacity as the problem, with the resolution being action to strengthen the social and economic fabric of the group or community. The civic model identifies the breakdown of social stability as causing inequality and prescribes finding new mechanisms to protect the public order. According to the women-centred model, the dichotomization of public and private spheres and the exclusion of women from the public sphere are the central problems. Its solutions range from reframing relations between the spheres to increasing women's participation in public spheres. Finally, the transformative model identifies existing systems as the problem and views conceptualizing alternative visions as the beginning of change.

Smock draws out a common core feature from the models, notably a shared view that community organizing builds both individual and community capacity. It develops local leaders, creates networks, and grows social capital. Social capital is built through patterns of informal and formal interaction that build relations of trust and reciprocity. And, in turn, this enhanced social capital allows for more effective collective action (Lowndes 2006; O'Neill and Gidengil 2006; Putnam 2001). Lowndes looks specifically at differences between the social capital of women and the social capital of men. She argues that "men and women tend to have different social capital profiles, with women's social capital more embedded in neighbourhood-specific networks of informal sociability" (224). The link is therefore made between stronger social capital and neighbourhood-level organization. For her part, Smock outlines four areas of activity that are useful to situate the work of women in community organizations: governance structure, diagnosis of community problems, collective action to bring about neighbourhood change, and, finally, widening the scope of work for broader change.

Susan Saegert builds on Smock's model in her analysis of civic capacity in urban neighbourhoods (Saegert 2006). Her point of departure is community capacity building, as distinct from community organizing and community development. She concludes that cooperative and confrontational approaches often coexist in specific organizations: "While the organizing strategies of consensus-oriented and confrontation/competition-oriented approaches differ, successful development of community civic capacity depends on using the right approach at the right time, in the right place, and with the right people. The attainment of civic capacity requires the ability to form distinct interests and goals, to develop shared agendas, and to act collectively. It requires cultivating strong and weak ties, recognizing allies and enemies, and changing the cast of characters as contingencies shift" (ibid., 291). Community building in general emphasizes "relationship building, leadership development, increasing relational and organizational skills of residents and organizations, sustaining stakeholder engagement, developing a sense of common purpose and an action agenda, and increased local institutional capacity" (ibid., 275-76). This approach parallels the importance attached by women-led organizations to "the human and relational development of community members and organizations" (ibid., 279).

Several conclusions follow from Saegert's analysis, and they relate directly to the importance of empirical research on community-based organizations. Detailed studies are necessary to better understand the ways in which cooperative and confrontational strategies interrelate in practice and to comprehend how individual relationship building and collective capacity building fit together in practice. Once more, this underlines the importance of Flyvbjerg's argument that case studies provide a depth of knowledge that is difficult to achieve using other methodologies.

This background helps to inform our interest in women's community-based leadership. The question of cooperation versus confrontation is often linked to gender, especially women's association with cooperative methods and men's association with confrontational ones. Saegert suggests this assumption needs to be studied in real-world organizations. In addition, she posits that the association between women's leadership and attention to individual-level relationships within organizations must be empirically investigated.

Gerda Wekerle's (2000) analysis of women's organizations in cities looks less at the structures of organizations, which is the focus of both Smock and Saegert's analyses, and instead concentrates on the content and basis of group claims. In Wekerle's words, "In cities throughout the world, women are invoking the language of rights and citizenship in making a multiplicity of collective claims on the city for the fulfillment of basic needs, space and inclusion ... resistance and mobilization from below that provide us with alternative models of urban citizenship rooted in women's multiple identities of class, race, ethnicity and sexual orientation" (203). She goes on to discuss different bases for women's claims to equal urban citizenship. Wekerle shows how rights arguments can be framed either within the discourse of human rights or as part of a gendered perspective that confronts both the advantages and limits of the "mobilization potential of maternalism" (ibid., 208). She develops a detailed description of rights claims that are based on "the life spaces of daily life": "Women are also making rights claims as gendered subjects that demand spatial-temporal spaces that support everyday life. They argue that their standpoint and gendered experiences have been excluded and denied by decision-makers, politicians and corporations that shape cities as growth machines, or the global nodes for the accumulation and flow of international capital" (ibid., 209). The political practice that emerges from this last approach is, according to Wekerle, "an alternative politics that is pragmatic and rooted in daily life" (ibid., 214). Again, this view needs to be investigated empirically in order to understand how the transformative potential of alternative politics can be linked with the pragmatics of daily life.

Wekerle's analysis also recognizes the importance of overlaps or intersections between gender and diversity, particularly since women's community organizing is rooted in the specific circumstances of daily life. This acknowledgment of intersectionality recalls the work of Olena Hankivsky (2005), who criticizes gender mainstreaming because of a failure to investigate "the complex circumstances involving gender differences and intersectionalities and multiple identities" (977). Hankivsky proposes a "more expansive diversity mainstreaming framework" (ibid., 987) that would take better account of advances in feminist theory, as well as the complexities of HIV/AIDS, sex trafficking, and other issues in which gender, class, race, and international boundaries are all implicated. Her conclusion, which is very similar to that of Wekerle, is as follows: "If the promise of GM (gender mainstreaming) – that is, social justice – is to be realized, there is a pressing need to integrate present feminist knowledge about the context of lives and experiences, structured inequalities in the public and private spheres, and gender with all its intersectionalities" (ibid., 996). This literature underpins our case study of women's community leadership. Writers in this field substantially agree that women's community leadership is marked by what Wekerle describes as "an alternative politics that is pragmatic and rooted in daily life" (2000, 214). Smock and Saegert emphasize the importance of governance structures, strategic action choices, and relations between individual and collective capacity building. Hankivsky's focus on the importance of using a diversity of lenses supports Wekerle's argument that women's preoccupation with daily life necessarily places intersectionality in a central position. Women's daily lives do not segment or isolate multiple identities; rather, race, class, language, gender, sexual orientation, and age are only some of the dimensions that shape their particular forms of community leadership. So now, back to Ottawa.

**City for All Women**

The CAWI is the second phase of a project in Ottawa that links women and local politics (Andrew and Klodawsky 2006; Andrew et al. 2004). The first phase began in 1998 with the decision by the Regional Council of Ottawa-Carleton to endorse the International Union of Local Authorities' (IULA) Declaration on Women in Local Government and to create a Working Group of Women's Access to Municipal Services. Although Ottawa-Carleton offered no funding and no staff positions, the working group eventually obtained funds for femocratic staff appointments from Status of Women Canada. Staff members organized focus groups and, owing to their energy and commitment, took very seriously the working group's declared intention to include a full range of diverse women in them. Somewhat to our surprise, the focus groups were splendidly diverse. They led to a report, a response from Ottawa-Carleton, and the project ending with the lesson that, although some interesting and innovative activities were going on, no consistent integration of women in their full diversity existed in the city.

The second project, the CAWI, took off in 2004 from this starting point. Participants were determined to learn from the lessons of the earlier project, in which city staff members engaged only on a volunteer basis. This had been unsatisfactory from a civil service point of view, because it led to increased workloads and, even more importantly, because it reflected a view that integrating diverse women was neither important work nor the main business of the city. For the CAWI to succeed, city staff would need to be paid for their efforts so that the project would become part of the regular municipal workload.

Yet, a looming budget crisis meant the city was too busy to think about the CAWI. This impasse led to a very innovative element within the CAWI: training in civic engagement, which came about once community-based women's group representatives expressed their desire for municipal government training. In interviews, diverse women said they knew nothing about how the city operated and found city hall an alien environment. They felt they did not belong in city hall and city hall did not belong to them – this was the recurring theme. So the CAWI decided to set up training programs for women from community groups to learn about municipal policy making and policy advocacy. Ottawa's budget crisis lent itself very nicely to the practical exercises, and the women, in small groups, prepared policy proposals and met with local councillors to present their proposals.

The highpoint of the process came when CAWI trainees made a presentation to the Ottawa City Council during public hearings on the budget. A group of sixteen women, all wearing peach-coloured scarves, stood up, sang a song, and then made two hard-hitting presentations on the detrimental social impact of increasing public transit fares and the importance of restoring community funding grants. The group – in terms of size, colour, and dress – was wonderfully diverse, and their presentation made an impact, if one can judge from the remarks of the elected officials immediately afterward and in the months that followed. In part, the fact that they were noticed was luck – they appeared after a long series of elderly, white, affluent residents called for decreased services, increased public transit fares, and, more generally, a reduction in the quality of urban public services. The contrast was striking and, in visual terms, showed the difference between an Ottawa of the past and a new Ottawa in the making.

The CAWI subsequently launched a second round of training and worked with the city to develop and test a gender equality guide for use by city managers. This work involved both city staff members designated to work with the CAWI and other city staff. The CAWI also undertook a pilot project with Community and Protective Services, the largest city department. Ottawa City Council voted to implement the CAWI's gender equality guide city wide in 2007, following a positive evaluation of the pilot project (City of Ottawa, CAWI, 2005, 2006). This decision was endorsed by senior management in June 2007.

The fact that the City of Ottawa was starting at such a basic level might be viewed as surprising, given that it had a history of inclusive practices. For example, the former mayor, Marian Dewar, worked to welcome and integrate Vietnamese boat people. Yet, the subsequent Harris years at the provincial level led to cuts in funding for urban diversity programs, leaving Ottawa in a position in which it more or less had to begin from zero.

The gender equality guide built on the 2002 Equity and Diversity policy of the City of Ottawa, which recognized as designated groups women; visible minorities; people with disabilities; gay, lesbian, bisexual, or transgendered citizens; and Aboriginal people. The policy related both to the municipal workforce and to incorporating the spirit of equity and diversity into municipal policies and programs. The gender equality guide was organized around seven phases of policy formulation: research or information gathering, consultation, policy development, project/program development, communication, service delivery, and evaluation. At each stage, the text raised questions about relevant social differences and inequalities that needed to be considered. Examples included family responsibility, unpaid work, time use, personal mobility, safety, and discrimination.

Following from the designated groups list, basic dimensions of difference were identified as follows: Aboriginal ancestry, income, race or ethnicity, language, physical and mental disability, marital status, family status and dependents, age, religion/culture, geographic location, length of time in Canada, and sexual orientation or identity. In fall 2006, the guide was evaluated to assess its usefulness; preliminary results indicated a positive evaluation from those city managers who had initially been trained in its application. Interestingly, some managers indicated that the material had been new and valuable to them, whereas others felt they were already aware of the content. The latter said they could see the material presented in a systematic way, and they therefore found that the guide was useful to them as well.

The CAWI's equality guide (2006) is based on the importance of including women's experiences in urban policy making: "Women are experts in day-to-day living, as a large majority of them juggle family and work demands. Women from equity-seeking groups have particular perspectives to bring in creating a more inclusive Ottawa. The experience of the full diversity of women and their organizations will not be fully considered unless specific steps are taken to ensure their inclusion" (8). The guide and its evaluation framework were developed through committees set up by the CAWI steering committee. Some committee members were from women's community groups, while others, including women who worked as training and evaluation professionals, were from the city at large. The latter were chosen carefully so as to represent the diversity of women as much as possible. The categories that were particularly salient to the CAWI were women from francophone, visible minority, and Aboriginal backgrounds. The delicate balancing of professional skills and community women's voices within the overall structure of the CAWI was crucial not only to embrace different perspectives, resources, and time dynamics but also to ensure that both constituencies learned about community capacity building and policy advocacy.

The transition or bridge from community leadership to municipal policy advocacy needs to be looked at in more detail. Local group activists were still involved in community leadership activities, but, via the CAWI, their work took on an additional dimension of formal politics. Community leadership varies in its forms but reveals the striking archetype of the woman leading a women's committee in an ethno-specific organization. The formal leadership of the larger group is male, but the real work is done by the women's committee. Women involved in the CAWI training initiative did remarkable amounts of community work, from organizing major fundraising events to solving endless individual-level problems that smoothed interactions between bureaucracies of the host society and members of their particular community (for example, to obtain public health cards). This problem solving extended the traditional female role of caring to an immigrant settlement context where the volume of necessary caring work had dramatically increased. Children – the women's own children and others in the community – needed help to negotiate the school system.

Many of the CAWI women faced their own economic and, especially, employment difficulties. In a number of cases, they juggled part-time employment and extensive community work with education and training. They shouldered these burdens quietly and almost invisibly – the formal leadership of their community-based organizations was male, while women described their contributions as merely carrying out community wishes in a collective way as part of the women's committee. Overall, their caring work in the community was usually described as doing things that needed to be done.

The settlement context in Ottawa transformed the traditional caring roles of these women into more substantial leadership roles. They became the mainstay of their families, extended families, and communities. They were involved both in building a specific community and in building bridges to the structures of the host society. In quiet ways, they acted with great competence and were aware of the skills they brought to work within their communities. They knew why the official leadership of their communities was male, and they were aware of the contradiction between the Canadian discourse of equality on gender and ethno-cultural grounds, on one side, and the realities of life as recently settled women in Canada, on the other.

**Assessing the Transition**

How did these women deal with the transition from community activity to engagement with formal politics? One dimension of this process for many was a move from acting principally within a single ethno-cultural community to acting in a multicultural environment. This part of the transition brought both challenges and positive energy to the training program. For many CAWI participants, the experience of acting in a group composed of both Canadian- and foreign-born women was a first. There was a sense that this represented Canada at its best, as an egalitarian, diverse community in which participants reached beyond the already intricate circles of people they cared for and cared about in their immediate families, extended families, and communities to embrace diverse women in Ottawa. This process illustrated the complex web of relations between individual and collective levels of capacity building and demonstrated that, for women in the CAWI project, concern for each other was integrally connected to views about collective action – the two were inseparable.

At the same time, the process brought with it the challenges of inclusionary development work. Differences between communities are often large, and skill is required to avoid making some bases of equality seem more important or valid than others. Luckily for the CAWI, the staff person was extremely skilled and highly sensitive to the potential for destructive hierarchies. Thanks to her abilities, the process was inclusive, and positive energy prevailed, despite a number of tense moments.

It must nevertheless be recognized that many women felt intimidated when they interacted with formal politics. For most, the first reaction was to retreat to the position that they knew nothing, whereas the politician and staff were all-knowing and all-powerful; according to this view, the imbalance of power was a fixed given. This was a first reaction, which prompted an interesting collective decision by community women about how to present themselves in the mainstream political arena. Their presentation to Ottawa City Council during the budget debates was a carefully thought-out performance that was grounded in remaining true to the values of community leadership while intervening effectively in official politics. This approach followed a long discussion about how to organize the presentation. Because the women were comfortable with their community roots and not committed to playing exactly by the mainstream rules, the decision to start with a song reflected their commitment to a different form of leadership. At Ottawa City Council the rules allow two speakers to have five minutes each, not sixteen women singing. The CAWI chose to sing in order to make the point that their expertise and legitimacy were community-based. Plus, they also wanted to have surprise value and attract attention. The song was also deliberate in that it made the points that life is holistic and culture is an integral part of community life; formal politics, by contrast, is one isolated area of activity in the modern hyper-segmented world. For CAWI participants, if the world of formal politics divides life into five-minute pieces, then the world of community leadership does not.

The song itself was clever. The music was slightly romantic but the lyrics were not; they said, "Please listen to us because if you don't, we'll remember this at the next election." These words reflected the same kind of deliberate transgressing of boundaries as the strategy of singing. Both were part of a conscious political choice and a commitment on the part of the women to remain true to themselves. The CAWI, in short, not only built community leadership but also leadership for municipal policy advocacy. It entailed confrontation, of a particular sort, as well as cooperation.

The city council intervention required effort, organization, and nervous energy. Participants planned to follow the song with two short presentations by two different women, and much coaching and practising was done for them to feel at ease at city hall. In this case, group action via song was easier than individual action via spoken word, since, for these women, playing an individual and publicly visible role was much more difficult than exercising community leadership. But their pleasure in succeeding carried with it a lesson that the transition was both possible and fruitful.

**Conclusion**

What are the lessons learned in terms of women's engagement? Three come to mind: first, changing politics and being changed by politics; second, the potential for transforming leadership skills from community to mainstream political bases; and third, the need for a deliberate process.

We can start with the question that is central to the study of women and politics: Does bringing women into formal politics change women or change politics? The fact that this is a slippery research question does not make it any less important, but rather more challenging and complex. The CAWI story suggests both processes can occur at the same time; that is, changes are made to politics but also to women's political behaviour. In this sense, in answer to the question posed in the introduction to this volume, one could conclude that the doors to participation are open wider than in the past. Following Arjun Appadurai's (2001) study of the organization of India's urban poor, we can think of small changes to the political process as precedent setting. This may be an overly optimistic view of the cumulative effects of small changes, and it certainly is a different position from that of authors who insist on the path-dependent nature of formal politics. However, according to Appadurai's analysis, this view comes from group recognition that political change is a very long-term process and that patience must remain the fundamental political position. Appadurai also links patience with good humour: if you take the long view of political change, then short-term problems illustrate the absurdities of life and can be seen as amusing. Indeed, laughing together also illustrates interrelations between individual and collective levels of capacity building – it builds inclusion on an individual level while at the same time creating a common perspective that supports collective action.

This is an appropriate perspective to apply to the CAWI. Can singing before Ottawa City Council be seen as setting a precedent for a more inclusive public space? At another city council committee meeting, CAWI members gave roses to staff members and elected councillors who had supported the gender equality guide. This behaviour transgressed the formal political process, but it did so in a way that had multiple references: it evoked women's traditional roles (loving flowers, appreciating beauty) in addition to the reverse of these roles (women giving flowers to men rather than receiving them from men). It also spoke to women's political militancy (by referencing "bread and roses"). The CAWI's behaviour at the council and committee meetings provided either one significant step towards a more egalitarian relationship between ordinary citizens and the formal political arena or such a small step as to be insignificant.

If the argument about women changing politics is best cast in a long-term perspective, then what about the argument that politics changes women? This is also a long-term process, one made up of many small steps.

For example, once individual women became known through their CAWI activity, important political and bureaucratic actors began to recognize and talk to them. These women were able to grasp opportunities to lobby significant political actors for their proposals. As former "outsiders," they took on attributes of political "insiders" and thus held a changed position. This constitutes but one small paving stone on the path to political engagement.

Our second consideration focuses on the potential for transferring leadership skills from community to political bases. Again, the CAWI case provides complex and nuanced perspectives. I observed no automatic transfer: women who behaved in leadership roles in their particular communities often saw themselves as knowing nothing about formal politics and as having no resources to bring to the formal political process. Yet, as their deliberations before the budget presentation indicate, CAWI participants demonstrated their ability to think strategically about how to convert community leadership skills into mainstream advocacy skills. Once they framed the question of how to make the most effective presentation with an appropriate level of comfort and good performance, they felt more competent and experienced. Clearly, their performance successfully combined community leadership skills with political leadership skills.

This brings us to the third and final point, which concerns the necessity to deliberately develop political leadership skills in women now active at the community level in Canada. This echoes the second question raised in the introduction, how can the doors to participation be opened even wider? This question is, of course, particularly important in the case of women coming from marginalized or "racialized" communities, a theme which is also treated in Chapter 3 on NAC by Mary-Jo Nadeau. There are, of course, women who have done this on their own, but, as a society, Canada will waste huge amounts of human talent if political integration processes are simply left to chance. A number of training programs are already in place at different spaces in the political continuum, but we need a great many more.

The CAWI project showed that many other areas of training would be useful and important. They include training for community-based women on how to interact with school teachers, school principals, social workers, and other front-line workers in the institutions of the host society; building on training in civic engagement in order to develop policy advocacy skills; offering learning opportunities for women who are thinking about running for public office; and training female candidates who have declared their intentions. Training requires a specific focus, and that focus has to square with how potential participants understand their needs at a precise moment in time.

The CAWI experience suggests training must be context-specific, and it shows how much can be learned from contacts between different groups. There are many experiences to share, a fact that recalls the literature on community work. In the CAWI, participants learned how to integrate intersectionality (defined here as multiple group identities or affiliations held by single individuals), construct alternative visions in a pragmatic way, present views clearly to people who oppose those views, build capacity on individual and collective levels, build coalitions around the issues of daily life, and sustain these coalitions across a diverse range of women and women's groups.

This chapter set out to advance our collective understanding of women and political leadership. Its particular contribution is to illuminate the enormous amount of community leadership that is undertaken by women in contemporary Canada, particularly among recently settled immigrant groups. Women in the CAWI cared for individual members of their communities, for their communities as collectivities, and for their communities' connections to the host society. The case study confirms two core themes. First, it is possible to combine political leadership roles with community leadership roles. Second, to do this well, Canada needs an explicitly planned process and a long-term horizon, since, to properly empower community-based women, training must respect and engage the lives of the participants.

The case study also raises significant questions. Is Appadurai right to suggest that small precedents can slowly produce a major transformation of politics? Can training alone allow community-based women to engage more effectively in formal politics? Or are more open and porous political systems a prerequisite for successful integration? These questions lead us to the next chapters in the book, notably towards their insights into how women's political engagement is both enabled and limited in contemporary Canada.

**Notes**

1 The work of the CAWI-IVTF was funded by Status of Women Canada, the Trillium Foundation, and United Way of Ottawa.

2 The style of community leadership exercised by immigrant women in Ottawa is not unique, however. One comparative example comes from a chance encounter, in the Zurich airport, on a stopover from Toronto to Delhi. I met a woman from Calgary who was president of the Canada-Tibet Women's Association. Her community work in Calgary was strikingly similar to that of the CAWI women in Ottawa, which is detailed later in this chapter. She helped obtain driver's licences for other people, did their shopping, dealt with medical problems, and assisted with other interactions with the host society that required language skills. At the same time, she organized major fundraising events in Calgary to aid Tibetans living in refugee camps, and she mirrored the CAWI women in projecting a quiet sense of her own competence and an understanding of the importance of her community work. In the middle of writing this chapter, I was particularly struck by the similarities between community leadership in Calgary and that of the CAWI women in Ottawa.

3 I am aware that this review of sources neglects the rich feminist literature on grassroots organizations. It focuses instead on studies of community-based organizing, especially women's role in the organizing process.

**References**

Andrew, Caroline, and Fran Klodawsky. 2006. "New Voices: New Politics." *Women and Environments International* 70/71: 66-67.

Andrew, Caroline, Pat Harewood, Fran Klodawsky, and Alette Willis. 2004. "Accessing City Hall." *Women and Environments International* 62/63: 49-50.

Appadurai, Arjun. 2001. "Deep Democracy: Urban Governmentality and the Horizon of Politics." *Environment and Urbanization* 13, 2: 23-43.

City of Ottawa. CAWI (City for All Women Initiative). 2005. *Planning an Effective Consultation: A Guide to Ensuring Inclusion of Diverse Women.* Ottawa: City of Ottawa and City for All Women Initiative.

–. 2006. *Gender Equality Guide.* Ottawa: Community and Protection Services Department.

Community Foundation of Ottawa. 2006. *Ottawa's Vital Signs: The City's Annual Checkup.* Ottawa: Community Foundation of Ottawa.

Flyvbjerg, Bent. 2001. *Making Social Science Matter.* Cambridge: Cambridge University Press.

Hankivsky, Olena. 2005. "Gender vs. Diversity Mainstreaming: A Preliminary Examination of the Role and Transformation Potential of Feminist Theory." *Canadian Journal of Political Science* 38, 4: 937-1001.

Lowndes, Vivien. 2006. "It's Not What You've Got, But What You Do With It: Women, Social Capital, and Political Participation." In *Gender and Social Capital,* ed. Brenda O'Neill and Elisabeth Gidengil, 213-40. New York: Routledge.

O'Neill, Brenda, and Elisabeth Gidengil, eds. 2006. *Gender and Social Capital.* New York: Routledge.

Putnam, Robert. 2001. "Social Capital: Measurement and Consequences." *Isuma: Canadian Journal of Policy Research* 2, 1: 41-51.

Saegert, Susan. 2006. "Building Civic Capacity in Urban Neighbourhoods: An Empirically Grounded Anatomy." *Journal of Urban Affairs* 28, 3: 275-94.

Smock, Kristina. 2004. *Democracy in Action: Community Organizing and Urban Change.* New York: Columbia University Press.

Wekerle, Gerda R. 2000. "Women's Rights to the City: Gendered Spaces of a Pluralistic Citizenship." In *Democracy, Citizenship and the Global City,* ed. Engin F. Isin, 203-7. New York: Routledge.

# 3
# Rebuilding the House of Canadian Feminism: NAC and the Racial Politics of Participation

*Mary-Jo Nadeau*

In 1992, the National Action Committee on the Status of Women (NAC) was definitively transformed "from a lobby group, to a group ... attempting to be a national representation of the women's movement in its broadest sense" (Rebick, as quoted in Gottlieb 1993, 381). Twenty years after its establishment as the largest umbrella for post-1960s Canadian feminist organizations, NAC's founding identity as a "new parliament of women" was permanently challenged and reconstituted, bringing the group into a new political terrain of "strong, extra-parliamentary movements" (NAC 1990, 3).

Anti-racism was a core demand in this "dramatic shift" (FitzGerald, as quoted in Gottlieb 1993, 377) and was pivotal in opening NAC's doors in ways that permanently transformed the organization. Indeed, a key gain of the period was exposing racism in NAC, an accomplishment that required opening doors that had remained closed for too long. This shift forced an examination of entrenched white feminist institutional practices and normative political cultures that had produced multiple, long-standing exclusions and hierarchies in NAC. In the process, NAC's political agenda, culture, and boundaries of participation broadened substantially.

As former NAC president Sunera Thobani has noted, this struggle breathed new life into NAC in the 1990s and "saved it from total irrelevance" (quoted in Rebick 2002, 74). Among other changes in this major institutional overhaul, NAC's constitution was revised to incorporate an "anti-racist, anti-heterosexist" agenda; an internal affirmative action policy was implemented at all levels; and a multi-racial national politic (while contested) was adopted to re-centre the participation of Aboriginal women and women of colour (Nadeau 2005). And, for the first time, feminists of colour took a dominant leadership position within NAC, advancing the key political aim to broaden participation by "integrat[ing] concerns of visible minority and immigrant women into the fabric of the organization" (NAC, VMIW, 1989, 3).

This chapter revisits the struggle to make NAC "truly representative of women in Canada" (NAC 1989). As a transformative moment, the period under discussion offers a critical entry point for analyzing the making and unmaking of internal hierarchies of racialized participation in second-wave Canadian feminist organizations. Arguably the most substantial transformation in NAC's history, activism in this period opened the organization's doors in unprecedented ways. It exposed the racial hierarchies of inclusion/exclusion that had privileged the participation of white feminists and, simultaneously, operated to place limits on participation for women of colour since the organization's creation in 1972.

Despite the significance of these developments, little research has probed the dynamics of anti-racism that ultimately decentred white hegemony as a formative power relation in Canada's second-wave "house" of national feminism. This chapter addresses that analytic gap by focusing on the anti-racist challenge to white feminism in NAC as a pivotal site for transforming its politics of participation. It also suggests alternate research routes and a new narrative strategy for understanding women's movement organizations in which whiteness figures as a central power relation.

I argue here that the struggle against racism in NAC revealed that both its founding political culture and organizational structure, which were grounded in the pursuit of parliamentary activism, naturalized white women as the presumed national leadership and "spokeswomen for feminism" (Duclos, cited in Jhappan 1996, 26) and authorized their privileged participation in "governmental belonging" (Hage 2000). Despite an increased focus on inclusivity during NAC's first twenty years, this white feminist "somatic norm" (Puwar 2004) in the organization's formative political culture continued to assert unacknowledged borders of racial participation. A resistant (white) centre continued to legitimate forms of unmarked white normativity and placed limits on broad-based multi-racial participation, which kept NAC's doors effectively closed (or barely ajar) to anti-racist feminist organizing (despite claims to openness and inclusivity). Indeed, even at the height of the dramatic shift, many feminists of colour expressed concern that white feminism's political culture persisted in forms of "subtle exclusion" (Bain, as quoted in Gottlieb 1993, 373) and exerted an entrenched "sense of proprietorship" over NAC (Roach, as quoted in Rebick and Roach 1996, 111).

To explore this line of argument, the chapter unfolds in four sections. The first section maps out the history of anti-racist research on NAC, identifying gaps in the literature and addressing some troubling legacies of white feminist frameworks. The second section argues for a definitive shift to intersectional analysis and offers some theoretical vocabulary in this direction (thus building on the discussion of intersectionality initiated by Andrew in Chapter 2). The third section extends and applies this analysis by articulating a new framework for narrating the history of NAC's racial politics of participation. This reframing views NAC's history as being formed and contested from the outset by hierarchies of participation that are, fundamentally, struggles over the intertwined terms of racial, political, and national belonging. The final section reflects on how obstacles and openings to participation can inform current struggles in social movement organizations.

## Literature on NAC and Anti-Racist Feminism

Despite the impact of the dramatic shift more than fifteen years ago, no reliable, well-documented history of NAC's racial politics of participation has been written. Three broad gaps continue to mark research about NAC: first, little systematic research probes the dramatic shift; second, limited vocabulary has been developed for analyzing the operations of white hegemony in NAC; and third, narrative frameworks for a critical race analysis of NAC remain undeveloped. Without addressing these gaps, white feminist formations remain positioned as core or essential agents of NAC's history, and white feminist narratives of participation remain naturalized (Brodie 1995; Molgat 1992, 1997; Vickers, Rankin, and Appelle 1993).

It is widely recognized that, "until the 1990s, NAC was dominated by white, English-Canadian women" (Vickers 2000, 140; see also Lee and Cardinal 1998). This racial dominance in the organization is reflected in the white feminist literature on NAC, most of which focuses on gender (and sometimes class), with little or no analysis of racial hierarchies inside NAC (Begin 1992; Brodie 1995; de Seve 1992; Dumont 1992; Greaves 1991; Vickers 1991, 1992; Vickers, Rankin, and Appelle 1993).

Anti-racist feminist writings about NAC emerged in the 1990s and challenged existing analyses by introducing critical reflections on the dramatic shift underway in the organization (see Armstrong 1994; Gottlieb 1993; Huang and Jaffer 1993; Rebick and Roach 1996). Much of this early work foregrounded the more general "crisis of legitimation" that centred on racism in the Canadian women's movement (Mukherjee 1992, 165; Simms 1992) and provided anti-racist reconsiderations of the document that NAC was established to implement, the 1970 Report of the Royal Commission on the Status of Women (see St. Lewis 1997; Turpel-Lafond 1997; Williams 1990). After more than two decades of anti-racist feminist organizing and writing, contemporary feminist accounts typically offer a far more inclusive history of NAC, including an acknowledgment of its early history as "an organization dominated by White middle-class women" (Coomber 1997, 50; see also Cohen 1993; Dobrowolsky 2000; Gottlieb 1993; Luxton 2001; MacDonald 2002; Molgat 1992; Rebick 2005). Studies tend to identify as key markers of change Sunera Thobani's election as NAC's first woman of colour president and the 1996 NAC-CLC Women's March Against Poverty. In this sense, an important and necessary shift towards an anti-racist feminist narrative has occurred in the field.

At the same time, two historiographical gaps remain. First, the documentation and interpretation of the history of anti-racist feminist struggle in NAC remains incomplete because it has mostly been recorded in round-table discussions, dialogues, interviews, and speeches by women who were directly involved in the struggle (Armstrong 1994; Gottlieb 1993; Jones and Stephen 1988; Rebick 2005; Rebick and Roach 1996; Robertson 1999). While these documents are indispensable resources for mapping out key sites of struggle over racism in NAC, they need to be supplemented by additional research and analysis. Second, even less research has been undertaken to document and interpret NAC's white feminist history, dating from 1972 when the country's demographic diversity was measurably less than it became in subsequent years. Although some work of this type has begun in recent years (Lee and Cardinal 1998; Stasiulis 1999; Vickers 2000), the bulk of studies fail to account for whiteness, leaving unexamined its many naturalized forms of racial participation.

On the whole, the field is not yet governed by the key premise in critical race theory that "an analysis of race that has nothing to say about whiteness is incomplete" (Knowles 2003, 174). Rather, racial participation is too often represented as an important but relatively insignificant part of the movement in NAC from white feminist exclusion (in the past) to anti-racist, feminist, pluralist inclusivity (in the present). On these terms, with NAC's white feminist history placed neatly in the past, there appears to be little need to interrogate the hierarchies of participation that historically shaped white feminism in NAC. And with the emphasis on the positive outcome of NAC's dramatic shift, the difficult story of the actual struggle to produce anti-racist change remains untold. On both counts, this narrative largely erases NAC's white normative foundations and their impact on the organization.

## Intersectional Analysis of Racial Participation in NAC

By the mid-1990s "gender essentialism" was widely identified as a foundational problem in feminist political science. Radha Jhappan's (1996, 17) pivotal article applied "critiques of white feminist theory levelled by women of colour" to this area of the discipline and outlined how gender was privileged above other forms of oppression. Writing in the same year, Taylor (1996, 892) noted the "continuing neglect" of race and ethnicity in political science and, like Jhappan, called for a comprehensive shift to intersectional analysis (see also Ship 1998).

Over time, writing about racial exclusion appeared more regularly (see Findlay 1998; Gabriel 1996; Tremblay and Andrew 1998; Williams 1998); it acknowledged that the "experiences of ethnic ... and racialized minority women ... have gone largely unexplored in key areas of the Canadian feminist scholarship on women and politics" (Ship 1998, 311). Analyses of race increasingly appeared where none had existed in the past, and some authors revisited earlier works through a lens focused on race. For example, in the anthology *Women and Political Representation in Canada,* Tremblay and Andrew (1998) took particular care to focus on the intersections of race and gender in the field. Other studies examined multiple, cross-cutting social relations and identities, including gender, race, class, and citizenship (see Gabriel 1996; Stasiulis 1999; Williams 1998).

Even with this shift, narrow interpretations of intersectionality have often prevailed, with the field tending not to push beyond minimal recognition of the "underrepresentation of women of colour" (Ship 1998, 12). Whiteness remains largely unexamined as a racial position. Moreover, class dimensions are neglected as writers collapse diverse racial groups into categories such as "women of colour" and "white women."

Fortunately, new theoretical and political vocabularies have emerged to expose, uncover, unpack, dislodge, and rewrite persistent forms of white normativity. Sheila Wilmot's (2005) work on white anti-racist theory and practice examines how and why this needs to be done from within the privileged location of whiteness. She argues that those located as white have a "social responsibility to challenge that notion of supremacy ... and the resulting racism" (Wilmot 2005, 12); they must also take direction from analyses developed by people of colour who "struggle with and resist multiple forms of oppression" (ibid., 21). Although white feminist political science has moved towards "taking responsibility" and "taking direction" by incorporating analyses of race, further work is needed in order to enrich the theoretical terrain.

This chapter takes up the challenge of applying intersectional theorizing to the analysis of NAC's history. It explicitly identifies white feminism as a *founding* power relation, and as central to intersectional analysis. Implicitly, white feminist hegemony remains in place because white feminist conventions, premises, and narratives remain unacknowledged *as* white feminism. In Judy Rebick's 2005 book, for example, the origins of second-wave feminism are described as follows: "By the end of the 1960s, there were three streams of feminism in Canada: VOW peace activists; the middle-class mothers and career women who belonged to established groups ... and the young radicals ... As the new decade dawned, the three streams of feminism flowed together to form the second wave of the Canadian women's movement" (Rebick 2005, 13). While the book includes important race analysis for the later decades, this part of the account renders racism in the movement and white feminism invisible as formative processes of NAC's creation (see also Vosko 2003).

This chapter also directs attention towards the implicit "white/non-white dichotomy" that is the hallmark of race essentialism (Jhappan 1996, 32). Full intersectional analysis calls for a more robust analysis of "intracategorical complexity" (McCall 2005, 1773), meaning the range of differences and hierarchies within each category of the white women/women of colour dichotomy. Recent work in transnational feminism is useful in this regard, particularly the concept of "relational positionalities," which is defined by Daiva Stasiulis (1999, 194) as "the multiple relations of power that intersect in complex ways to position individuals and collectivities in shifting and often contradictory locations within geopolitical spaces, historical narratives, and movement politics." This framing permits us to see power relations as complex and contradictory, a focus that is necessary for analyzing the power of whiteness as it operates simultaneously with lived experiences of gender and other forms of oppression and privilege.

This discussion adopts and expands upon the language of "modes," primarily to unsettle unmarked and unacknowledged white normative frameworks. My analysis of NAC uses an overarching framework of "white feminist" and "anti-racist feminist" modes, each of which is understood as complex and diverse. "Mode" is used here as an interpretive device, a method for identifying broad tendencies within and across multiple (and sometimes conflicting) feminist political formations and narrative traditions (Shohat 1998). What distinguishes a mode is the character of its knowledge claims and practices, rather than an essentialized racial position.

As a mode, then, white feminism has historically emerged at the core or centre of Canadian feminism. This has typically been accomplished by invoking a singular hegemonic historical trajectory for Canadian feminism that is often expressed in generational and national terms, as in the historically persistent "nationalizing desire to unify all women under a single Anglo-Canadian banner" (Lee and Cardinal 1998, 217). White feminist formations also distinctively define their position, and the hierarchical terms of participation in Canadian feminism, through an unquestioned sense of entitlement to a position of governance or leadership (especially in the national space). This is facilitated by privileging gender hierarchies as primary and treating race as secondary or non-essential – a practice that often results in the production of whiteness through unmarked racial categories, including "Canadian women." While such categories are seen as natural and uncontested entities, they are actually formed through struggle and in hierarchical relation to racial categories of belonging constructed as "other" including immigrant women (see Thobani 2007). Ultimately, by failing to engage with or incorporate relevant anti-racist critiques, the white feminist mode reproduces the range of problems just described.

## Opening Closed Doors in NAC, 1966-92

While NAC's doors have always been formally open to broad participation, the organization presented barriers to women from diverse backgrounds. How was whiteness entrenched as a somatic norm? How was it challenged by the anti-racist women's movement?

This section reviews three broad moments of struggle that significantly shaped the racial politics of participation in NAC: the formation of a national white feminist agenda during the royal commission period from 1966 to 1970, the consolidation of NAC through whiteness as a new parliament of women from 1972 to 1984, and the reconstitution of the group via anti-racist feminist politics from 1985 to 1992. The last period was followed by the implementation of an anti-racist constitution and political culture in NAC after 1993. The organization's history in this rendering becomes an ongoing struggle over "governmental belonging" (Hage 2000, 59) and the (re)articulation of participation in racial/national terms. Each moment encapsulates a particular dynamic of struggle over defining and participating in the "national we," or the governing voice of women as a national constituency. Ghassan Hage's work provides a vocabulary for this analysis, permitting us to see the making of white feminist hegemony as the mobilization of a "national will" and to examine how an organized anti-racist women's movement subsequently challenged this by mobilizing a national "counter-will."

**Formation, 1966-70**

In the mid-1960s the Committee for the Equality of Women (CEW) formed with the sole aim of lobbying the federal government to create a royal commission on the status of women. Although the CEW contained "varying political hues" (Morris 1982, 113), most activists were white, well educated, English Canadian, upper-middle-class married women active in "women's clubs and organizations that had been founded over 50 years earlier" (Freeman 2001, 22).

Hage's work is useful for illuminating the centrality of racial location to the group's primary agenda of institutionalizing white liberal feminist ideals into a mode of national leadership. He asserts that those who occupy the dominant racial location (whiteness) "assume that it is their very natural right to take up the position of governmentality within the nation and become the national managers" (Hage 2000, 62). Indeed, in assuming a place of governmental belonging, the CEW successfully positioned itself as a legitimate elite player in the broader (male-dominated) white nationalist project that was underway, while also claiming a position as the voice of organized feminism. These overlapping claims reinforced the CEW's formal political legitimacy, permitting it to be seen as representative of a national constituency (i.e., Canadian women, through the Royal Commission on the Status of Women [RCSW]) and as the voice of official leadership in the women's movement (by situating the RCSW as NAC's founding document).

Three meetings held in the spring and summer of 1966 were attended by women from about thirty established national and provincial women's organizations. While CEW activists debated *how* to proceed, none questioned the rightness of doing so on national terms (CEW 1966, 16 May, 28 June, 17 September). In asserting itself as a "national we," the CEW assumed a role as the natural group to represent Canadian women, took control of the terms on which this would occur, and pursued a national agenda to secure women's "full participation" within a human rights framework (reflecting the dominant white, liberal discourse of the period). Through whiteness, then, the CEW entrenched a position of governmental belonging by claiming to represent the women of Canada. Whiteness thus became entrenched as a somatic norm in emergent second-wave Canadian feminism.

It is crucial to recognize that this pattern of participation was not simply exclusionary. Rather, it established a *hierarchy of inclusion* in which "a tacit reservation of privileged positions" for white women simultaneously positioned women of colour as "out of place" or non-representative as national feminist leaders (Puwar 2004, 10). Indeed, NAC's presidents were exclusively white until 1993, when Sunera Thobani became president.[1] This hierarchy of inclusion had a broader resonance as well, creating a climate of participation marked by an elite, club-based, white, leadership-centred ideal that was substantially (if not formally) exclusionary in its social and spatial composition. For example, CEW meetings were not public: they were held at the University Women's Club in Toronto, and most of the organizing was done by elite representatives of established women's groups, many of whom had social class connections to government officials.

That being said, the CEW's legitimacy also rested on support from the broad constituency of "Canadian women." The group employed a strategy of managed inclusivity, in which "ordinary women" were frequently addressed in the public domain, at the same time as leadership positions were reserved for group insiders (see Nadeau forthcoming). This pattern of white feminist governmental belonging continued as a legacy in NAC, whereby formalized inclusivity coexisted with racial (and other) hierarchies of exclusion.

## Consolidation, 1972-84

Once formed, governmental belonging must be reinforced through an ongoing "struggle to impose" and naturalize its dominant position (Hage 2000, 66). This struggle continued in the years following 1972 as NAC's leaders sought to consolidate their legitimacy as a new parliament of women. Secure in the terrain of elite national feminist politics, NAC's first president and CEW founder Laura Sabia, along with others of her cohort, asserted parliamentary structures as the most legitimate organizational form. While overtly inclusive in its attempt to encourage "participation," this model privileged and centred hegemonic national, racial, class, and political identities, thus reinforcing a hierarchy of inclusion at the leadership level.

NAC's first newsletter, *Status of Women News,* provides a glimpse into early struggles to produce a sense of governmental belonging through whiteness.

The newsletter's content, which included photos of women parliamentarians and textual emphases on parliamentary activism, reflected parliamentary iconography. Through frequent "suggestions, reminders and guidelines" (NAC 1977b, 9), NAC members were encouraged to participate in formal political channels and in this normative white Canadian identity. Newsletters also honoured and celebrated particular elements of feminist history. "Pioneer feminists" of the first wave were represented in benevolent and familial terms as the women of Canada who, according to one article, "blazed the path from the prairies to Parliament Hill" for "our daughters' future" (NAC 1978, 10).

Further reinforcing these norms of participation were descriptions of NAC that paralleled prevailing white, Eurocentric talk of "two founding nations," which referred to "*the two* ethnic groups" and "*our two* cultures" (NAC 1977a, 4). The initial volume of *Status of Women News,* published in 1974-75, employed this discourse to present NAC's "official" terms of national belonging and participation. In all of these ways, the organization absorbed and projected the era's signature non-racial language of (white) Canadian unity and the liberal mode of pluralist inclusivity. This representational terrain persisted in *Status* until about 1978, at which time a more working-class, grassroots, and movement-based approach emerged.

White feminist modes remained in place at NAC until the mid-1980s (Nadeau 2005). As time passed, socialist and working-class feminists began "playing a more central role in NAC," partly to displace liberal feminist hegemony but also to challenge "the increasingly conservative politics of the federal government" (Findlay 1998, 297; see also Bashevkin 1989; Brodie 1995; Jones and Stephen 1988; Luxton 2001; MacDonald 2002). While this shift did not disrupt NAC's parliamentary framework that had developed since 1972, it helped open the organization's participatory structures by bringing in more movement-based activists and constituent groups (some of which would later form alliances with anti-racist feminism).

**Reconstitution, 1985-92**

With the dramatic shift of the late 1980s, NAC's claims to inclusivity were challenged in unprecedented and foundational ways. Indeed, a new meaning of inclusivity emerged, often expressed in calls for "*real* inclusion" (Roach, in Rebick and Roach 1996, 106) and for making NAC truly representative (NAC 1989). In particular, the organization was increasingly described as a space of systematic racial exclusion and marginalization. Growing challenges to NAC's established governing mode from "historically excluded" women exposed the racialized norm of whiteness that had been able to "pass as the universal figure of leadership" (Puwar 2004, 5).

To grasp the dynamics of this struggle, we need to cast an analytic gaze in two directions: first, towards the emergence of a "national counter-will" in the form of an anti-racist feminist movement; and second, to the managerial response by dominant white feminists to contain it (see Nadeau 2005, ch. 7). The reconstitution period began with the formation, in 1985, of NAC's Visible Minority and Immigrant Women Committee (VMIW), which came out of the 1985 annual general meeting. That session marked a historic moment in the formation of an anti-racist feminist movement within NAC: a "real groundswell became apparent" (NAC 1985c, point 9) as feminists of colour and their allies pressed for the creation of a Standing Committee on Visible Minority Women in Canada (NAC 1985a). This committee became the first legitimate site in NAC's administrative apparatus for organizing and making anti-racist claims.

According to Jon Leah Hopkins, the first chair of the VMIW, "it was tough in those days," and women of colour activists were frequently ignored by the majority of white feminists (quoted in Rebick and Roach 1996, 107). Although the committee's initial focus was external lobbying to address issues of racism in "employment, immigration, housing, education, social aid, place in the economy, earning power and political power" (NAC 1985b, 3), this mandate expanded to critique racism "on the homefront" – NAC itself was brought into the struggle (NAC 1987b, 10).

One year later, delegates to NAC's 1986 annual general meeting voted to launch an organizational review. Their decision can be read in part as a white feminist response to the rise of an anti-racist national counter-will in NAC, which was beginning to make claims on the "national we" (Jones and Stephen 1988, 4). This internal formation was part of a broader terrain in which anti-racist activists were asserting a claim on the national feminist voice, as was reflected in the founding of the National Organization of Immigrant and Visible Minority Women (NOIVMW) as a new umbrella organization. During a period when relations between organized feminism and the Mulroney government grew increasingly tense (Bashevkin 1989), anti-racist feminists were increasingly perceived from within white feminism as a threat to NAC's established mode of national political leadership (Sweet 1987).

In this context, white feminist leaders exercised far more control over NAC's organizational review than did anti-racist feminists. The former's ability to express a managerial "national will" ultimately obscured this white dominance by setting the agenda using a language of inclusivity and diversity rather than racism, and by failing to implement internal affirmative action for categories of identity other than the territorially based ones of region and language. For example, the review initially constructed a representational schema that prioritized Quebec francophone women as having "rightful" claims to NAC leadership. At the same time, it undermined other claims that were generally not territorially based, by lumping together a disparate array of "groups traditionally underrepresented in NAC – women of colour, low income women, disabled women, immigrant and native women" (NAC 1987a, 42).

By 1987, however, women of colour began to consolidate as a national counter-will and staked out claims to leadership in the national space "[a]s the women of Canada" (NAC 1987c, 2). The 1988 NAC annual general meeting was a key turning point in the struggle to overturn white feminism as the only legitimate national leadership voice (Jones and Stephen 1988). The VMIW committee reported that "our voices were heard and we had some impact and success" at this annual general meeting (NAC, VMIW 1988, 14). Indeed, affirmative action guidelines were set in place for the next organizational review committee that included francophones from Quebec and the rest of Canada, as well as visible minority, immigrant, and NAC staff women. The 1988 meeting can therefore be read as a moment of collective "disorientation" for white feminism, as it was displaced by interests that had historically "been constructed out of the imagination of authority" (Puwar 2004, 42).

The 1988 annual meeting was thus remarkable as a decisive moment when a national counter-will effectively implemented the shift to an anti-racist feminist mode of leadership in NAC. Collectively, feminists of colour and their allies successfully asserted a position of governmental belonging and claimed the "national we" as a legitimate space from which to speak. At that point, NAC's leaders could no longer operate under the cover of neutral or non-racial leadership. The persistent anti-racist feminist project of naming normative whiteness as a specific mode was eventually able to undermine and displace that same mode. As part of the larger shift to an extra-parliamentary agenda, the racial politics of participation in NAC were permanently reconfigured and doors opened wider.

## Conclusion

This chapter has offered a general framework for reinterpreting NAC's history in order to illuminate the racial dynamics of organizational participation during NAC's formation and its first twenty years. The following provides a brief sketch of some of the issues that emerged from the implementation of anti-racist feminist practice and multi-racial organizing in the years after 1992. These years correspond with a definitive and sustained displacement of whiteness as the unspoken somatic norm. Extending this analysis into the current period, however, requires a further expansion of analytical terms – none of which can be adequately developed here but are necessary to address new forms of white hegemony and racial exclusion.

Judy Rebick (2002, 74) argues that while many "white middle-class professionals departed" during the 1990s, NAC continued to grow as an important anti-racist, grassroots, extra-parliamentary organization. The 1996 cross-Canada Women's March Against Poverty, organized jointly by NAC and the Canadian Labour Congress, is viewed by many as an exemplary moment in this shift because it "provided access points for women who are working on the grassroots who have never been involved" in national movement organizations (Ladd, as quoted in Robertson 1999, 318). Whiteness as the somatic norm was displaced within NAC and in the public sphere more generally as organizing continued in both the national context and on the world stage via anti-globalization and global justice activism, the 1998 World March of Women, and the 2001 World Conference against Racism.

At the same time, the era could be seen as marking a moment of demobilization for many women of colour, as efforts to mobilize were curtailed by political backlash, cuts to NAC's funding, and the absence of a unifying organizational strategy (Rebick 2002; Robertson 1999). The latter area needs further interrogation and will likely hold many lessons for efforts to reinvigorate and reorganize under the NAC banner.

Scholars have also begun to probe the homogenization of the categories "feminists of colour" and "white feminists." During the period of struggle against white feminism, it was difficult for activists to consider divisions among women of colour. Yet, as a former NAC executive member and anti-racist activist noted in her keynote address to the organization's 2006 annual general meeting, these debates need to occur with respect to questions of sexuality, class, citizenship, and political position (Bain 2006). A more difficult politics of intersectionality, on the ground, needs to be forged in order to open some doors wider and to pass through new ones.

The same meeting was the setting for a difficult debate over the regularization of refugee, migrant, and non-status workers in Canada. The subject was so contentious that a resolution about it barely reached the floor for discussion. These difficult debates reveal the need for an intersectional analysis of race, gender, and national belonging, and they require a new political vocabulary that moves beyond the categories and analyses that have been employed during the past decade.

On the question of citizenship, NAC remains committed to a three-nations approach that views Canada as "three nations or national communities, each of which is multicultural and multiracial: the aboriginal nations, Quebec and the rest of Canada" (Rebick and Roach 1996, 147). While this idea was adopted during a specific moment in the early 1990s as part of an important alliance between NAC and the Native Women's Association of Canada, it was also contested (Sharma 2003; Vickers 2000). The range and bases of this contestation need to be examined, alongside newer debates about national belonging and especially state actions that narrow legitimate claims to citizenship. NAC's work needs to be informed by indigenous peoples' organizing and decolonization struggles, and by Open Borders campaigns that have moved towards the centre of grassroots organizing (Blaney 2003). These two streams sometimes occur in alliances that draw together migrant rights, open borders, and indigenous organizing, while at other times they take place in tension with each other. Indeed, this debate may prove to be the measure of whether NAC can claim to be a truly multi-racial organization.

Finally, it remains to be seen how NAC will evolve on the ideological spectrum. Socialist feminism no longer unites women's movement activists in Canada, as witnessed by the fact that recent NAC meetings have drawn only a small representation of trade union women. Anti-capitalist organizing, however, has emerged as a viable site of movement building and intersects with NAC's efforts since 2006 to challenge federal government directions under the Harper Conservatives. NAC's earlier history of coalition building suggests forms of leadership that not only struggle against hierarchies that divide and exclude women but also take on broader external challenges affecting women in Canada and internationally.

Some of these questions were addressed at the 2006 NAC meeting (NAC 2006). Activists debated the viability of renewal and raised many difficult questions, including how to grapple with organizational leadership, capacity building, and structure. Time will tell whether older debates converge with newer ones as NAC struggles to rebuild a scaled-down organizational structure with few resources and clear demands that it make gains for a fragmented movement in a hostile neoliberal environment (Grant-Cummings 1998; Arat-Koc 2005, 32). Analyzing earlier anti-racist struggles can be instructive as NAC attempts to build alliances and develop a new politics of participation.

**Note**

1 The reception to Sunera Thobani's election itself indicates the strength of the association between whiteness and leadership in Canada's foremost national women's movement organization. Thobani's right to leadership was challenged in the public domain on racial and national terms once she was (inaccurately) identified as an "illegal immigrant." This instance reveals the unsettling dynamic of protecting white governing positions in the national space through the evocation of "racist discourses articulated to the practices of nationalist exclusion" (Hage 2000, 40). It is also a disciplinary move that dissuades other "others" from participating in leadership positions that were historically coded as white.

**References**

Arat-Koc, Sedef. 2005. "The Disciplinary Boundaries of Canadian Identity after September 11: Civilizational Identity, Multiculturalism, and the Challenge of Anti-Imperialist Feminism." *Social Justice* 32, 4: 32-49.

Armstrong, Pat. 1994. "Interview with Judy Rebick." *Studies in Political Economy* 44: 39–71.

Bain, Beverly. 2006. "NAC and the Women's Equality Seeking Movement." Keynote address, *NAC AGM*, 30 September.

Bashevkin, Sylvia. 1989. "Free Trade and Canadian Feminism: The Case of the National Action Committee on the Status of Women." *Canadian Public Policy* 15, 4: 363-75.

Begin, Monique. 1992. "The Royal Commission on the Status of Women in Canada: Twenty Years Later." In *Challenging Times: The Women's Movement in Canada and the United States,* ed. Constance Backhouse and D. H. Flaherty, 21-38. Montreal and Kingston: McGill-Queen's University Press.

Blaney, Fay. 2003. "Aboriginal Women's Action Network." In *Strong Women Stories: Native Vision and Community Survival*, ed., K. Anderson and B. Lawrence, 156-70. Toronto: Sumach Press, 2003.

Brodie, Janine. 1995. *Politics on the Margins: Restructuring and the Canadian Women's Movement.* Halifax: Fernwood Publishing.

CEW (Committee for the Equality of Women). 1966. Minutes. Various dates.

Cohen, Marjorie Griffin. 1993. "The Canadian Women's Movement." In *Canadian Women's Issues*. Vol. 1, *Strong Voices,* ed. Ruth Roach Pierson, Marjorie Griffin Cohen, Paula Bourne, and Philinda Masters, 1-31. Toronto: James Lorimer and Company.

Coomber, Jan. 1997. *Women: Changing Canada.* Don Mills: Oxford University Press Canada.

de Seve, Micheline. 1992. "The Perspectives of Quebec Feminists." In *Challenging Times: The Women's Movement in Canada and the United States,* ed. Constance Backhouse and D.H. Flaherty, 110-16. Montreal and Kingston: McGill-Queen's University Press.

Dobrowolsky, Alexandre. 2000. *The Politics of Pragmatism: Women, Representation and Constitutionalism in Canada.* Don Mills: Oxford University Press.

Dumont, Micheline. 1992. "The Origins of the Women's Movement in Quebec." In *Challenging Times: The Women's Movement in Canada and the United States,* ed. Constance Backhouse and D.H. Flaherty, 72-89. Montreal and Kingston: McGill-Queen's University Press.

Findlay, Sue. 1998. "Representation and the Struggle for Women's Equality: Issues for Feminist Practice." In *Women and Political Representation in Canada,* ed. Manon Tremblay and Caroline Andrew, 293-310. Ottawa: University of Ottawa Press.

Freeman, Barbara. 2001. *The Satellite Sex: The Media and Women's Issues in English Canada, 1966-1971.* Waterloo: Wilfrid Laurier University Press.

Gabriel, Christina. 1996. "One or the Other? 'Race,' Gender, and the Limits of Official Multiculturalism." In *Women and Canadian Public Policy,* ed. Janine Brodie, 173-98. Toronto: Harcourt Brace.

Gottlieb, Amy, ed. 1993. "What about Us? Organizing Inclusively in the National Action Committee on the Status of Women." In *And Still We Rise: Feminist Political Mobilizing in Contemporary Canada,* ed. Linda Carty, 371-85. Toronto: Women's Press.

Grant-Cummings, Joan. 1998. "The Global Capitalist Economic Agenda: Impact on Women's Human Rights." *Canadian Woman Studies* 18, 1 (Spring 1998): 6-10.

Greaves, Lorraine. 1991. "Reorganizing the National Action Committee on the Status of Women 1986-1988." In *Women and Social Change: Feminist Activism in Canada,* ed. Jeri Dawn Wine and J.L. Ristock, 101-16. Toronto: James Lorimer and Company.

Hage, Ghassan. 2000. *White Nation: Fantasies of White Supremacy in a Multicultural Society.* New York: Routledge.

Huang, Agnes, and Fatima Jaffer. 1993. "Interview with Judy Rebick: It's Been a Slice." *Kinesis* (June): 10-11.

Jhappan, Radha. 1996. "Post-Modern Race and Gender Essentialism or a Post-Mortem of Scholarship." *Studies in Political Economy* 51 (Fall): 15-63.

Jones, Miriam, and Jennifer Stephen. 1988. "Tempest in a Teapot: NAC Annual General Meeting." *Rebel Girls Rag* 2, 4: 4-5.

Knowles, Caroline. 2003. *Race and Social Analysis.* London: Sage.

Lee, Jo-Anne, and Linda Cardinal. 1998. "Hegemonic Nationalism and the Politics of Feminism and Multiculturalism in Canada." In *Painting the Maple: Essays on Race, Gender, and the Construction of Canada,* ed. Veronica Strong-Boag, Joan Anderson, Sherrill Grace, and Avigail Eisenberg, 215-41. Vancouver: UBC Press.

Luxton, Meg. 2001. "Feminism as a Class Act: Working-Class Feminism and the Women's Movement in Canada." *Labour/Le Travail* 48 (Fall): 63-88.

MacDonald, Laura. 2002. "Globalization and Social Movements: Comparing Women's Movements' Responses to NAFTA in Mexico, the USA and Canada." *International Feminist Journal of Politics* 4, 2: 151-72.

McCall, Leslie. 2005. "The Complexity of Intersectionality." *Signs* 30, 3: 1771-800.
Molgat, Anne, with additions by Joan Grant-Cummings. 1992. "'An Action That Will Not Be Allowed to Subside': NAC's First Twenty Years." Toronto: National Action Committee on the Status of Women, 1992.
–. 1997. "'An Action That Will Not Be Allowed to Subside': NAC's First Twenty-Five Years." National Action Committee on the Status of Women. http://www.nac-cca.ca/about/his_e.htm.
Morris, Cerise. 1982. "No More Than Simple Justice: The Royal Commission on the Status of Women and Social Change in Canada." PhD diss., McGill University.
Mukherjee, Arun. 1992. "A House Divided: Women of Colour and American Feminist Theory." In *Challenging Times: The Women's Movement in Canada and the United States,* ed. Constance Backhouse and D.H. Flaherty, 165-74. Montreal and Kingston: McGill-Queen's University Press.
NAC (National Action Committee on the Status of Women). 1977a. *Status of Women News* (May): 4.
–. 1977b. *Status of Women News* (July): 9.
–. 1978. *Status of Women News* (March): 10.
–. 1985a. "Memo." Executive Board. 14 June.
–. 1985b. "NAC Adopts Committee Membership Policy, Third World, Visible Minority Committees." *Feminist Action Feministe* 1, 1 (July): 3.
–. 1985c. "Memo." Table Officers. 18 July.
–. 1986. "President's Report." *AGM Annual Report.* May-June.
–. 1987a. "Committee Report." Organizational Review. April.
–. 1987b. "AGM Annual Report." Visible Minority and Immigrant Women Committee. May.
–. 1987c. "Fighting Racism Is '80s Biggest Challenge, Sims [sic] Says." *Feminist Action Feministe* 2, 5 (July): 2.
–. 1989. "Minutes." Executive Board Meeting. November.
–. 1990. "Report." Annual General Meeting. May.
NAC. Visible Minority and Immigrant Women. 1988. *Feminist Action Feministe* 3, 4, and 5 (September): 14.
–. 1989. "NAC Committee Reports." *Feminist Action Feministe* 3, 6 (April): 3.
Nadeau, Mary-Jo. 2005. "The Making and Unmaking of a Parliament of Women: Nation, Race and the Politics of the National Action Committee on the Status of Women, 1972-1992." PhD diss., York University.
–. Forthcoming. "'Enterprising Nationals': The Committee for the Equality of Women of Canada and the Racial Politics of Managed Dissent in the Women's Movement." In *Debating Dissent: Canada and the Sixties,* ed. G. Kealey, D. Clément, and L. Campbell. Toronto: University of Toronto Press.
Persad, Judy Vashti. 1992. "Let the Links Be Made." *Feminist Action Feministe* 6, 2: 8-9, 12.
Puwar, Nirmal. 2004. *Space Invaders: Race, Gender and Bodies Out of Place.* Oxford: Berg Publishers, 2004.
Rebick, Judy. 2002. "Disappearing Act." *Elm Street* (Summer): 74.
–. 2005. *Ten Thousand Roses: The Making of a Feminist Revolution.* Toronto: Penguin Canada.
Rebick, Judy, and Kike Roach. 1996. *Politically Speaking.* Vancouver: Douglas and McIntyre.
Robertson, Angela. 1999. "Continuing on the Ground: Feminists of Colour Discuss Organizing." In *Scratching the Surface: Canadian Anti-Racist Feminist Thought,* ed. E. Dua and A. Robertson, 309-29. Toronto: Women's Press.
St. Lewis, Joanne. 1997. "The Entire Woman: Immigrant and Visible-Minority Women." In *Women and the Canadian State,* ed. Caroline Andrew and Sanda Rodgers, 262-67. Montreal and Kingston: McGill-Queen's University Press.
Sharma, Nandita. 2003. "No Borders Movements and the Rejection of Left Nationalism." *Canadian Dimension* 37, 3 (May-June): 37-39.
Ship, Susan Judith. 1998. "Problematizing Ethnicity and 'Race' in Feminist Scholarship on Women and Politics." In *Women and Political Representation in Canada,* ed. Manon Tremblay and Caroline Andrew, 311-40. Ottawa: University of Ottawa Press.

Shohat, Ella, ed. 1998. *Talking Visions: Multicultural Feminism in a Transnational Age.* New York: MIT Press.
Simms, Glenda. 1992. "Beyond the White Veil." In *Challenging Times: The Women's Movement in Canada and the United States,* ed. Constance Backhouse and D.H. Flaherty, 175-81. Montreal and Kingston: McGill-Queen's University Press.
Stasiulis, Daiva. 1999. "Relational Positionalities of Nationalisms, Racisms, and Feminisms." In *Between Woman and Nation: Nationalisms, Transnational Feminisms, and the State,* ed. Caren Kaplan, Norma Alarcon, and Minoo Moallem, 182-218. Durham: Duke University Press.
Sweet, Lois. 1987. "Minority Women's Group Welcome." *Toronto Star,* 23 January: B2.
Taylor, Rupert. 1996. "Political Science Encounters 'Race' and 'Ethnicity.'" *Ethnic and Racial Studies* 19, 4 (October): 884-95.
Tremblay, Manon, and Caroline Andrew, eds. 1998. *Women and Political Representation in Canada.* Ottawa: University of Ottawa Press.
Turpel-Lafond, Mary Ellen. 1997. "Patriarchy and Paternalism: The Legacy of the Canadian State for First Nations Women." In *Women and the Canadian State,* ed. Caroline Andrew and Sanda Rodgers, 64-78. Montreal and Kingston: McGill-Queen's University Press.
–. 2000. "Feminisms and Nationalisms in English Canada." *Journal of Canadian Studies* 35, 2 (Summer): 128-48.
Vickers, Jill. 1991. "Bending the Iron Law of Oligarchy: Debates on the Feminization of Organization and Political Process in the English Canadian Women's Movement, 1970-1988." In *Women and Social Change: Feminist Activism in Canada,* ed. Jeri Dawn Wine and J. Ristock, 75-94. Toronto: J. Lorimer and Company, 1991.
–. 1992. "The Intellectual Origins of the Women's Movements in Canada." In *Challenging Times: The Women's Movement in Canada and the United States,* ed. Constance Backhouse and D.H. Flaherty, 39-60. Montreal and Kingston: McGill-Queen's University Press.
Vickers, Jill, Pauline Rankin, and Christine Appelle. 1993. *Politics as if Women Mattered: A Political Analysis of the National Action Committee on the Status of Women.* Toronto: University of Toronto Press.
Vosko, Leah F. 2003. "The Pasts (and Futures) of Feminist Political Economy in Canada: Reviving the Debate." In *Studies in Political Economy: Developments in Feminism,* ed. Caroline Andrew, Pat Armstrong, Hugh Armstrong, Wallace Clement, and Leah F. Vosko, 305-32. Toronto: Women's Press.
Williams, Fiona. 1998. "Reflections on the Intersections of Social Relations in the New Political Economy." *Studies in Political Economy* 55 (Spring): 173-90.
Williams, Toni. 1990. "Re-Forming 'Women's' Truth: A Critique of the Report of the Royal Commission on the Status of Women in Canada." *Ottawa Law Review* 22, 3: 726-59.
Wilmot, Sheila. 2005. *Taking Responsibility, Taking Direction: White Anti-Racism in Canada.* Winnipeg: Arbeiter Ring Publishing.

# Part 2
# Winning Legislative Seats

# 4

# Women in the Quebec National Assembly: Why So Many?

*Manon Tremblay, with the assistance of Stephanie Mullen*

Writing in 1994, Wilma Rule laid out the case for electoral system barriers to women's political participation. In her words, "Electoral systems explain almost 30 percent of the varying proportions of women in democracies' national legislatures. 'Woman-friendly' electoral systems are very significant but insufficient for explaining women's successes. Sixty percent is generally due to political, socioeconomic, and cultural factors, while 10 percent is unexplained. However, favorable societal conditions will not substitute for unfavorable electoral systems relative to women reaching their optimum representation in parliament" (Rule 1994, 16).

The case of Quebec is particularly intriguing in light of this statement. In fact, despite first-past-the-post (FPTP) or single-member plurality (SMP) election rules, 32 percent of the members of the National Assembly (MNAs) in that province in 2006 were women.[1] With roughly one-third female members, Quebec's legislature can, according to a classification system established by the Inter-Parliamentary Union, be compared with some of the most feminized nation-state parliaments in the world, including those of Germany (31.6 percent), New Zealand (32.2 percent), and Iceland (31.7 percent) (Inter-Parliamentary Union 2008). Quebec is also not far behind the nation-state front-runners (for several decades) in women's legislative representation, namely Sweden (47 percent), Norway (37.9 percent), Finland (42 percent), and Denmark (36.9 percent). Unlike Quebec, which employs FPTP rules, all of the countries that have national parliaments composed of at least 30 percent women mix FPTP with proportional or list proportional voting systems for legislative elections.[2]

Applying Rule's observation to the situation in Quebec raises the following question. Are political, socioeconomic, and cultural circumstances in Quebec so formidable as to compensate for a voting method that limits women's election to parliament? How, in short, can we explain women's success in winning National Assembly seats?

The objective of this chapter is to explain the relatively high proportion of women in Quebec's National Assembly, despite the use of FPTP rules that are reputedly unfavourable to such an outcome. The hypothesis that animates this discussion attributes women's success in Quebec to a high turnover rate of MNAs and to a willingness among political parties to position women candidates in competitive constituencies. In addition, in another article Rule (1987) suggests that women's political mobilization may overcome certain impediments that electoral systems sometimes raise against the election of women. We believe that this partially explains the presence of women in the Quebec National Assembly; that is, for decades women have been a relevant constituency for both the federalist Parti libéral du Québec (PLQ) and the independentist Parti Québécois (PQ). We will first paint a broad portrait of the factors affecting women's access to legislatures. The goal of this section is to identify relevant circumstances and contribute a more comparative perspective on the Quebec case, notably to identify what conditions appear to favour women's election to the National Assembly. We then describe the methodology of this study, present the results of our analysis of the electoral results, and, in conclusion, attempt to explain women's unexpectedly high representation as MNAs.

## Review of the Literature

Researchers in this area have identified three main groups of factors affecting women's participation: cultural, socioeconomic, and political. The first group of factors, cultural, is seen as being superimposed on the other two factors, since culture comprises society's values, beliefs, and attitudes (Paxton and Kunovich 2003). They, in turn, affect the social views of women, as well as the structure of parties and other political institutions. In fact, many studies have shown that religion, education, and views about women's roles are key variables shaping the proportion of women in a given parliament (see Inglehart 1981; Inglehart and Norris 2003, 140-41; Mateo Diaz 2005, 64; Norris 1985, 1997a; Norris and Inglehart 2001; Nowacki 2003; Paxton 1997; Peschard 2003; Reynolds 1999; Rule 1987; Saint-Germain 1994).

The second group of factors influencing engagement is socioeconomic, since occupation, education, and income directly affect women's ability to volunteer in party organizations, run as candidates, and hold public office. Darcy, Welch, and Clark (1994, 104-5) explain women's political underrepresentation with reference to their limited numbers in affluent socioeconomic circles that provide a primary recruitment pool for legislative candidates. According to Norris and Lovenduski (1995, 14-15), the supply of women candidates should be greater in post-industrial than agricultural or industrial societies since the former offer opportunities based more on knowledge and education than on physical strength. Research supports this conclusion and identifies other related variables, including robust social policy provision via a well-developed welfare state (see Matland 1998, 2005; Moore and Shackman 1996; Norris 1985, 1987, 122; 2004, 186; Oakes and Almquist 1993; Reynolds 1999; Rosenbluth, Salmond, and Thies 2006; Rule 1987, 1988; Siaroff 2000; United Nations Office at Vienna 1992, 30-31).

The final group of explanatory factors is political, and they include both the political rights of women that enable them to be selected as legislative candidates and the political regime that enables women candidates to be elected to a legislature. When examining political rights, one key indicator stands out – namely the year women were enfranchised at the national level. As a general trend, the longer women have had the right to vote in a national election, the higher their proportion in parliament (Kenworthy and Malami 1999; Mateo Diaz 2005, 67; McAllister and Studlar 2002; Norris 2004, 186; Siaroff 2000; United Nations Office at Vienna 1992, 99). Research on the political regime dimension suggests that voting systems, party systems, and structures of parliament matter to women's participation. For participation, the type of voting system, the characteristics of electoral districts, and whether party lists are open (voters can reorder names on the party list) are important voting system characteristics. Significant party system variables include how candidates are selected, the number of parties contesting elections, and the ideology of the party or parties that form the government. Studies that examine the structure of parliament have considered the number of seats in a legislature and the maximum length of a government term.

Voting systems have, without a doubt, generated the richest literature on proportions of women in legislative assemblies (for a summary of these studies, see Tremblay 2008). Parliaments elected by proportional representation (PR) generally have higher percentages of women members than those based on FPTP systems (Matland 2005; McAllister and Studlar 2002; Norris 2004, 187; Paxton 1997; Reynolds, Reilly, and Ellis 2005, 60-61; Rule 1987, 1994; Rule and Norris 1992; Sawer 1997; Squires and Wickham-Jones 2001, 10). Nonetheless, there are many nuances in the association between PR and women's presence in parliaments (Darcy, Welch, and Clark 1994, 147; Kunovich and Paxton 2005; Mateo Diaz 2005, 51, 81; Salmond 2006).

Two mechanisms in a PR voting system have been found to influence women's ability to be elected. The first is the threshold of representation; the second is district magnitude. When parties require a significant share of votes in order to win seats, the threshold of representation is high and fewer parties hold parliamentary seats than when the threshold is low. Since each party in a high threshold legislature has a good share of seats, they tend to assign significant numbers of seats to women (Matland 2003, 2005; Mateo Diaz 2005, 87-93; Meier 2005).[3] District magnitude (the number of parliamentary seats per constituency) also influences women's ability to win in a

PR voting system. Simply put, the more candidate openings that exist in an election, the more opportunities there are for women to win (Engstrom 1987; Matland 1993; Matland and Brown 1992; Reynolds, Reilly, and Ellis 2005, 121; Rule 1987; Studlar and Welch 1991).

Parties play a key role in electing women to legislatures: they are the gatekeepers responsible for selecting candidates. Matland and Montgomery (2003, 31-32) report that electoral systems influence party strategies for candidate nomination, which in turn affect female parliamentary representation. Indeed, David Farrell (2001, 167) argues that "it is not the electoral system which is at fault [for the under-representation of women in parliaments] so much as the party selection committees" (see also Gallagher 2005; Norris et al. 1990).

Unlike in the United States, where open primaries give parties little control over candidate selection, Westminster-style systems in countries such as Australia, Britain, and Canada give political parties a great deal of control over candidate nominations. The amount of influence a party has in candidate nominations therefore varies greatly according to the voting system and its particular characteristics (Carey and Shugart 1995; Norris 1997b). Several studies suggest that a standardized and centralized selection process for party candidates may increase the number of women nominees each party puts forward because it eases the ability of parties to adopt positive action or affirmative action measures that encourage women to run and quotas that mandate percentages of women candidates. Centralized nominations permit party leaders to impose their will on both uncooperative local constituency organizations as well as on maverick legislators, who risk not being renominated if they cross swords with party elites (Caul Kittilson 2006, 127; Matland and Studlar 1996; Norris 1992; Pitre 2003; Randall 1982, 141-42). Similarly, in terms of participation, centralized selection processes offer central party executives as an obvious target for the lobbying efforts of women's movements.

Conversely, decentralized selection processes may help to explain low proportions of women elected. In Canada, the existence of one of the world's most decentralized selection arrangements predicts few women in Parliament (Sayers 1999). Yet, in 2006, the Canadian House of Commons had slightly more women than its British counterpart (20.8 percent versus 19.7 percent) – even though considerably more centralized nomination practices were employed in the United Kingdom.

An important element in understanding the proportion of women in the Canadian House of Commons is the parliamentary turnover rate. Upon analyzing more than 116 elections in 25 democracies between 1973 and 1994, Richard Matland and Donley Studlar (2004) found that, on average, two-thirds of incumbent parliamentarians won re-election. However, Canada had the lowest re-election rate for incumbent legislators, 53 percent, compared with 85 percent in the US Congress between 1980 and 1994, 80 percent in the Australian parliament between 1980 and 1993, and 76 percent in the British House of Commons between 1979 and 1992. Although the Progressive Conservative Party was reduced to only two seats in 1993, which dramatically depressed incumbent re-election levels, Canadian general elections during the twentieth century resulted in an average of only 60 percent of veteran MPs returning to the House of Commons (Laponce 1994). Canada's high turnover rate has led many scholars to conclude that the House of Commons is characterized by low levels of parliamentary professionalism or, conversely, high levels of amateurism (Atkinson and Docherty 1992; Docherty 1997, 36-59; 2002; Franks 1987, 72-79).

This same pattern may explain the relatively high percentage of women MPs. In a text published in 1991, Lisa Young argued that high turnover and low incumbency rates offered women an opportunity to step into the Canadian House of Commons, an opportunity that was not available to the same extent in the United States, the United Kingdom, or Australia (see also Norris 1996). Young (1991) adds, however, that institutional factors alone cannot bring gender parity to the Canadian House of Commons, since the supply of and demand for candidates is also relevant. Seats in Parliament may be available, but women need to manifest a desire to occupy them (by first considering a candidacy and then deciding to run; see Lawless and Fox 2005) and political parties must be willing to consider seriously their candidacies. A mobilized and parliamentary-focused women's movement, which Mary-Jo Nadeau's chapter indicates NAC was, to some degree, during its early years, can clearly stimulate both the supply of and demand for female candidates. Moreover, voters must elect women candidates.

This chapter examines the following hypothesis: the relatively strong presence of women in Quebec's National Assembly follows from a high parliamentary turnover rate and parties' willingness to position women candidates in competitive constituencies. Parties may be willing to nominate women candidates in winnable seats because this is a low-cost way of signalling to the female electorate that parties are sensitive to the concerns of those voters. Significant legislative representation may also follow from women's movement mobilization on the electoral scene. Before examining this hypothesis, we present the methodology behind our research and briefly describe the voting system used to elect MNAs.

## Methodology

Like most other Canadian legislatures, the Quebec National Assembly uses the FPTP system, in which candidates win if they receive the largest number of valid votes cast in their constituency. First past the post is also known as single-member plurality, since only one candidate is elected per constituency and that candidate usually holds a plurality rather than a majority of the votes cast. First past the post is often seen as unfavourable to women because its recruitment and candidate selection processes require a supply of female candidates and a demand for them from the parties (Norris and Lovenduski 1995, 14-15). The supply of women candidates depends on their ability to contest party nominations in winnable seats; they must have particular cultural and socioeconomic attributes in order to be noticed, recruited, and seen as credible by parties and voters.

In the context of Quebec, background factors favour women's access to parliamentary representation. Alhough traditional Catholicism long distanced women from political life relative to the rest of Canada and led to far later enfranchisement in Quebec than in other provinces (Tremblay 2005, 19-82), contemporary Quebec is, for the most part, a modern, secular society in which church and state are clearly separated. In terms of higher education, women have taken huge steps in the past two decades, so much so that, in 2001, 16.7 percent of Quebec women (as compared to 17.1 percent of their male counterparts) held a university certificate or degree (Government of Quebec, Institut de la statistique 2003a). Quebec culture clearly is also open to gender equality in attitudinal terms. In a November 2004 survey by Environics, which was based on a sample of 3,200 Canadians, 92 percent of Quebec interviewees endorsed increased numbers of women political leaders as a way to improve governance.

In Quebec, the rate of employment of women in 2007 was 57.2 percent (Government of Quebec, Institut de la statistique 2008). Although females constituted 46 percent of the members in good standing of the Quebec bar, most working women were not in law or other so-called trampoline professions to a political career (Barreau du Québec 2008).[4] Instead, most held traditional clerical and other low-paid jobs, often on a part-time basis (Government of Quebec, Institut de la statistique 2003b). The average income for part-time and full-time working women in Quebec in 2005 was only 67.5 percent that of working men (Government of Quebec, Institut de la statistique 2007). However, this gap was not much different from elsewhere, including in Denmark, where women's income was 71 percent of men's. The percentages for Iceland were 63 percent, for Norway, 65 percent, and for New Zealand and Sweden, 68 percent (PNUD 2001, Table 23). This last group of countries had relatively high proportions of women parliamentarians and used PR or mixed voting systems. In short, Quebec's cultural and socioeconomic context generally favoured women's legislative presence.[5]

Parties express their openness towards women via their recruitment, nomination, and selection processes. The FPTP voting system used for Quebec legislative elections implies that each political party nominates one candidate per constituency, unlike in list PR systems where each party offers several names per electoral district. In Quebec, the local constituency association is expected to select a candidate who is most acceptable to the largest number of voters. In this scenario, not all candidates are equal since not all pass what researchers refer to as the *homo politicus* test (see Norris and Lovenduski 1989; Reynolds, Reilly, and Ellis 2005, 37, 61). An informal sense of who is a winning candidate informs gatekeepers or recruiters in local constituency associations: as they choose the person who will represent their organization on election day, partisans may avoid diverse candidates, including women. But the relatively high proportion of women in the National Assembly suggests that gatekeepers in Quebec are sympathetic rather than hostile to female candidates.

This study used a quantitative methodology to analyze electoral competition in provincial constituencies in the general elections of 1976, 1981, 1985, 1989, 1994, 1998 and 2003.[6] Which parties ran against one another, and what were the competitive circumstances of the Parti libéral du Québec (PLQ) and the Parti Québécois (PQ)? Our decision to begin the analysis in 1976 follows from the fact that multiple women (five to be precise) were elected as MNAs in that year. Moreover, the 1976 election crystallized an electoral realignment that had been in gestation since the early 1970s and continues to mark the Quebec political scene (at least until the 2007 elections). Not only did the Union Nationale disappear, but also the PQ was elected to power. Thus began an alternation in office of the PLQ and the PQ that generally follows a cycle of every two general elections. This study only considers PLQ and PQ candidates. Of the 144 women MNAs elected between 1976 and 2003, all but one belonged to the PLQ or the PQ.[7] From 1976 until 2003, Liberals and Péquistes monopolized 97.3 percent of National Assembly seats. These two parties, in short, held the keys to open the doors to legislative participation by women.[8]

In questioning why, despite a voting system reputed to be disadvantageous, roughly a third of the MNAs are female, we divided all legislative candidates into winners and losers and asked, what particular features characterized women MNAs? Our analysis compares winning female and male candidates and losing female and male candidates. We analyze the losing candidates to establish if, as we sometimes hear, disproportionate numbers of women run in especially difficult constituencies for their parties (as compared with unsuccessful male candidates). Data on party, percentage of valid votes obtained, sex of candidate, and the win or loss in the seat were collected for each Quebec constituency in each election and for each Liberal or PQ candidate between 1976 and 2003.

As Table 4.1 indicates, a total of 317 PLQ and PQ female candidates ran as candidates during this period, compared with 1,344 male candidates.[9] Men thus monopolized 80.9 percent of Liberal and Péquiste candidacies for the period 1976-2003; however, the proportion of male candidates declined from 94.8 percent in 1976 to 69 percent in 2003. Of the women candidates, 143 became MNAs, for a success rate of 45.1 percent (143/317).[10] Men's success

*Table 4.1*

**Success rates of PLQ and PQ candidates in Quebec elections, by sex and status, 1976-2003***

| | Women | | | Men | | |
|---|---|---|---|---|---|---|
| Status | *N* | Elected | Success rate (%) | *N* | Elected | Success rate (%) |
| Challengers | 139 | 23 | 16.5 | 533 | 142 | 26.6 |
| Dissidents | 34 | 11 | 32.3 | 122 | 57 | 46.7 |
| Inheritors | 49 | 29 | 59.2 | 141 | 76 | 53.9 |
| *Sub-total* | *222* | *63* | *28.4* | *796* | *275* | *34.5* |
| Incumbents | 95 | 80 | 84.2 | 548 | 413 | 75.4 |
| *Total* | *317* | *143* | *45.1* | *1,344* | *688* | *51.2* |

* $p \leq .05$.

rate was 6 percent higher. The proportion of winning female candidates to losing female candidates was thus within a plus or minus 5 percent margin of the half and half point, since 45.1 percent of PLQ and PQ female candidates won seats in the National Assembly while 54.9 percent (174/317) lost their bids for election (Quebec National Assembly 2004).[11]

## Parliamentary Turnover and Competition

Previous studies argue that low rates of parliamentary turnover impede women's access to parliamentary office (see, for example, Norris 1993; Schwindt-Bayer 2005; Thompson and Moncrief 1993). However, as noted above, turnover is relatively high in both the Canadian House of Commons and the Canadian provincial legislatures (Moncrief 1998). As Matland and Studlar (2004) observe, MPs may leave their seats voluntarily because they do not seek a new mandate or resign between elections, or they may resign their seats involuntarily because of death or, more frequently, electoral defeat. Women candidates can take advantage of voluntary departures by stating their interest in seeking a given seat.[12] If the party has been successful in that constituency, the woman candidate can hope to inherit a strong constituency association and a robust volunteer base (Pelletier and Tremblay 1992).

How powerful is incumbency in Quebec provincial politics? Do female MNAs come disproportionately from constituencies in which their party's previous candidate was also an MNA? On average, 61 percent of MNAs who sought another term between 1976 and 2003 were re-elected.[13] This means that each legislative sitting contained about 40 percent new faces during this period, which is comparable to the percentage at the Canadian federal level (Laponce 1994) but high by international standards (Matland and

Studlar 2004). The highest proportions of new MNAs of both genders arrived with changes in government, including in 1976 when the PQ won its first majority. The lowest percentage of new MNAs, 17 percent, was elected in 1998. New MNAs often had to defeat the other party's incumbent, although some inherited a constituency left vacant by the retirement of an MNA from their own party.[14]

Table 4.1 shows the success rate of Liberal and Péquiste candidates in elections from 1976 to 2003. They are grouped by sex and status, with the status category divided among incumbents, inheritors (candidates who inherited a constituency left vacant by an MNA from their own party), dissidents (candidates who ran against inheritors), and challengers (candidates who ran against incumbents).

Not surprisingly, success rates for both women and men varied according to status: incumbents had the highest success rates and challengers the lowest. For non-incumbents, the best way to become an MNA was to run as an inheritor candidate. Women were advantaged on two levels. First, of the 222 female candidates who were not incumbents, 22 percent (49) ran as inheritors compared with 17.7 percent (141/796) of the male candidates. Second, the success rate of female inheritors was 59.2 percent (29/49) compared to 53.9 percent for male inheritors (76/141). Although the proportion of female and male dissidents was the same at 15 percent, proportionately fewer women than men ran against incumbents when first elected to the legislature.

The data also show that female MNAs and inheritor candidates were significantly more likely to win than their male counterparts, although men were significantly more successful as dissidents and challengers. These results do not confirm the view that women are more likely than men to run in lost-cause constitutencies, since, if that were true, female inheritors would not have been more likely to win than their male counterparts. On the other hand, lower success rates among women challengers and dissidents may indicate that, in certain circumstances, female candidates are discriminated against by parties and voters.

One way to explore this issue more deeply is to examine the composition of individual consitutencies in which women and men ran for office. Clearly, open seats vary in the degree to which they are competitive for parties; we therefore distinguish among seats, using the margin of victory in the last election (measured by the percentage of votes separating PLQ and PQ candidates) and the past performance of the party in that constituency in the three previous general elections.[15] These criteria allowed us to identify the three types of constitutencies that candidates can inherit – safe, winnable, and marginal – which are distinguished by their differing levels of competitiveness (for further details, see appendix at end of chapter).

*Table 4.2*

**Win/loss margin in previous elections for PLQ and PQ candidates, by sex and status, 1976-2003**

| | Winners | | | | Losers | | | |
|---|---|---|---|---|---|---|---|---|
| | Women | *(N)* | Men | *(N)* | Women | *(N)* | Men | *(N)* |
| Challengers | 15.4% | (22) | 15.2% | (132) | 21.3% | (110) | 22.1% | (362) |
| Dissidents | 9.9% | (11) | 14.0% | (56) | 20.7% | (21) | 25.6% | (65) |
| Inheritors | 21.8% | (22) | 25.2% | (64) | 7.3%* | (17) | 15.4% | (50) |

* $p \leq .01$.

As Table 4.2 shows, women seeking their first term in the National Assembly did not benefit from running in highly winnable constituencies, but men did. The same pattern held among female dissidents and challengers, who did not necessarily run where their party had been weak in the last election. However, female inheritors who lost experienced more disadvantageous conditions than their male counterparts; that is, unsuccessful women inheritors ran for parties whose average margin of victory in the last election was 7.3 percent. In contrast, unsuccessful male inheritors ran for parties whose average margin of victory in the last election was 15.4 percent. In fact, more than a third (35.4 percent or 6/17) of female inheritors who lost, compared with only 18 percent (9/50) of men in that category, ran in constituencies in which their party's last margin of victory was less than 5 percent. Moreover, even after removing these six cases with a narrow margin from the analysis, female inheritors remained significantly disadvantaged relative to male inheritors.

What particular electoral conditions were experienced by "sacrificial lamb" female candidates? In every case, they inherited a constituency nomination for the wrong party, the party likely to end up in opposition after the next election. These sacrificial lamb candidates included two PQ candidates in 1985 (when the PLQ returned to power), seven Liberal candidates in 1994 (when the PQ won), and eight Péquistes in 2003 (when the Liberals won). Six of these seventeen female inheritors faced a star male candidate running for the other party, while three confronted races that involved a third party, the ADQ – which pushed female PQ candidates into third place. Clearly, these women inheritors inherited a Trojan horse rather than a safe legislative seat.

If we consider the margins of victory that parties had from previous elections, we find that female inheritors did not benefit disproportionately from contesting strong open seats. As Table 4.3 demonstrates, women who lost seats their parties had won in the past experienced a double disadvantage: first, their parties had a significantly weaker margin of victory in the last

*Table 4.3*

**Competitiveness of open seats for PLQ and PQ candidates, by sex and status, 1976-2003**

| | Winners | | | | Losers | | | |
|---|---|---|---|---|---|---|---|---|
| | Women | *(N)* | Men | *(N)* | Women | *(N)* | Men | *(N)* |
| Inheritors | | | | | | | | |
| Safe | 89.7% | (26) | 90.8% | (69) | 20.0%* | (4) | 36.9% | (24) |
| Winnable | 10.3% | (3) | 9.2% | (7) | 80.0% | (16) | 63.1% | (41) |
| Dissidents | | | | | | | | |
| Winnable | 100.0% | (11) | 82.5% | (47) | 13.0% | (3) | 10.8% | (7) |
| Marginal | 0.0% | (0) | 17.5% | (10) | 87.0% | (20) | 89.2% | (58) |

* $p = .13$.

election than did the parties of male inheritors; and second, few women were nominated in the most promising inheritor seats. In contrast, women dissidents who won all ran for office where they had the best chances of winning, where they were not constrained by the usual norms of party recruitment and deference to a party incumbent.

As is shown in Table 4.4, female and male challengers ran against similarly experienced incumbents; for example, the women did not confront unusually secure MNAs. Nonetheless, female challengers who won were slightly less likely than their male counterparts to run against an MNA with modest legislative experience. On the other side of the spectrum, female challengers who lost ran against less experienced incumbents than did the male challengers who lost. The former often confronted a novice MP with only one term of service in the National Assembly.

Finally, first-past-the-post rules are such that, in situations where PQ and PLQ women run against each other, the result will, at most, result in one woman being elected. If, on the other hand, these two women candidates campaigned in different constituencies, they could, theoretically, both sit as

*Table 4.4*

**Number of incumbent MNA terms facing challenger PLQ and PQ candidates, 1976-2003**

| | Winners | | | | Losers | | | |
|---|---|---|---|---|---|---|---|---|
| | Women | *(N)* | Men | *(N)* | Women | *(N)* | Men | *(N)* |
| One | 40.9% | (9) | 52.0% | (66) | 67.0% | (77) | 57.8% | (218) |
| Two | 50.0% | (11) | 37.0% | (47) | 15.7% | (18) | 23.3% | (88) |
| Three or more | 9.1% | (2) | 11.0% | (14) | 17.4% | (20) | 18.8% | (71) |

MNAs. In other words, maximizing the odds of electing female candidates in Quebec requires that women not run against each other. Of the 830 candidacies analyzed in this study, only 36 (or 4.3 percent) involved Liberal and Péquiste women contesting the same seat in the same election. This very low percentage provides another reason for the relatively high percentage of women MNAs.

## Conclusion

What circumstances advantage women in Quebec provincial politics? The results of this study support the hypothesis that high rates of legislative turnover combined with the positioning of female candidates in competitive constituencies help to explain the relatively strong representation of women in the National Assembly. With an average of nearly 40 percent of new faces in the legislative chamber after each election between 1976 and 2003, the National Assembly had a high turnover of members when compared with the British House of Commons or the US House of Representatives.

Moreover, most Liberal and Péquiste women who sought seats ran in competitive constituencies that, from a statistical point of view, offered the same potential for winning as did the constituencies in which men ran. Although a subset of female candidates were inheritors who, in almost one-third of cases, contested seats in which the competitive circumstances were not promising (because their party's margin of victory in the preceding elections was narrow or because the party was unlikely to win the election), female inheritors as a group were more successful in elections than male inheritors.

What can we conclude? First, our data disconfirm arguments that women were more likley than men to contest lost-cause constituencies. This conclusion echoes Studlar and Matland's (1996) finding from a study of more than eleven thousand Canadian provincial candidacies between 1975 and 1994. However, the fact that a third of women inheritors in Quebec experienced conditions that made their election improbable leads us to view the PLQ and PQ as still somewhat resistant to the full integration of women, especially if women aspire to be MNAs or party leaders (on the PQ, see Praud 2003).

In some provinces, including Ontario, women have led mainstream parties that had a reasonable chance of winning power, although the norm has been for them to lead less competitive parties (see chapters in this volume on federal politics by Bashevkin and on the New Brunswick NDP by Everitt and Camp). It is only very recently, however, when Pauline Marois won the top position in the Parti Québécois by acclamation in the spring of 2007, that a major Quebec party has been led by a woman. However, reaching the peak of the PQ hierarchy was no easy task for Marois, who had already run twice previously (in 1985 and 2005) before she succeeded to the leadership in 2007 in the absence of any other declared candidates.

Second, this analysis shows that the first-past-the-post electoral system is not systematically unfavourable to women. The Quebec case illustrates that women can reach a level of legislative representation comparable to that achieved in countries using proportional representation or mixed-member proportional representation. As Farrell (2001, 167) reminds us, "it is not the electoral system which is at fault [for the under-representation of women in parliaments] so much as the party selection committees." The results of the 2007 Quebec election demonstrate the importance of the candidate selection process for the feminization of legislative assemblies: the proportion of women in the National Assembly dropped in large part because of the electoral success of the ADQ, a right-wing, primarily rural party that nominated far fewer female candidates than the PLQ and the PQ (20.8 percent, compared with 35.2 percent for the PLQ and 32.8 percent for the PQ).

Third, data from Quebec show women can play the electoral game strategically to increase their presence in legislatures. In particular, this case study encourages a further and deeper exploration of feminist movement mobilization in the electoral field, both within parties and outside them, to understand women's electoral success. Caul Kittilson (2006, 126) has already demonstrated that the presence of women in party elites had positive effects on the legislative representation of women, although Tremblay and Pelletier (2001) reach a more nuanced conclusion. Previous studies have shed light on the importance of women's movement mobilization to increasing the number of women parliamentarians (Lovenduski 2005; Matland 2003). Rule (1987) goes as far as stating that feminist mobilization can be a counterweight to the resistance certain voting systems offer to the election of women; in her words, "negative electoral system features have been overcome by women's political mobilization" (495).

From this perspective, we hypothesize that the Yvette Affair during the 1980 Quebec referendum campaign mobilized Quebec women, which in turn defined them as a significant interest on the public agenda.[16] Given that sovereignty remains a contested issue in Quebec politics, this mobilization persists, and political parties have had no choice but to take women into account in their political platforms. To do so in a credible way, they must remain visibly sensitive to claims made by women in their party ranks and in civil society generally. The two main Quebec parties since 1976 have indeed nominated more female candidates over time in competitive constituencies.

Future research might investigate the role of organized feminism in mobilizing women to seek open seats in Quebec and question whether this has occurred primarily in urban areas such as Montreal and Quebec City, as Louise Carbert's chapter, which follows, suggests. In response to Mary-Jo Nadeau's contribution to this volume, scholars could also probe the extent to which Quebec feminism's primary focus, since the 1970s, on the political executive, legislature, and civil service in Quebec City – in contrast to the divided attention that English Canadian women's movements have devoted to the federal capital and multiple provincial and territorial capitals – has advantaged that movement.

Finally, politics in Quebec has been dominated by centrist political parties since the 1970s. However, the recent success of the ADQ may change the political opportunity structure for women's legislative representation. On the one hand, the ADQ's gains may translate into stagnation, or even a pronounced decrease, in the proportion of women in the National Assembly. On the other hand, these reversals may serve to mobilize the women's movement, creating a renewed commitment to the parliamentary and, especially, electoral project. Quebec women's groups may use the outcome of the 2007 provincial election as an opportunity to press the PLQ and the PQ to open their doors further to women. In short, the next few years provide an exceptional chance for scholars to assess the consequences of shifts in party standings, notably the rise of a provincial right-wing party in Quebec, for women's engagement.

### Appendix: Explanation of Constituency Categories

*Safe constituencies* are defined either as those in which a party won the three last general elections, thus resisting the usual PLQ-PQ alternation, or those in which a party holds the constituency at election time and the alternation appears to be in its favour. We focus on the number of consecutive mandates in the National Assembly rather than in any given constituency for two reasons: first, the periodic revision of the borders of electoral constituencies sometimes requires MNAs to run in a new constituency; second, and more fundamentally, the measurement also presumes that a female or male MNA will be all the more difficult to beat if she or he has been in the National Assembly for a long time and, especially, survived the PLQ/PQ alternation.

*Winnable constituencies* are defined either as those in which a party holds the constituency at election time but the PLQ-PQ alternation appears not to be in its favour or where a party does not hold the constituency at election time but the alternation appears to be in its favour.

*Marginal constituencies* are defined either as those in which a party has consistently lost in the last three general elections or where a party does not hold the constituency at election time and the PLQ-PQ alternation appears to be not in its favour.

### Notes

1 This percentage decreased to 25.6 percent following the 2007 elections.
2 Cuba, which uses two-round majority voting, is an exception.
3 The opposite, however, can also be argued: a low threshold of representation favours the parliamentary representation of fringe parties, for which women are often candidates.
4 Statistics obtained from the Barreau du Québec in September 2008.
5 Other patterns that support this proposition include Quebec's public child care system, which costs $7 per day per child, as well as the province's low fertility rate and high level of urbanization. Each of these trends is associated in the literature with higher proportions of women in parliaments.
6 This study does not consider the 2007 elections, since several indicators suggest a new party system may be emerging as of that date. First, the PLQ and the PQ no longer held a monopoly on representation in the National Assembly as of 2007, when the PLQ won forty-eight

seats, the Action démocratique du Québec (ADQ) forty-one, and the PQ only thirty-six. Second, the ADQ became the official opposition, while the PQ was reduced to operating as a second opposition party. Third, unlike in elections held between 1976 and 2003, when votes were divided for the most part between the PLQ and the PQ, three parties shared the votes in 2007, with 33.1 percent for the PLQ, 30.8 percent for the ADQ, and 28.4 percent for the PQ.

7 Sylvie Roy was elected in the 2003 general elections under the banner of the ADQ.

8 This statement must be nuanced in light of the elections of 2007, since the ADQ now offers women another avenue for accessing the National Assembly. However, this political formation's rightist ideology suggests that the ADQ is less open to women than the PLQ or the PQ. Among other things, the ADQ electoral base is primarily rural rather than urban, a factor that Louise Carbert's chapter (Chapter 5 in this volume) suggests is unlikely to contribute to the election of female candidates.

9 This is the number of candidatures and not the number of women, since one woman could have been a candidate several times.

10 Five women became MNAs in 1976, eight in 1981, eighteen in 1985, twenty-three in 1989, twenty-three in 1994, twenty-nine in 1998, and thirty-seven in 2003.

11 These data are drawn from the Quebec National Assembly website. We occasionally used the services of the Directeur général des élections du Québec (DGÉQ) to specify the gender of candidates. We would like to thank the DGÉQ staff for their kind collaboration.

12 The supply of female candidates can depend on many factors, including mobilization inside local constituency associations. This factor is not addressed in the present study.

13 Figures were obtained from research services at the Bibliothèque de l'Assemblée nationale du Québec.

14 Elections from 1976 to 2003 saw 173 MNAs inheriting constituencies, with this number varying between 16 in 1976 and 41 in 1994.

15 Measurements of party competitiveness go back three elections except for the year 1981, for which our calculation uses only the election results from 1973 and 1976, and the year 1976, for which we consider only 1973 results. Going back further than 1973 would distort measures of PQ competitiveness, given that the party won only seven seats in the 1970 election.

16 This refers to the major mobilization of federalist women in Quebec in response to a comment by Lise Payette, a cabinet minister in René Lévesque's PQ government. During the 1980 referendum campaign, Payette described Madeleine Ryan, wife of Liberal leader Claude Ryan, as an Yvette, a traditional female character in schoolbooks. See Godin (2004).

**References**

Atkinson, Michael M., and David C. Docherty. 1992. "Moving Right Along: The Roots of Amateurism in the Canadian House of Commons." *Canadian Journal of Political Science* 25, 2: 295-318.

Barreau du Québec. 2008. "Tout sur le Barreau." http://www.barreau.qc.ca/barreau/index.html.

Carey, John M., and Matthew Soberg Shugart. 1995. "Incentives to Cultivate a Personal Vote: A Rank Ordering of Electoral Formulas." *Electoral Studies* 14, 4: 417-39.

Caul Kittilson, Miki. 2006. *Challenging Parties, Changing Parliaments: Women and Elected Office in Contemporary Western Europe*. Columbus: Ohio State University Press.

Darcy, R., Susan Welch, and Janet Clark. 1994. *Women, Elections, and Representation*. 2nd ed. Lincoln: University of Nebraska Press.

Docherty, David C. 1997. *Mr. Smith Goes to Ottawa*. Vancouver: UBC Press.

–. 2002. "Political Careers in Canada." In *Citizen Politics*, ed. Joanna Everitt and Brenda O'Neill, 338-54. Don Mills: Oxford University Press.

Engstrom, Richard L. 1987. "District Magnitudes and the Election of Women to the Irish Dail." *Electoral Studies* 6, 2: 123-32.

Farrell, David M. 2001. *Electoral Systems: A Comparative Introduction*. Houndmills: Palgrave.

Franks, C.E.S. 1987. *The Parliament of Canada*. Toronto: University of Toronto Press.

Gallagher, Michael. 2005. "Conclusion." In *The Politics of Electoral Systems,* ed. Michael Gallagher and Paul Mitchell, 535-78. Oxford: Oxford University Press.
Godin, Stéphanie. 2004. "Les Yvettes comme l'expression d'un féminisme fédéraliste au Québec." *Mens. Revue d'histoire intellectuelle de l'Amérique française* 5, 1: 73-117.
Government of Quebec. Institut de la statistique. 2003a. "Taux d'obtention d'un certificat ou d'un grade universitaire, population de 15 ans et plus selon le groupe d'âge, le sexe et le principal domaine d'études, Québec, 2001." http://stat.gouv.qc.ca/donstat/societe/education/etat_scolr/11dom_uni_taux.htm.
–. 2003b. "Les 20 principales professions féminines et masculines, Québec, 1991 et 2001." http://stat.gouv.qc.ca/donstat/societe/march_travl_remnr/cat_profs_sectr_activ/professions/recens2001/tabwebprof_juin03-1.htm.
–. 2007. "Revenu d'emploi moyen des hommes et des femmes gagnant un revenu, Québec, 1996 à 2005." http://www.stat.gouv.qc.ca/donstat/societe/famls_mengs_niv_vie/revenus_depense/revenus/gainspart96_2005.htm.
–. 2008. "Taux d'emploi des femmes selon certains groupes d'âge, moyennes annuelles, Québec, Ontario, Canada, 1976 à 2007." http://www.stat.gouv.qc.ca/donstat/societe/march_travl_remnr/parnt_etudn_march_travl/pop_active/tab15.htm.
Inglehart, Margaret L. 1981. "Political Interest in West European Women: An Historical and Empirical Comparative Analysis." *Comparative Political Studies* 14, 3: 299-326.
Inglehart, Ronald, and Pippa Norris. 2003. *Rising Tide.* Cambridge: Cambridge University Press.
Inter-Parliamentary Union. 2008. "Les femmes dans les parlements nationaux." Inter-Parliamentary Union. http://www.ipu.org/wmn-f/classif.htm.
Kenworthy, Lane, and Melissa Malami. 1999. "Gender Inequality in Political Representation: A Worldwide Comparative Analysis." *Social Forces* 78, 1: 235-68.
Kunovich, Sheri, and Pamela Paxton. 2005. "Pathways to Power: The Role of Political Parties in Women's National Political Representation." *American Journal of Sociology* 111, 2: 505-52.
Laponce, Jean A. 1994. "Democracy and Incumbency: The Canadian Case." In *The Victorious Incumbent: A Threat to Democracy?* ed. Albert Somit, Rudolf Wildenmann, Bernhard Bell, and Andrea Rommel, 122-49. Aldershot: Dartmouth.
Lawless, Jennifer L., and Richard L. Fox. 2005. *It Takes a Candidate: Why Women Don't Run for Office.* New York: Cambridge University Press.
Lovenduski, Joni, ed. 2005. *State Feminism and Political Representation.* Cambridge: Cambridge University Press.
Mateo Diaz, Mercedes. 2005. *Representing Women? Female Legislators in West European Parliaments.* Colchester: ECPR Press.
Matland, Richard E. 1993. "Institutional Variables Affecting Female Representation in National Legislatures: The Case of Norway." *Journal of Politics* 55, 3: 737-55.
–. 1998. "Women's Representation in National Legislatures: Developed and Developing Countries." *Legislative Studies Quarterly* 23, 1: 109-25.
–. 2003. "Women's Representation in Post-Communist Europe." In *Women's Access to Political Power in Post-Communist Europe,* ed. Richard E. Matland and Kathleen A. Montgomery, 321-42. Oxford: Oxford University Press.
–. 2005. "Enhancing Women's Political Participation: Legislative Recruitment and Electoral Systems." In *Women in Parliament: Beyond Numbers – A Revised Version,* ed. Julie Ballington and Azza Karam, 93-111. Stockholm: International IDEA.
Matland, Richard E., and Deborah Dwight Brown. 1992. "District Magnitude's Effect on Female Representation in U.S. State Legislatures." *Legislative Studies Quarterly* 17, 4: 469-92.
Matland, Richard E., and Donley T. Studlar. 1996. "The Contagion of Women Candidates in Single-Member District and Proportional Representation Electoral Systems: Canada and Norway." *Journal of Politics* 58, 3: 707-33.
–. 2004. "Determinants of Legislative Turnover: A Cross-National Analysis." *British Journal of Political Science* 34, 1: 87-108.

Matland, Richard E., and Kathleen A. Montgomery. 2003. "Recruiting Women to National Legislatures: A General Framework with Applications to Post-Communist Democracies." In *Women's Access to Political Power in Post-Communist Europe,* ed. Richard E. Matland and Kathleen A. Montgomery, 19-42. Oxford: Oxford University Press.
McAllister, Ian, and Donley T. Studlar. 2002. "Electoral Systems and Women's Representation: A Long-Term Perspective." *Representation* 39, 1: 3-14.
Meier, Petra. 2005. "Le système électoral belge et les rapports de genre." In *Genre et politique en Belgique et en francophonie,* ed. Bérengère Marques-Pereira and Petra Meier, 23-34. Louvain-La-Neuve: Bruylant-Academia s.a.
Moncrief, Gary F. 1998. "Terminating the Provincial Career: Retirement and Electoral Defeat in Canadian Provincial Legislatures, 1960-1997." *Canadian Journal of Political Science* 31, 2: 359-72.
Moore, Gwen, and Gene Shackman. 1996. "Gender and Authority: A Cross-National Study." *Social Science Quarterly* 77, 2: 275-88.
Norris, Pippa. 1985. "Women's Legislative Participation in Western Europe." *West European Politics* 8, 4: 90-101.
–. 1987. *Politics and Sexual Equality: The Comparative Position of Women in Western Democracies.* Boulder: Rienner.
–. 1992. "Electoral Systems and the Parliamentary Recruitment of Women." In *Political Leadership in Democratic Societies,* ed. Anthony Mughan and Samuel C. Patterson, 136-45. Chicago: Nelson-Hall.
–. 1993. "Conclusions: Comparing Legislative Recruitment." In *Gender and Party Politics,* ed. Joni Lovenduski and Pippa Norris, 309-39. London: Sage.
–. 1996. "Legislative Recruitment." In *Comparing Democracies: Elections and Voting in Global Perspective,* ed. Lawrence LeDuc, Richard G. Niemi, and Pippa Norris, 184-215. Thousand Oaks: Sage.
–. 1997a. "Conclusions: Comparing Passages to Power." In *Passages to Power,* ed. Pippa Norris, 209-31. Cambridge: Cambridge University Press.
–, ed. 1997b. *Passages to Power.* Cambridge: Cambridge University Press.
–. 2004. *Electoral Engineering.* Cambridge: Cambridge University Press.
Norris, Pippa, and Joni Lovenduski. 1989. "Pathways to Parliament." *Talking Politics* 1, 3: 90-94.
–. 1995. *Political Recruitment.* Cambridge: Cambridge University Press.
Norris, Pippa, R.J. Carty, Lynda Erickson, Joni Lovenduski, and Marian Simms. 1990. "Party Selectorates in Australia, Britain and Canada: Prolegomena for Research in the 1990s." *Journal of Commonwealth and Comparative Politics* 28, 2: 219-45.
Norris, Pippa, and Ronald Inglehart. 2001. "Cultural Obstacles to Equal Representation." *Journal of Democracy* 12, 3: 126-40.
Nowacki, Dawn. 2003. "Women in Russian Regional Assemblies: Losing Ground." In *Women's Access to Political Power in Post-Communist Europe,* ed. Richard E. Matland and Kathleen A. Montgomery, 173-95. Oxford: Oxford University Press.
Oakes, Ann, and Elizabeth Almquist. 1993. "Women in National Legislatures." *Population Research and Policy Review* 12, 1: 71-81.
Paxton, Pamela. 1997. "Women in National Legislatures: A Cross-National Analysis." *Social Science Research* 26, 4: 442-64.
Paxton, Pamela, and Sheri Kunovich. 2003. "Women's Political Representation: The Importance of Ideology." *Social Forces* 82, 1: 87-114.
Pelletier, Réjean, and Manon Tremblay. 1992. "Les femmes sont-elles candidates dans des circonscriptions perdues d'avance? De l'examen d'une croyance." *Revue canadienne de science politique* 25, 2: 249-67.
Peschard, Jacqueline. 2003. "The Quota System in Latin America: General Overview." In *The Implementation of Quotas: Latin American Experiences,* International IDEA, 20-29. Stockholm: International IDEA.
Pitre, Sonia. 2003. "Political Parties and Female Candidates: Is There Resistance in New Brunswick?" In *Women and Electoral Politics in Canada,* ed. Manon Tremblay and Linda Trimble, 109-24. Don Mills: Oxford University Press.

PNUD. 2001. *Rapport mondial sur le développement humain 2001*. Bruxelles: De Boeck and Larcier s.a.

Praud, Jocelyne. 2003. "The Parti Québécois, Its Women's Committee and the Feminization of the Quebec Electoral Arena." In *Women and Electoral Politics in Canada*, ed. Manon Tremblay and Linda Trimble, 125-37. Don Mills: Oxford University Press.

Quebec National Assembly. 2004. "Informations historiques: Les résultats électoraux depuis 1867." Quebec National Assembly. http://www.assnat.qc.ca/fra/patrimoine/resultatselec/index.html.

Randall, Vicky. 1982. *Women and Politics*. London: Macmillan.

Reynolds, Andrew. 1999. "Women in the Legislatures and Executives of the World: Knocking at the Highest Glass Ceiling." *World Politics* 51, 4: 547-72.

Reynolds, Andrew, Ben Reilly, and Andrew Ellis. 2005. *Electoral System Design: The New International IDEA Handbook*. Stockholm: International IDEA.

Rosenbluth, Frances, Rob Salmond, and Michael F. Thies. 2006. "Welfare Works: Explaining Female Legislative Representation." *Politics and Gender* 2, 2: 165-92.

Rule, Wilma. 1987. "Electoral Systems, Contextual Factors and Women's Opportunity for Election to Parliament in Twenty-Three Democracies." *Western Political Quarterly* 40, 3: 477-98.

–. 1988. "Why Women Don't Run: The Critical Contextual Factors in Women's Legislative Recruitment." *Western Political Quarterly* 34, 1: 60-77.

–. 1994. "Parliaments of, by, and for the People: Except for Women?" In *Electoral Systems in Comparative Perspective: Their Impact on Women and Minorities*, ed. Wilma Rule and Joseph F. Zimmerman, 15-30. Westport: Greenwood Press.

Rule, Wilma, and Pippa Norris. 1992. "Anglo and Minority Women's Underrepresentation in Congress: Is the Electoral System the Culprit?" In *United States Electoral Systems: Their Impact on Women and Minorites*, ed. Wilma Rule and Joseph F. Zimmerman, 41-54. New York: Praeger.

Saint-Germain, Michelle A. 1994. "The Representation of Women and Minorities in the National Legislatures of Costa Rica and Nicaragua." In *Electoral Systems in Comparative Perspective: Their Impact on Women and Minorities*, ed. Wilma Rule and Joseph F. Zimmerman, 211-21. Westport: Greenwood Press.

Salmond, Rob. 2006. "Proportional Representation and Female Parliamentarians." *Legislative Studies Quarterly* 31, 2: 175-204.

Sawer, Marian. 1997. "Mirroring the Nation? Electoral Systems and the Representation of Women." *Current Affairs Bulletin* 73, 5: 8-12.

Sayers, Anthony M. 1999. *Parties, Candidates, and Constituency Campaigns in Canadian Elections*. Vancouver: UBC Press.

Schwindt-Bayer, Leslie A. 2005. "The Incumbency Disadvantage and Women's Election to Legislative Office." *Electoral Studies* 24, 2: 227-44.

Siaroff, Alan. 2000. "Women's Representation in Legislatures and Cabinets in Industrial Democracies." *International Political Science Review* 21, 2: 197-215.

Squires, Judith, and Mark Wickham-Jones. 2001. *Women in Parliament: A Comparative Analysis*, Research Discussion Series. Manchester: Equal Opportunities Commission.

Studlar, Donley T., and Richard E. Matland. 1996. "The Dynamics of Women's Representation in the Canadian Provinces, 1975-1994." *Canadian Journal of Political Science* 29, 2: 269-93.

Studlar, Donley T., and Susan Welch. 1991. "Does District Magnitude Matter? Women Candidates in London Local Elections." *Western Political Quarterly* 44, 2: 457-66.

Thompson, J.A., and Gary F. Moncrief. 1993. "The Implications of Term Limits for Women and Minorities: Some Evidence from the States." *Social Science Quarterly* 74, 2: 300-9.

Tremblay, Manon. 2005. *Québécoises et représentation parlementaire*. Sainte-Foy: Les Presses de l'Université Laval.

–. 2008. "Introduction." In *Women and Legislative Representation: Electoral Systems, Political Parties, and Sex Quotas*, ed. Manon Tremblay, 1-22. New York: Palgrave Macmillan.

Tremblay, Manon, and Réjean Pelletier. 2001. "More Women Constituency Party Presidents: A Strategy for Increasing the Number of Women Candidates in Canada?" *Party Politics* 7, 2: 157-90.

United Nations Office at Vienna. 1992. *Women in Politics and Decision-Making in the Late Twentieth Century*. Dordrecht: Martinus Nijhoff Publishers.

Young, Lisa. 1991. "Legislative Turnover and the Election of Women to the Canadian House of Commons." In *Women in Canadian Politics: Toward Equity in Representation,* ed. Kathy Megyery, 81-99. Toronto: Dundurn.

# 5

# Are Cities More Congenial? Tracking the Rural Deficit of Women in the House of Commons

*Louise Carbert*

It is well known that the proportion of seats held by women in Canada's House of Commons lags far behind levels typically found in European legislatures with proportional representation. This difference, as Manon Tremblay notes in the previous chapter, is consistent with comparative research on the implications of Canada's single-member, plurality-based (SMP) electoral system. While electoral rules work well to explain cross-national differences, this factor does not necessarily play out the same way within a single system. In fact, Tremblay's discussion in Chapter 4 documents how an entire province has, to a notable extent, overcome the challenges of an SMP electoral system.

This chapter examines a significant dimension of the Canadian story that has thus far been overlooked: a strong rural-urban divide. By grouping Canada's federal electoral districts by population density, this chapter shows that female MPs are overwhelmingly drawn from metropolitan constituencies, notably the Toronto and Montreal areas, where the proportions of seats held by women are not far below those found in Nordic countries. Conversely, very few women MPs hold seats outside Canada's largest cities. This chapter examines the origins and characteristics of this pattern, which crosses regional and partisan divides. This discussion recognizes the rural deficit in female MPs as a separate, pervasive, and durable pattern that impedes women's political representation at the federal level in Canada.

In 2006, women held 21 percent of the seats in the House of Commons. Although this proportion has come a long way since the 1960s, as has women's representation at other levels of Canadian government, a more careful look at the historical record reveals a troubling development. It has become increasingly apparent since the mid-1990s that the long-standing pattern of overall gains in women's participation has stalled, at both national and provincial levels, with proportions of women stagnating near the 20 percent mark nation-wide. This plateau can be seen in both curves of Figure

*Figure 5.1*

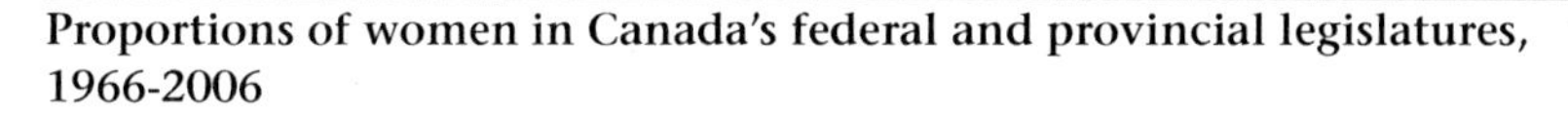

**Proportions of women in Canada's federal and provincial legislatures, 1966-2006**

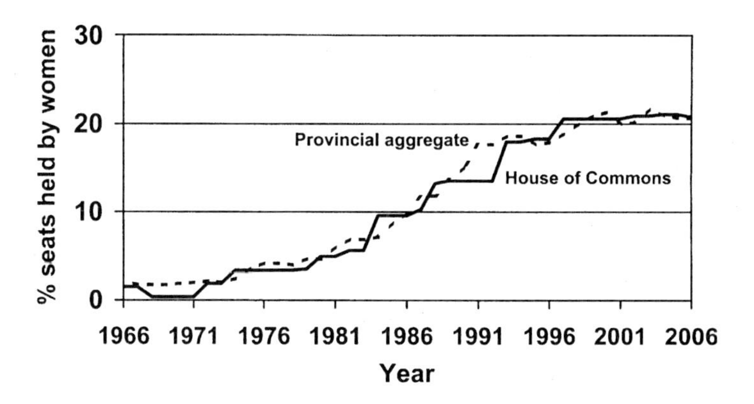


*Note:* The provincial aggregate shown is calculated by assigning equal weight to all seats in provincial legislatures in the ten Canadian provinces

5.1, which illustrates the proportions of seats held by women over the past few decades in the House of Commons and in provincial legislatures. From a base of less than 5 percent during the 1960s and 1970s, the two proportions rose nearly in tandem during this period. Increases were most rapid during the 1980s, as women's representation approached 15 percent by the end of that decade. The rate of growth slowed during the 1990s, a decade that saw the implosion of the federal Progressive Conservative party and the rise of regionalist organizations, including the Reform party and Bloc Québécois. Both curves reached a plateau thereafter: numbers of seats held by women languished near the 20 percent mark, with no further significant increases. The federal election of 2006 only confirmed this pattern: the number of women elected to Parliament decreased by one and the proportion of women remained at 21 percent.

While many people are aware of the overall gender imbalance in the House of Commons, few appreciate just how much the numbers of women elected have been held back by an extreme dearth outside Canada's largest cities. To get a feel for the scale of this contrast, consider that in the 2004 federal election women won 36 percent of the densely populated urban constituencies in and around Toronto, Canada's largest city.[1] Female MPs were also elected in 38 percent of the urban seats in and around Montreal, the second largest city.[2] These proportions eclipse the nation-wide average of 21 percent, which suggests that there is limited potential for further increases in women's representation in metropolitan constituencies.[3]

If the metropolitan centres of Toronto and Montreal are so far above the national average in electing women, it follows that districts elsewhere must be below average. Quantitative studies have consistently found that fewer women hold elected office at all levels in rural areas than do women in metropolitan centres (see Brodie 1977; Matland and Studlar 1998; Moncrief and Thompson 1991).

This chapter tracks how the metropolitan concentration in the election of women has played out over three consecutive federal elections, and it puts this story in a contemporary political context. It illustrates just how strong and persistent this pattern has been and shows that the deficit of women MPs outside large cities can neither be viewed as a regional characteristic nor as a reflection of partisan preferences. Of course, the under-representation of urban MPs relative to urban population in the House of Commons does not help; simple calculations will clarify the extent and location of rural over-representation. Further calculations will be used to analyze women's candidacies at the constituency level over the same three federal elections in order to compare the relative impact of voter and party activist preferences in determining whether women become MPs. The results show that voter hostility plays, at most, a secondary role. The election of women is limited primarily by the small numbers of female candidates who are nominated for winnable seats.

Asking why a rural constituency association did *not* choose a woman as its federal candidate invokes issues that go far beyond the closed-door vote that completes the nomination process. In many cases, no woman declared an interest in running. Far more to the point is the difficult and open-ended question about events that preceded the nomination meeting: Who else could have been chosen instead of the eventual candidate? The pool of potential nominees goes beyond those who actually put their names forward.

It is sometimes useful to frame the recruitment process with an analogy to market forces of supply and demand, in which women's candidacy is conceptualized as the "product" under consideration (Lovenduski 2005, 64). A good deal of research has addressed the demand-side constraints – that is, the role of party gatekeepers in excluding women as candidates (Bashevkin 1985; Niven 1998). Who was qualified and available but was not groomed? Whose qualifications went unrecognized?

Far less effort has been directed to supply-side questions. Do rural districts produce too few qualified women to supply a significant number of women candidates? Another possibility is that some women might exclude themselves: Who was qualified but unwilling to step forward? Perhaps the greatest challenge in understanding why there are so few women candidates in winnable rural seats is trying to learn about the pool of potential candidates.

My own field-based research on rural women's leadership has attempted to address this gap in knowledge by gathering together small groups of rural community leaders, both in the Atlantic region and in the western provinces, and interviewing them about their experiences and perceptions of leadership, public life, and running for elected office. The fieldwork confirms that sufficient numbers of qualified rural women leaders exist to supply significantly more female candidates outside Canada's largest cities. The interviews revealed that low candidacy levels to date have been driven by local resistance to recruiting more women and by reluctance on the part of women themselves. They provide first-hand accounts of the underlying reasons behind low rates of women's candidacy that move well beyond stereotypes of rural traditionalism (see Carbert 2006). The implications of those interview results for the prospects of women's representation in the House of Commons are discussed in the concluding section of this chapter.

## Locating the Rural Deficit of Women

A brief glance at the electoral map of Canada reveals a large number of highly urban districts that are concentrated in very small spatial areas and a large number of less densely populated districts that are geographically much larger and encompass substantial rural areas. Between the two is a middle range of constituencies that contain both smaller cities and rural areas. Rather than designating each district as either rural or urban, we used district population density to formulate a continuous spectrum and examined how women's representation varied along that spectrum.

Although population density measures can miss some important nuances in a few mixed districts (notably those in and around Saskatoon), this indicator, for the most part, provides consistent and objective categorization of federal ridings. As will be shown, the relationships being studied are strong enough to be illustrated clearly without the need to probe smaller differences.[4] For the sake of convenience, we refer to districts with low population densities as "more rural," and those with high population densities as "more urban." This is not meant to reduce all of the complex characteristics of rurality and urbanity to a single measure, but simply to get a handle on population density variation. As the empirical section of this chapter reveals, the relationship between population density and the probability of electing a woman MP in Canada is strong and straightforward, but the underlying explanations are more complex.

For the 2004 and 2006 elections, population data for 308 federal constituencies (based on the 2001 Canadian census) were obtained from Elections Canada. They show that the least densely populated seat was Nunavut (where fewer than twenty-seven thousand people lived on more than 2 million square kilometres of land), while the most densely populated seat was Papineau in the Montreal area (with more than eleven thousand people per square kilometre). For the 2000 election, population information about 301 constituencies was drawn from historical district profiles provided by Elections Canada.

We began with a simple contrast that lists all federal electoral districts in order of population density and then compares the top and bottom halves of the list.[5] The dividing line between the two parts of the list is approximately 160 people per square kilometre, which is equivalent to approximately 1.4 acres (or a square plot with 75 metres on each side) per person. Specific examples help to characterize the two types of districts. As of 2006, Fundy Royal in New Brunswick had the median density for the bottom half of the list, at nine people per square kilometre (or 27 acres per person). In the middle of the top half of the list was London North Centre, which is located in a fairly large city in southwestern Ontario, with 1,680 people per square kilometre (or about seven people per acre).

The 2006 election results reveal a stark contrast between the two halves of the list. Looking first at the more urban seats, we found that women MPs were elected in 29 percent (44/154) of the most densely populated constituencies. In the more rural half, we found that women won in only 13 percent (20/154) of the districts. According to this simple estimate, urban constituencies were more than twice as likely as rural ones to elect female MPs in 2006.

Figure 5.2 illustrates this contrast and offers the same comparison for the two preceding elections. It shows that the 2006 results paralleled those of 2004 and 2000, since, in all three cases, far more women were elected from densely, as opposed to more sparsely, populated constituencies. In short, the rural-urban contrast was a robust feature of recent Canadian elections, which produced very different partisan results – a Liberal majority government in 2000, a Liberal minority government in 2004, and a Conservative minority government in 2006. If anything, the rural-urban contrast was somewhat more extreme in 2000 than in 2006. Further research is required to determine the contours of the contrast in elections before 2000.

Did all constituencies in the more rural half of the list share equally in the shortfall of female MPs? Or is this pattern confined to the most sparsely populated, highly rural areas? To address these questions, we subdivided the two halves of federal electoral districts, again according to population density. Some specific examples help to give a concrete sense of what these four groupings represent. The median constituency in the most highly rural quartile is Bonavista-Gander-Grand Falls-Windsor in central Newfoundland, while the median constituency in the less rural category is Stormont-Dundas-South Glengarry in eastern Ontario. Hull-Aylmer, a sprawling suburban constituency north of Ottawa, is in the middle of the next most urban group of districts, while the top quartile of the list includes such densely populated

*Figure 5.2*

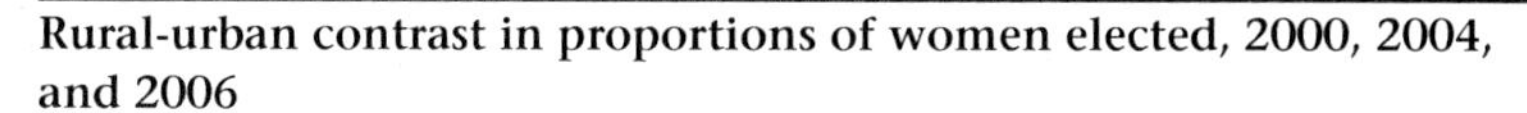

**Rural-urban contrast in proportions of women elected, 2000, 2004, and 2006**

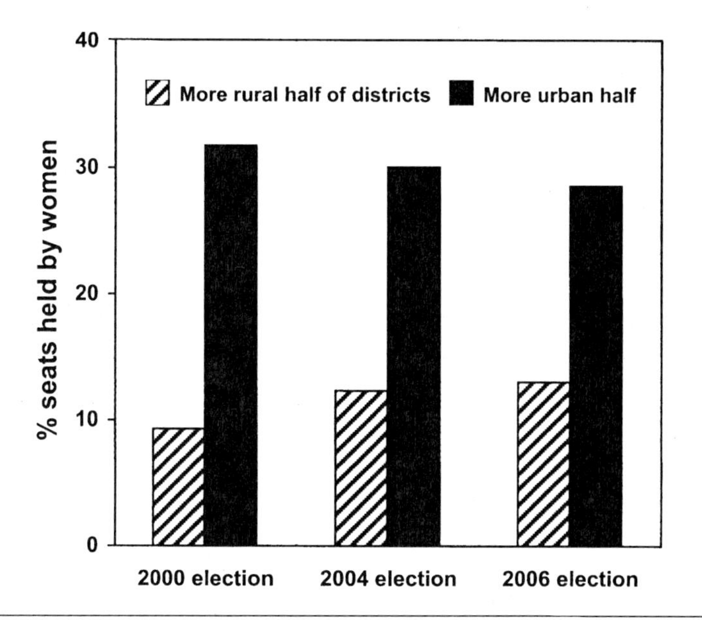


*Note:* Districts were divided into two equal groups by population density.

seats as Winnipeg Centre, Calgary Centre, Etobicoke Centre, and, of course, downtown Toronto and Montreal districts, which are at the top.

Figure 5.3 illustrates the proportions of women elected to each quartile of districts since 2000. In each case, the number of seats held by women decreased monotonically with decreasing population density. As expected, the most rural quartile elected the fewest women – 10 percent or lower in all three elections. While the shortfall in the second-sparsest quartile was not as marked, this category of constituencies played an important role in depressing the overall numbers of female MPs. In each election year – 2000, 2004, and 2006 – the proportion of seats won by women in the second-sparsest group of districts was well below the national average and less than half the level found in the most urban quartile.

These results helped us to refine the description of which sorts of ridings have been more, rather than less, likely to elect women MPs. The districts throughout the top half of the population-density list have sent proportions of women well above the national average over all three elections. These are overwhelmingly the urban districts within Statistics Canada's census metropolitan areas (Mendelson and Lefebvre 2003).[6] Hence, it makes sense to refer

*Figure 5.3*

**Rural-urban contrast in proportions of women elected, 2000, 2004, and 2006**

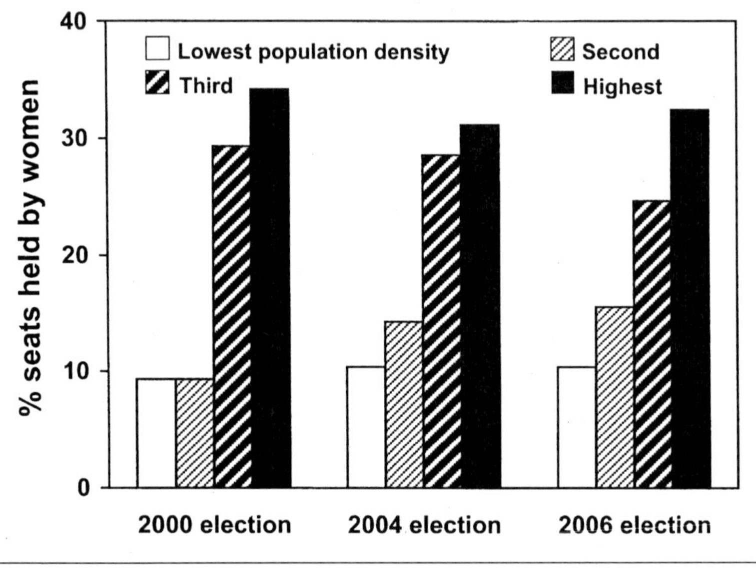


*Note:* Districts were divided into four equal groups by population density.

to a "metropolitan concentration" of women in the House of Commons. Conversely, the deficit in women MPs extends throughout the least densely populated half of federal constituencies, which is home to about 14 million people, or 46 percent of Canada's total population. Roughly speaking, this half of federal districts covers most of Canada outside major cities. While the shortfall in women MPs is greatest in the most sparsely populated areas, its reach extends quite strongly to districts containing small- and medium-sized cities. The phenomenon is clearly a rural deficit, in the sense that the probability of a woman being sent to Ottawa decreases with the increasing rurality of the district. However, we need to bear in mind that what we term "the rural deficit of women" extends well beyond narrow definitions of what constitutes a rural riding.[7]

The impact of this deficit is magnified by an over-representation of rural voters that has been a long-standing feature of Canada's electoral system. Based on the 2001 census, the more densely populated half of districts contained approximately 16 million people, or 54 percent of Canada's population, as compared to 14 million people, or 46 percent of Canada's population in the less densely populated half. Elections Canada has drawn the electoral boundaries in such a way that not every district contains the national median of 102,000 people per constituency; instead, this number is lower in rural areas and higher in metropolitan centres. Hence, the more densely populated half of ridings – roughly speaking the urban metropolitan districts – had a median population of about 106,000. The more rural half of ridings had a median population of about 95,000, which is approximately 10 percent lower than that of urban metropolitan districts. These numbers suggest that if rural over-representation were removed, the number of women sitting in the House of Commons would be somewhat higher than it is today – with perhaps an additional two or three women, judging from the patterns illustrated above. Nevertheless, under the hypothetical scenario of strict representation by population, the rural deficit of women MPs would still remain as a major factor holding back women's representation in the House of Commons.

Even the incremental gain of two or three women is elusive, considering how difficult it would be to achieve equal district populations in Canada's electoral system. Much of the rural over-representation is contained in the lowest-population-density quartile of districts, for which the median population is about 84,000. The other three quartiles have median populations ranging from 102,000 to 108,000 – much closer to the national median. Even within the most rural quartile, a good deal of the over-representation is confined to a few districts – the remote northern districts of Nunavut, Labrador, Yukon, and Western Arctic, as well as Prince Edward Island's four constitutionally protected seats – each of which has a population of less than 40,000. The deeply entrenched political and constitutional issues at stake in these and other over-represented districts would certainly be invoked to oppose any redrawing of electoral boundaries that threatened to reduce their voting power.

Taken together, Figures 5.2 and 5.3 show a stark contrast in women elected across the rural-urban spectrum. The dearth of women MPs outside Canada's largest cities is perhaps the single largest factor limiting the number of women in Parliament. Women do not hold half the seats in major urban centres, but metropolitan areas have come far closer to parity than less densely populated areas. It would therefore be unrealistic to expect large cities by themselves to raise significantly the entire national average in the near future. We know that the overall proportion of female MPs has stalled at less than halfway to parity. Bluntly stated, Canada's more rural districts need to elect greater numbers of female MPs in order for the country to climb above this plateau and thus achieve meaningful gains in House of Commons representation.

## Tracking Regional Effects

Is the rural deficit an artifact of regional differences? To address this possibility, we divided federal electoral districts in each region into two groups: one more rural and the other more urban. To ensure that a standard measure

*Figure 5.4*

**Rural deficit by region, 2000, 2004, and 2006 elections**

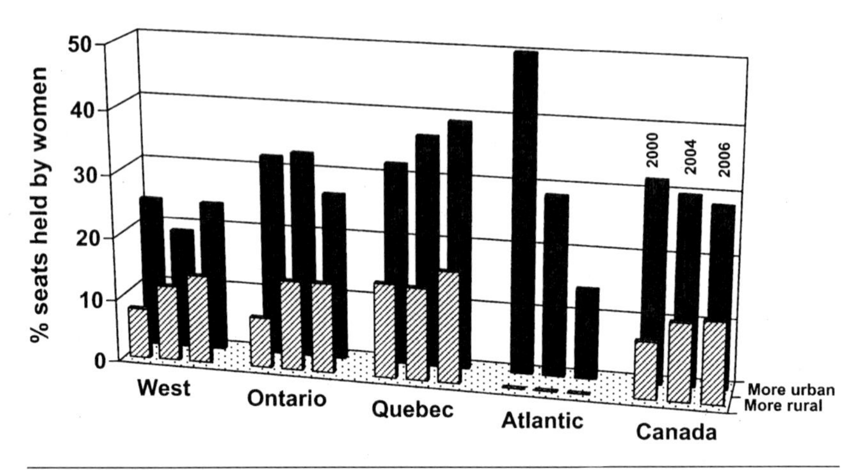


*Note:* Districts were divided into two groups according to whether their population density is above or below the national median.

was employed for each region, we used the same criterion as in the preceding section, namely national median population density across all House of Commons constituencies.[8] In any given region, the number of districts in the more urban category was not necessarily the same as the number in the more rural category because some regions were more highly urbanized than others.

Figure 5.4 shows results for the same three elections. Each region has its own set of three pairs of bars, and the national results from Figure 5.2 are repeated on the right for reference. In Ontario in 2004, women won 14 percent (6/42) of the seats in the more sparsely populated group, compared with 33 percent (21/64) in the more urban districts. These two levels are illustrated by the middle two bars in the Ontario series in Figure 5.4, with the more rural proportion in front of the more urban proportion. The 2000 election result is represented by the two bars to the left, and the 2006 result is represented by the two bars on the right.

The overwhelming pattern in this figure is that, in every region in all three elections, the rear-most bar is higher than the front-most bar, indicating that the proportion of women elected to the more urban seats is consistently above that in the more rural ones. Hence, the rural deficit in the election of women extends to every region of Canada. In a country with such enormous geographical scale and regional diversity, this degree of uniformity across regions, over three elections that produced divergent political results, is remarkable.

It cannot be concluded, however, that there were no regional differences or temporal variations. The Atlantic region (including New Brunswick, Nova Scotia, Prince Edward Island, and Newfoundland and Labrador) did not elect any women in rural constituencies in 2000, 2004, or 2006, and the proportion of urban women MPs declined precipitously over time. This drop-off was actually a coincidence of small numbers: since only seven Atlantic seats fell in the urban half of the national list, the retirements of Elsie Wayne from Saint John, Wendy Lill from Dartmouth, and Claudette Bradshaw from Moncton-Riverview-Dieppe had a major impact on the percentages. In light of Manon Tremblay's research on Quebec inheritor candidates in Chapter 4, it is notable that Wayne, Lill, and Bradshaw were not succeeded by women running for the same party.[9]

Figure 5.4 also shows that Quebec elected more women MPs than other regions. Part of this distinction is simply due to the fact that this province is more highly urbanized than either the West or the Atlantic region.[10] There is more to it, however, as Quebec's proportions of women MPs exceed those of Ontario, which is even more highly urbanized. Furthermore, Quebec's numbers are elevated in both urban and rural districts. Combining the present results from the House of Commons with those from the National Assembly in the preceding chapter, we can infer that Quebec's political environment has strongly favoured the election of women at both levels of government. In Chapter 4, Tremblay highlighted the role of organized feminism at the provincial level, with its ties to mainstream political parties. Her argument about the specificity of Quebec seems applicable to the federal level as well, where the Bloc Québécois (BQ) has dominated since 1993. These partisan effects are considered in more detail in the following section.

Although percentages of women MPs from Quebec are higher than those from other regions, the rural-urban contrast exists there as elsewhere. Figure 5.4 shows that the proportion of women MPs in Quebec's metropolitan districts was more than twice that found in relatively rural ones (39 percent versus 18 percent in 2006, with similar ratios in the two earlier elections). Furthermore, the percentage of female MPs from rural Quebec was below the overall Canadian national average across all districts.

Cities in western Canada elected fewer women than cities in other regions, as is seen in Figure 5.4. The partisan dimension of this distinction is discussed in the next section. At the same time, rural districts in the West elected similar proportions of women as rural districts in Ontario or Canada as a whole. Hence, the rural-urban contrast in the West, while still marked, was less stark than in other regions.

Overall, Figure 5.4 shows a striking uniformity across Canada's regions. Relatively rural districts in each region elected fewer women MPs than metropolitan districts in that same region. This does not mean that the different regions sent similar proportions of women to the House of Commons, because some regions were more rural than others. Geography thus flavours the rural-urban mix for female parliamentarians in Canada.

## Tracking Partisan Effects

Observers might, at first glance, suspect that the rural-urban contrast follows from partisan preferences, since it is well known that Conservative Party support is concentrated in rural areas, and previous studies have demonstrated a link between the strength of Canadian parties on the right and low numbers of women legislators (Young 2003, 87-88).

To address this part of the puzzle, the parliamentary caucuses of each major federal political party were divided into two groups. The split was done according to whether MPs were from the more or less densely populated halves of Canada's three hundred-plus electoral districts. Following the 2000, 2004, and 2006 elections, the gender balance in each party's rural caucus was compared with that of its urban caucus.

Figure 5.5 illustrates the results. In the 2004 election, the Conservative Party won 70 out of a possible 154 seats in the less densely populated half of federal districts. Eight of these constituencies elected women, for a Conservative rural yield of 11 percent. In the more densely populated half of districts, the Conservatives took 29 of 154 seats, with four women elected, for a yield of 14 percent. As might be expected for a party that has not actively promoted women candidates, both of these proportions fell below the national average. These ratios can be seen in the middle two bars in the Conservative series in Figure 5.5, with the rural proportion in front of the urban one. Results from 2000 are represented by the two bars to the left, while results from 2006 are represented by the two bars on the right.[11] In all three elections, the proportion of women in the Conservative urban caucus was much lower than for the other parties. This result helps to explain why western Canadian cities elected somewhat fewer women than did urban constituencies elsewhere (see Figure 5.4). Western cities, simply put, have favoured the Conservative Party more than cities have elsewhere, and that party has not favoured women candidates.

A different result emerges in the more rural ridings. Figure 5.5 shows that the Liberals fared no better than Conservatives in electing rural women in recent elections. For example, in 2004, Liberal candidates won forty-six seats in the less densely populated half of Canadian districts, of which only four, or 9 percent, were women. This level is slightly lower than the rural Conservative result of eight women in seventy seats, or 11 percent. The same pattern was repeated in the elections of 2000 and 2006, when women made up no more than 9 percent of rural MPs in the Liberal caucus.

In contrast, the Liberal Party was much more adept at nominating and electing women in urban seats. In 2004, women won one-third of urban seats

*Figure 5.5*

**Rural deficit by party caucus, 2000, 2004, and 2006 elections**

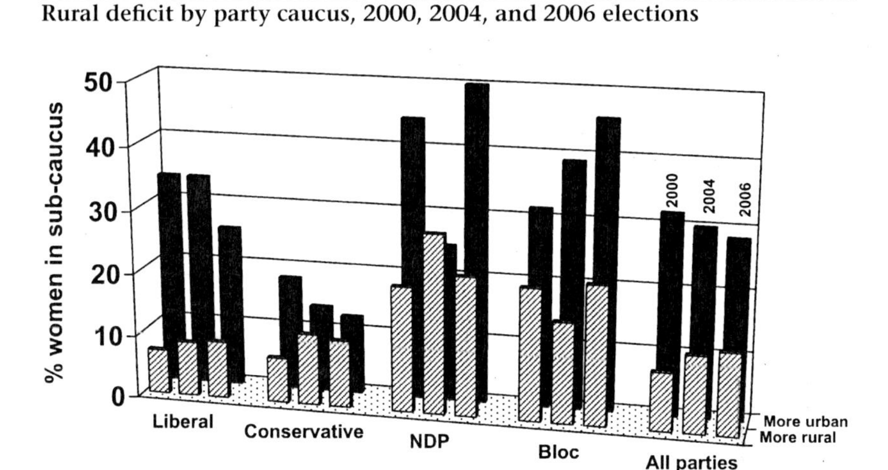


*Note:* Each caucus was divided into two groups according to whether the district population density is above or below the national median.

held by the Liberals (30/89), a pattern that paralleled results in 2000 and 2006. In short, the rural deficit in the Liberal caucus after each of the three elections was at least as large as in the rest of the House of Commons.

Since neither the Liberals nor Conservatives elected many women in rural seats, the main difference between them in regard to women's representation rests in urban districts. When Conservative candidates wrested control of a number of urban seats from the Liberals in 2006, they defeated four women MPs from Ontario. In each case, Conservative men succeeded Liberal women: Pat Brown took Aileen Carroll's seat in Barrie, Mike Wallace replaced Paddy Tornsey in Burlington, John Baird defeated Marlene Catterall in Ottawa West-Nepean, and Jim Flaherty replaced Judi Longfield in Whitby-Oshawa. The resulting decrease in the proportion of women elected in urban Ontario can be discerned in Figure 5.4.

The Bloc Québécois (BQ) caucus included impressive numbers of women following the 2000, 2004, and 2006 elections. Their high levels, shown in Figure 5.5, are consistent with the relatively high proportions of female representatives in the PQ and PLQ caucuses in the Quebec National Assembly, as is discussed by Tremblay in the preceding chapter. At both levels of government, dominant parties have tended to advance progressive social agendas that in turn reinforce and foster linkages with organized feminism, which then elevate proportions of female legislators.

Despite this pattern, the rural deficit was clear in Bloc constituencies. For example, in the 2006 election, the Bloc won twenty-seven seats in less densely populated Quebec seats, and women held six, or 22 percent, of them. This figure stands at or above the national average, which is a significant achievement for the BQ. Still, women's representation was twice as high in urban Bloc ridings, where female MPs held 45 percent of seats (11/24). Similar results emerged for the Bloc in 2000 and 2004. Hence, even the woman-friendly Bloc featured a large rural deficit within its caucus.

The same conclusion holds for the New Democratic Party (NDP), except that the NDP did not have a rural deficit in 2004. This anomaly can be linked to the problem of small numbers: the NDP won only seven seats in the more rural half of Canadian districts that year. Although internal New Democratic policies have consistently promoted women candidates, and have contributed in significant ways to Canadian public life, the NDP's weak standing in less populated areas of Canada means the party has exerted little impact on the rural deficit of women MPs.

Overall, results in Figure 5.5 present a compelling pattern of rural-urban contrast across party lines. The bars in front, which depict women's representation in the more rural districts, are consistently much lower than the metropolitan levels shown in the bars behind. To be sure, the overall proportions of women elected from each party vary, as is described above. But it is equally important to recognize the pervasive cross-party headwind that impeded the election of women in rural areas. Taken together with the results reported in the previous section, these results support the conclusion that the rural deficit is an independent electoral pattern that is no less important for women's representation than regional and party differences.

## Tracking Federal Candidacies

What are the origins of this headwind? Are rural voters hostile to women candidates, or do parties fail to nominate women as rural candidates? To address these questions, we turn from elected MPs to party candidates. Party candidates were divided into two groups, according to whether the candidate's constituency was in the more or less densely populated half of Canadian districts. The gender balance in the two groups of districts over the three elections, which is illustrated on the left side of Figure 5.6, shows more women ran as candidates in urban than in rural districts. However, the rural-urban contrast in candidates in Figure 5.6 is much less stark than was the case for MPs.

Although this result initially suggests rural voters may be less likely than urban voters to vote for women candidates, a more careful analysis reveals a different picture. Inferring voter bias presumes that, apart from the gender of candidates, each major party had an equal chance of winning, which is an unrealistic presumption. Clearly, not all of the major parties are competitive in all districts. It turns out that a disproportionate number of women

*Figure 5.6*

**Women's candidacy in 2000, 2004, and 2006 federal elections**

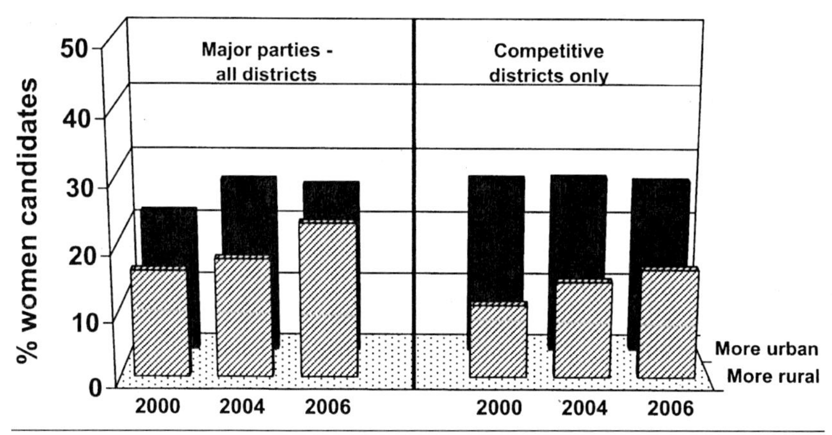


*Note:* All districts were divided into two equal groups by population density. In each district, a party is deemed competitive if its candidate wins more than half as many votes as the winner.

candidates in the rural districts ran for parties that stood no chance of winning in those constituencies. A fair comparison would exclude such lost-cause districts and consider only candidates whose parties stood a reasonable chance of winning their particular seats. This is not meant to diminish the contributions to public life made by candidates who act as standard-bearers for their parties in districts in which winning is a remote possibility; rather, it recognizes that voters in those districts are reluctant to vote for a locally unpopular party and are not necessarily expressing gender bias.

A simple way to consider competitiveness is to limit the analysis to candidates who finished reasonably close to the winner. In this section, we include candidates who won at least half as many votes as the winner in the same district.[12] The proportions of women candidates running for competitive parties in the two groups of districts over the past three elections are illustrated on the right side of Figure 5.6. Comparing the two sides of the figure, the proportion of women candidates in winnable seats in the more urban half of districts was about the same, or slightly higher, than in combined winnable plus lost-cause urban districts. If anything, women candidates in large cities were decidedly clustered in winnable districts.

In contrast, the proportion of women candidates in the more rural districts went down substantially when we excluded lost-cause constituencies in order to consider only winnable seats. The right side of Figure 5.6 thus gives a more realistic indication of what was presented to voters in each group of districts than does the left side; it shows that far fewer women ran as competitive

*Figure 5.7*

**Women candidates by party, 2000, 2004, and 2006 elections**

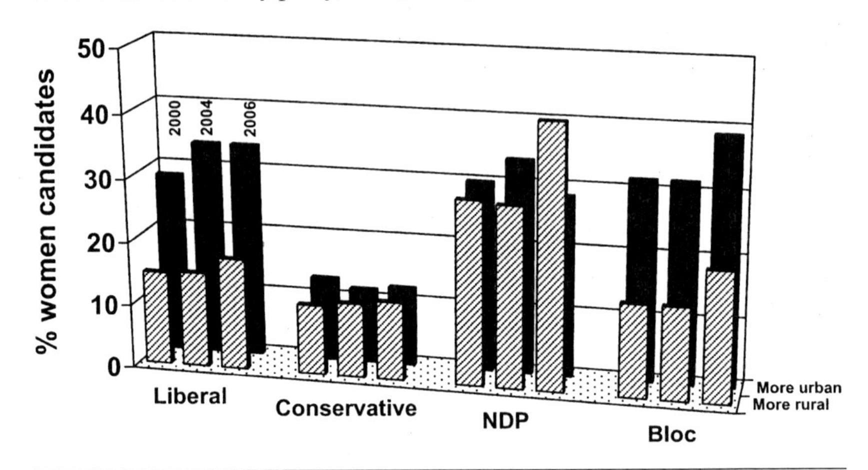


*Note:* Districts are divided into two groups according to whether their population density is above or below the national median.

candidates in rural than urban seats. The rural-urban contrast on this measure is clear and on the same scale as the contrast in electoral outcomes.

Why did so many women run in lost-cause rural districts? The answer to this question can be found in Figure 5.7, which shows proportions of women candidates nominated by each party. The most striking feature is just how many of the rural women ran for the NDP. In fact, the NDP contribution to the totals shown in Figure 5.6 is even greater than it appears in Figure 5.7 because the Bloc's contribution is confined to districts in Quebec. For example, fully 55 percent of female candidates in the more rural districts in 2006 (64/117) ran for the NDP. While the NDP promotes women candidates in both rural and urban districts, that party has enjoyed limited electoral success in less densely populated areas. Hence, the large numbers of NDP women running in rural areas have had little impact on the gender balance in the House of Commons.

Taking party competitiveness into account, these results indicate, first, that the election of women MPs is limited primarily by the small numbers of female candidates who contest winnable seats and, second, that voter hostility plays, at most, a secondary role. The party competitiveness factor also features in the story of women's success as party leadership candidates in Bashevkin's chapter in this volume. For election to the House of Commons, party fortunes matter in both urban and rural settings, but the shortfall of competitive female candidates is simply more extreme in rural areas. Numerous quantitative studies report a similar lack of voter hostility in

Britain (Lovenduski 2005, 64) and the United States, where Darcy, Welch, and Clark (1994, 73) examined candidate success rates in state elections and concluded that "voters were not discriminating against female candidates. There was little difference in voters' reactions to male and female candidates of similar party and incumbency status."

**Discussion**

The patterns presented here allow us to make educated guesses about what might happen in the future to the number of women in the House of Commons under various electoral scenarios. If the Conservatives increased their presence in the House, the number of women MPs might not simply continue to stagnate; it would likely decline significantly. The results presented in this chapter show that the relationship between the party in power and women's representation is not simple. If the Conservatives were to gain rural seats at the expense of the Liberals, the impact on the gender balance in the House would likely be negligible, since neither party has a record of electing many women in rural districts. Rural districts in Quebec are different in that the Bloc Québécois has elected somewhat higher numbers of rural women there than the Liberals and Conservatives have in the rest of Canada.

The real concern rests with metropolitan seats, especially those in Ontario and Quebec, where the Conservatives have nominated far fewer women candidates than other parties. Proportions of women elected in these major cities have exceeded 30 percent during the past few elections. In metropolitan districts that have favoured the Bloc and NDP, proportions of elected women and men have approached parity. If the Conservatives were to win significantly more of these city seats, without radically changing their approach to women candidates, the proportion of female MPs would almost certainly drop. A taste of this scenario was provided in the 2006 election, when the Conservatives made some gains in a few urban Ontario districts at the expense of the Liberals. This relatively modest change resulted in a noticeable decrease in the representation of women among Ontario MPs.

If the NDP were to win urban seats from the Liberals, this change might result in a few extra women MPs and could partially offset the losses from increased Conservative strength. For example, in the 2006 election, two Ontario urban seats previously held by Liberal men went to New Democratic women: Tony Ianno lost to Olivia Chow in Trinity-Spadina, and Pat O'Brien was defeated by Irene Mathyssen in London-Fanshawe. Two other seats held previously by Liberal women went to New Democratic women: Beth Phinney lost to Chris Charlton in Hamilton Mountain, and Sarmite Bulte was defeated by Peggy Nash in Parkdale-High Park. If, on the other hand, Liberal fortunes were to improve, the proportion of women in the House would not decline and might continue along the plateau shown in Figure 5.1.

For the most part, these scenarios for near-term partisan outcomes involve the loss or retention of women MPs in urban seats and no significant change in rural districts. The prospects for resuming the overall increases seen in the 1980s seem slim indeed. Fundamentally, this comes down to the rural deficit itself. Looking at recent election results, it seems clear that only incremental gains can be made in Canada's largest cities in the near future. Far more room exists for major gains in sparsely populated districts, where the proportions of women elected remain significantly below those in urban centres. However, such gains are rendered difficult by the rural headwind described earlier.

We have shown that the election of women is limited primarily by the small numbers of female candidates who are nominated for winnable seats. Voter hostility plays, at most, a secondary role. This turns our attention away from the vote itself and towards the same recruitment and nomination processes considered in the Tremblay and Byrne chapters in this volume. Unless massive numbers of rural voters turn to the NDP, it seems clear that, for sparsely populated districts to elect more women MPs, the Conservatives and Liberals need to nominate more women candidates in winnable seats outside major cities.

As is noted in the introductory section of this chapter, part of the rural headwind is due to demand-side constraints. Local riding executives lean heavily on (overwhelmingly male) incumbents or other well-regarded (again, overwhelmingly male) local figures with established networks whom party elites *feel* can be relied on to carry their weight in Ottawa and bring much needed resources to their constituency. But it is important to keep in mind that candidate demand does not emanate only from the local executive. Central leadership seeks in general to maintain and improve the public image of the party, and an increasingly glaring flaw in that image involves the numbers of women candidates. Lynda Erickson observed that, as far back as the early 1980s, "party leaders had voiced their support for increasing the number of women candidates, and parties had organized activities designed to do this, including, for example, workshops for women interested in party candidacies" (1998, 233). Lisa Young and William Cross found that the central leadership of most national parties continued to support measures to increase the number of women holding elected office (2003, 106). These measures can obviously lead to tension between central leadership and local executives, particularly outside metropolitan centres where remoteness and greater focus on local issues insulate riding associations from the ebbs and flows of national agendas (Carty and Eagles 2005, 149).

This sort of tension has been evident within the Liberal Party of Canada. Immediately after winning the 2006 Liberal party leadership convention, Stéphane Dion deplored the low numbers of female MPs and committed to having women make up at least one-third of his party's slate in the next election. To that end, he appointed Linda Julien as his women's candidate search director "to recruit prominent and successful women to run as Liberal candidates" (Liberal Party of Canada 2006). At that time, Dion did not rule out using his power as leader to appoint women as candidates in winnable ridings (Taber 2006). A year later, Dion followed through in the rural Saskatchewan seat of Desnethé-Missinippi-Churchill River by appointing Joan Beatty as the Liberal by-election candidate and dismissing local appeals for a nomination meeting. Another related act of central direction occurred in Central Nova, a rural district in Nova Scotia, where Dion pledged not to run a Liberal candidate against Green Party leader Elizabeth May, to the dismay of local Liberals.

On the political right, the Reform, Alliance, and merged Conservative parties have, in turn, demonstrated much less support for pro-women measures. The electoral results described here offer no indication that the Conservative Party has adopted a more pro-active role in women's empowerment than its earlier incarnations. Clearly, this party could go further than it has in recruiting more women candidates at the national level.

Nevertheless, wanting is not having. Carbert (2006) has shown that the rural headwind also includes formidable supply-side constraints. While the rural pool of potential female candidates is easily large enough to supply substantial increases in female MPs, it is not so large as to be able to do so in the face of limited enthusiasm among women themselves. An alarming majority of rural women leaders who were interviewed, especially in Atlantic Canada, expressed strong reluctance to stand for elected office. This reluctance was not typically linked to competing family responsibilities or traditional gender roles. More commonly, these women cited the dangers of partisan affiliation to their careers, or to the family's business.

Quite apart from such practical issues, interviewees also revealed a pervasive and deeply held disdain for political practices in their local environment. Rural politicians are often expected to take an active role in attracting external public sector resources to benefit their constituents and the local economy. In extreme cases of economic fragility, their role can verge on that of a patron to dependent clients. Many women leaders – especially those close enough to the centre of power to know how it is exercised in their communities – were not enthused with the idea of running for elected office in a system of which they disapprove, in a system in which they see the short-term interests of a few well-connected insiders being traded against long-term community viability. As a result, many rural women remain reluctant to embrace the moral ambiguities of elected office.

The resistance by local elites to recruiting women, and the reluctance of potential candidates to run, are both linked to economic and demographic structures that shape the relationship between rural politicians and their electorates. Carbert's interviews showed that communities that rely on a stagnant or declining single-commodity resource place heightened expectations on politicians. In this sort of environment, any political change, however small, is a potential risk. Not all rural communities are the same, however. As some commodity prices have rebounded sharply after decades of decline, rapidly expanding resource extraction industries have brought enhanced economic activity and an influx of new residents to many rural communities, especially (but not exclusively) in the West. This sort of environment, where change is pervasive and politics less urgent, may present new opportunities for women's empowerment by a motivated party.

This chapter has highlighted results from recent federal elections that show a strong and pervasive rural deficit in the election of women. Given that the rural deficit stands independent of partisan and regional characteristics, we are not hopeful that the next election, under any likely partisan outcome, will provide a quick and easy fix to stagnant levels of representation that have persisted during the past decade. It appears that one of the few available routes to open doors further to women's participation is for the parties, especially the Conservative and the Liberal, to groom and cultivate women's leadership outside major urban centres, with the goal of increasing numbers of women candidates in winnable constituencies.

**Notes**

1 This calculation includes thirty-nine urban and suburban ridings that form a geographically contiguous block of densely populated electoral districts from Scarborough in the east through Mississauga, Oakville, Burlington, and Hamilton in the west, and from Lake Ontario in the south to Richmond Hill in the north. The result, 36 percent (14/39), is not very sensitive to where one draws the line on the surrounding urban area: the percentage of Toronto-area seats held by women ranges from 32 percent to 40 percent, depending on which constituencies are included. Election results were obtained from Elections Canada.

2 This calculation includes thirty-four urban and suburban ridings that form a geographically contiguous block of densely populated electoral districts on and around the island of Montreal. The result, 38 percent (13/34), is not very sensitive to where one draws the line on the surrounding urban area: the percentage of Montreal-area seats held by women ranges from 36 percent to 40 percent, depending on which constituencies are included. Election results were obtained from Elections Canada.

3 One might contend that comparison to the 2004 national average is unfair, because Toronto and Montreal are located in provinces that elected relatively high proportions of women MPs: 25 percent in Ontario and 27 percent in Quebec. However, these relatively high province-wide numbers are almost entirely attributable to the particularly high numbers in Toronto and Montreal, respectively. If we exclude the thirty-nine Toronto and surrounding area ridings used in the previous calculation, we find that the "rest-of-Ontario" proportion drops to only 19 percent, which is near or below the national average. Similarly, the non-Montreal proportion of Quebec federal seats held by women was only 17 percent. It should be noted that these lower proportions include other urban centres, such as Ottawa and London in Ontario, as well as Quebec City and Hull in Quebec, so they should not be construed as rural proportions.

4 We have experimented with more complicated analyses that do a better job of ranking the oddly mixed districts within the rural-urban spectrum and have verified that such modifications have only negligible effects on the patterns presented in this chapter.

5 The main purpose of this analysis is to illustrate how the rural deficit has developed during recent years, and to place this pattern in the context of Canada's current federal political scene. Each of the figures in this chapter is designed to offer a visually clear presentation, understandable to as broad an audience as possible.

6 In drawing the boundaries for its census metropolitan areas (CMAs), Statistics Canada also includes rural areas that it deems to be influenced by the metropolitan centres. While 64 percent of Canada's 2001 census population lived within the overall boundaries of the CMAs, less than 60 percent lived in the urban parts of the CMAs. Hence, the percentage of Canadians living in cities like Toronto, Calgary, Halifax, and Thunder Bay is in the fifties. In a particularly lucid pair of articles, Roy MacGregor explained the discrepancy between this number and the oft-cited statistic that Canada is 80 percent urbanized. The resolution involves the large numbers of Canadians who live in smaller, technically urban, settings, including, as extreme examples, Arnold's Cove, Newfoundland; Val-Brillant, Quebec; Rodney, Ontario; Killam, Alberta; and Salmo, British Columbia. See MacGregor 2007a and 2007b.

7 In Canada, no official definition establishes what constitutes a rural electoral district. Statistics Canada designates its smallest unit – a census block – as either rural or urban based on a minimum community population of only one thousand. Fewer than one-quarter of federal electoral districts have a majority of people confined to communities that small. The remaining constituencies in the "more rural" half of Canadian districts have significant minorities of people in census blocks designated by Statistics Canada as rural and other people living in towns as well as small and medium-sized cities with populations over one thousand. Readers who wish to use the most exclusive definition of a rural constituency might prefer to call the phenomenon described in this chapter a "non-metropolitan deficit of women MPs" or, even, a "rural, town, and small- and medium-sized city deficit." However, these terms, in addition to being cumbersome, fail to convey the basic pattern, which is that women's parliamentary representation is directly related to population density. For these reasons we refer to a "rural deficit."

8 A two-way split in each region helps to simplify the presentation of results without washing out any of the strongest relationships. Breaking the results into two groups on either side of the national median is supported by the results presented in Figure 5.3, which show that both of the more sparsely populated quartiles elected significantly fewer women than the national average in all three elections, while both of the more densely populated quartiles elected significantly more women than the national average.

9 Due to the small number of federal districts in the Atlantic region, caution should be exercised when comparing proportions of women elected in that region with those in other regions. Research not reported here shows that cities in the Atlantic region tend to elect more women to provincial legislatures than do less densely populated areas (Carbert 2006, 13).

10 The western region comprises British Columbia, Alberta, Saskatchewan, and Manitoba.

11 The 2000 election preceded the merger between the Canadian Alliance and the Progressive Conservatives that formed the Conservative Party. The two caucuses were combined for the 2000 results shown in Figures 5.5 and 5.7.

12 We tested other possible indicators of competitiveness and found the result was not overly sensitive to how it was measured.

**References**


Bashevkin, Sylvia. 1985. *Toeing the Lines: Women in Party Politics in English Canada*. Toronto: University of Toronto Press.

Brodie, Janine. 1977. "The Recruitment of Canadian Women Provincial Legislators, 1950–1975." *Atlantis* 2, 2: 6-17.

Carbert, Louise. 2006. *Rural Women's Leadership in Atlantic Canada*. Toronto: University of Toronto Press.

Carty, R. Kenneth, and Munroe Eagles. 2005. *Politics Is Local: National Politics at the Grassroots*. Don Mills: Oxford University Press.

Darcy, Robert, Susan Welch, and Janet Clark. 1994. *Women, Elections, and Representation*. 2nd ed. Lincoln: University of Nebraska Press.

Erickson, Lynda. 1998. "Entry to the Commons: Parties, Recruitment and the Election of Women in 1993." In *Women and Political Representation in Canada,* ed. Manon Tremblay and Caroline Andrew, 219-56. Ottawa: University of Ottawa Press.
Liberal Party of Canada. 2006. "Liberals Announce Women's Candidate Search Director." Press Release. 13 December.
Lovenduski, Joni. 2005. *Feminizing Politics*. Cambridge: Polity Press.
Matland, Richard, and Donley Studlar. 1998. "Gender and the Electoral Opportunity Structure in the Canadian Provinces." *Political Research Quarterly* 5, 1: 117-40.
McGregor, Roy. 2007a. "Who Says We're an Urban Country?" *Globe and Mail,* 24 November: A2.
2007b. "Can We Really Call a Town without a Stoplight 'Urban'?" *Globe and Mail,* 10 December: A2.
Mendelson, Robert, and Janet Lefebvre. 2003. *Reviewing Census Metropolitan Areas (CMA) and Census Agglomerations (CA) in Canada According to Metropolitan Functionality.* Ottawa: Statistics Canada Geography Working Paper Series. Catalogue no. 92F0138MIE – no. 001.
Moncrief, Gary, and Joel Thompson. 1991. "Urban and Rural Ridings and Women in Provincial Politics: A Note on Female MLAs." *Canadian Journal of Political Science* 24, 4: 831-37.
Niven, David. 1998. *The Missing Majority: The Recruitment of Women as State Legislative Candidates*. Westport: Praeger.
Taber, Jane. 2006. "Don't Let Afghanistan Split Party, Ignatieff Warns Dion." *Globe and Mail,* 14 December.
Young, Lisa. 2003. "Can Feminists Transform Party Politics? The Canadian Experience." In *Women and Electoral Politics in Canada,* ed. Manon Tremblay and Linda Trimble, 76-91. Toronto: Oxford University Press.
Young, Lisa, and William Cross. 2003. "Women's Involvement in Canadian Political Parties." In *Women and Electoral Politics in Canada,* ed. Manon Tremblay and Linda Trimble, 92-109. Toronto: Oxford University Press.

# Part 3
# Cabinet and Party Leadership Experiences

# 6
# Making a Difference When the Doors Are Open: Women in the Ontario NDP Cabinet, 1990-95

*Lesley Byrne*

In September 1990, Ontario voters elected a New Democratic Party (NDP) majority government in Canada's wealthiest and most populous province. Of the NDP candidates who won that year, women formed a record proportion – 26 percent. Premier Bob Rae then appointed eleven women to his twenty-seven-member cabinet (42.3 percent). This was a groundbreaking move. No premier in Canadian history had ever formed a cabinet with such a high percentage of women, nor had any previous Ontario premier appointed near that level.

The Rae cabinet was a turning point on symbolic as well as substantive levels, since so many women in a single government held the potential to change public policy. For researchers, this period provided an ideal setting in which to study whether elected women could make a substantive difference.

While many American studies on the impact of women in politics focus on the legislative arena (Swers 2002; Thomas 1991; Welch 1985), analyses of parliamentary systems recognize that the political executive holds dominant policy power. The Canadian cabinet is known as the "focus and fulcrum" of the system, and provincial government has been called "cabinet government" (Dunn 1996). Cabinet ministers are so significant that one study uses appointments to that level to gauge the political influence of electoral districts (Walks 2004).

Moreover, examining the Ontario NDP experience permits us to probe questions of critical mass. Some scholars suggest that the proportion of women needed to change a decision-making culture rests in the range of 15 percent (Arscott and Trimble 1997) to 30 percent (Dahlerup 1988), while others argue that there is no direct correlation between the percentage of women in cabinet and the passage of legislation beneficial to women as a group (Childs and Krook 2006). Sandra Grey's analysis of women in the New Zealand legislature found that female MPs were strong advocates for women and women's issues, but their activism peaked at a representational level of 15 percent and declined once numbers reached 33 percent (Grey 2006).

Members of the Rae government came from a political party that had long placed women's issues at the forefront. In her study of the Alberta legislature, Trimble (1993) found that party affiliation was at least as influential as the election of more women: even male opposition MLAs (of the NDP) tended to be more pro-feminist in their policy interventions than female Conservatives. Young's (2000) comparative account of Canada and the United States noted the long-standing ideological convergence between women's movement and NDP perspectives.

The confluence of a pro-feminist party in power in 1990-95, alongside record numbers of elected as well as cabinet women, offers a chance to ask whether women changed the style and content of provincial government. An article in *Chatelaine* magazine named Rae's cabinet ministers "women of the year" (Gray 1991). Some of the individuals appointed to Ontario's political executive raised expectations even higher. "Women do things in a different, more consensual way," argued citizenship minister Elaine Ziemba. "Issues that affect women's lives will have a priority they never had before," promised Anne Swarbrick, minister responsible for women's issues (as quoted in Gray 1991, 22).

By 1995, the Rae government was history. The recession of the early 1990s, compounded by public perceptions that the NDP government could not manage these difficulties, helped elect a majority Conservative government with Mike Harris as premier. Only four New Democratic women were re-elected in 1995. Harris promised to abolish employment equity legislation, which had formed a cornerstone of the Rae government's feminist initiatives. Just four of the eighteen Harris-era Conservative cabinet ministers (22 percent) were women.

This reversal of fortunes also leads us to ask why the doors for women's elite-level participation seemed so open in 1990. What were the circumstances under which so many NDP women won legislative seats? Did their cabinet appointments make a difference, in the sense of speaking for or substantively representing the women of Ontario? Did they change the institution of government in any way, or did they have an appreciable impact on policy? And finally, are the doors opening wider over time in Ontario?

## Electing NDP Women in 1990

For the Ontario NDP, the 1990 provincial election was unique in a number of ways: a record number of women were running and no New Democrats expected their party to form a government. In 1982, the party passed an affirmative action resolution to improve women's representation on internal party bodies, and, in 1989, it was agreed that 50 percent of all constituencies

*Figure 6.1*

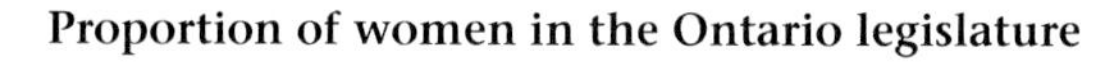

**Proportion of women in the Ontario legislature**

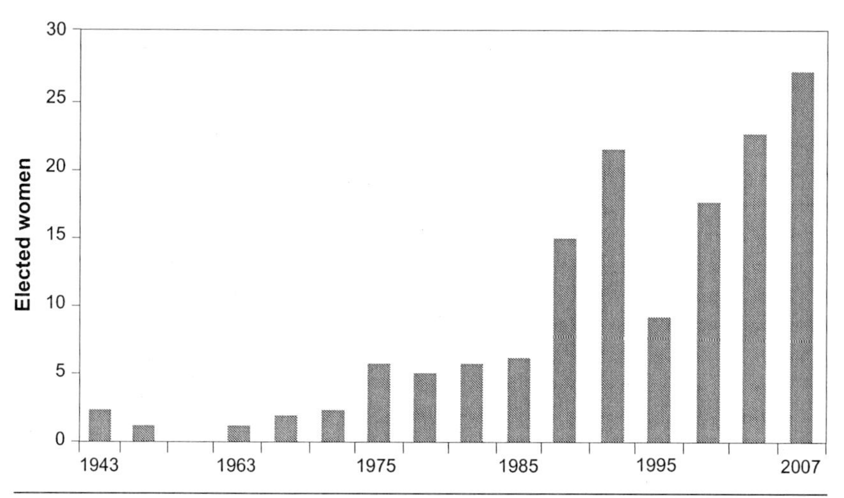


*Sources:* Elections Ontario (1999 and 2003); *Canadian Parliamentary Guide* (various years).

should have women candidates and 60 percent of winnable seats should have affirmative action nominees. The 1989 guidelines also stipulated that constituencies without an NDP incumbent could not hold a nomination meeting until at least one candidate was nominated from a "specific target group" (which included women, visible minorities, people with disabilities, and Aboriginal people; see Bashevkin 1993, 100). The party's proactive approach helps to explain why New Democrats nominated an unprecedented number of women candidates in 1990 (thirty-six, or 28 percent of Ontario candidates).

At the beginning of the 1990 campaign, the NDP was not considered likely to form the government, which meant some women agreed to run on the assumption that they would not become members of provincial parliament (MPPs). Once the party won a majority government with a minority of votes, nineteen women became MPPs.[1] As is shown in Figure 6.1, this same pattern caused a measurable jump in the percentage of women in the legislature – from 14.6 percent before the 1990 election to 21.5 percent afterward.

Before and during the 1990 provincial campaign, the NDP offered a number of specific supports for women candidates, including the following:

- a Women Candidate Support Committee – composed of women who had previously run and who mentored first-time candidates
- a Women Candidate Hotline – for problems and support

- a conference for women candidates – including a workshop on campaign survival
- $500 for child care expenses, if needed
- a Women's Canvas day across the province, with leaflets outlining each party's record on women's issues.

One important question remains, however. Did the NDP women who were elected in 1990 make significant changes to provincial politics, including the content of public policy or the tenor of legislative debate?

I addressed this question by interviewing women who served in the Rae cabinet, and I was able to meet with nine of the original eleven appointed in 1990, as well as one additional woman who was appointed later in the mandate. The interviews each lasted approximately sixty to ninety minutes and took place during the spring and summer of 1996, when almost all had left elected office. I asked cabinet ministers about their professional backgrounds, relationship to the party, self-identification as feminists, gender divisions in cabinet, the importance of critical mass, constraints on achieving a feminist agenda, and opinions about substantive representation. During a subsequent round of interviews in 2006-7, I met with seven women who served as cabinet ministers in the Harris/Eves Conservative governments from 1995 to 2003. In the summer of 2007, I also spoke to party officials from all three parties about their efforts – both current and historical – to help elect women.

**Why Expect Policy Impact?**

As is discussed in Bashevkin's introduction to this volume, substantive representatives have a special role in advocating for (or "acting for") women – and a commitment to feminism and feminist policy offers one clear indication of their intention to contribute in this way. Many NDP women elected and appointed as cabinet ministers in 1990 can be considered feminists on several grounds. First, they called themselves feminists, and prior to the election many pursued feminist objectives in women's organizations as well as in the NDP. Marion Boyd, who served as Ontario's attorney general, minister of education, minister of community and social services, and minister responsible for women's issues, discussed publicly the need to change the power relationships between men and women. Frances Lankin, who served in the Rae cabinet as chair of management board of cabinet, minister of government services, minister of health, and minister of economic development and trade, talked about the importance of social change in advancing the status of women. Jenny Carter, who was appointed minister of energy, described differences in how women and men experienced the world. Five women ministers in the Rae government had held prior public office: two had been municipal councillors, one served as a school trustee, and two were incumbent MPPs. Each of the women in the NDP cabinet had a long history of community involvement, either professionally or on a volunteer basis. Two had run women's shelters, several were trade union activists, and a number had led community agencies. More important for determining commitment to the values of the women's movement, all of them except one (Shelley Martel, who was only twenty-four when she was first elected) had worked either professionally or on a volunteer basis for a women's service organization or a feminist policy campaign (including child care and pay equity).

Second, as New Democrats, these women were guided by party principles that inclined them in a feminist direction. As noted above, the Ontario NDP had already adopted significant internal guidelines during the 1980s that were designed to attract more women to senior positions. Other explicitly feminist content can be found in party policies dating from 1980, including, for example, the area of post-secondary education, where women were described as "ghetto-ized in the traditional fields of study" (Ontario NDP 1996, n.p.). In 1988, in the midst of a heated national debate over reproductive choice, the Ontario NDP convention adopted a resolution that stated: "Whereas choice is an equality and economic issue facing women ... Therefore be it resolved that the Ontario New Democratic Party reaffirm a woman's freedom of choice by supporting the right of women to full access to abortion" (ibid.).

Each woman who served in the Rae cabinet saw herself as having a special responsibility to represent women and women's issues. In interviews, former ministers stated that they felt an "added responsibility" and an "awareness of our role" in the government and the legislature. Some viewed this role as being extremely important. For example, former attorney general Marion Boyd, speaking in 1996, argued: "I think the question about who's going to benefit and who will lose and that the cumulative benefit and loss to specific groups was looked at more carefully. Everybody would have said it was an overall perspective, but we as women know that the overall perspective is overwhelmingly a male perspective and it does not take into account the vulnerabilities of different groups. So absolutely, that made a difference. And it made a difference all the time because these questions were asked" (interview with Marion Boyd, 1996). Because of their perspectives and experience in the women's movement, combined with the NDP's own history and values, Rae-era cabinet women were not only expected to make a policy difference, they themselves expected to exert some influence.

## Measuring Policy Impact

Since cabinet members must vote with the government or else resign their positions, we cannot discern much from voting records at Queen's Park. A great deal of important policy discussion occurs in the privacy of cabinet and caucus meetings well before issues make it to the floor of the legislature. On the subject of gender divisions in cabinet, Rae-era ministers noted that women voted as a block on some issues, and they believed it made an enormous difference to have so many women at the table. "We were about to vote on an issue," said Evelyn Gigantes, former minister of housing, "and I just looked up and realized there were enough women to support it. We had the votes" (interview with Evelyn Gigantes, 1996).

Few respondents could recall specific issues that divided the cabinet along gender lines. Although none betrayed the principle of cabinet secrecy, many acknowledged that female ministers were generally less swayed than their male counterparts by calls for budget cuts and other anti-deficit steps. Some issues that ended up dividing the cabinet along gender lines were entirely unexpected, including the decision not to go ahead with committing provincial funds to an opera and ballet house in downtown Toronto. Male NDP ministers saw this as a good investment in tourism and culture. Women, on the other hand, argued that an economic recession was no time to build an elite cultural institution and maintained that the cabinet should focus on building affordable housing. The women won the vote.[2]

One of the most important tests of substantive representation is the extent to which women cabinet ministers affected public policy. While its impact was less profound than many Ontario women's groups had hoped and expected, the Rae government did enact important milestones in this area. Accomplishments included a job creation program with specified child care provisions, increases to the provincial minimum wage, extended parental leave provisions, protection for home workers, employment equity legislation that required employers to ensure that their workforces reflected the diversity of the larger community, pay equity laws that raised the pay of more than a million women, enhanced funding for violence against women programs (including prevention, treatment, and education), child care initiatives, legalized midwifery, and full public health insurance coverage for abortions performed in private clinics (Ontario 1994).

Some of these policies were equity-oriented, notably pay equity and employment equity. They sought to address what many New Democrats viewed as institutionalized and measurable inequalities. These polices were the first to be overturned by the Harris government, although the Ontario courts denied the Conservatives the right to rescind pay equity. Other initiatives, notably those in the areas of midwifery, preventing violence against women, and access to abortion, went beyond an equal rights framework. Ironically, many of the latter survived the subsequent Conservative government.

One of the factors that may have helped advance this agenda was the presence of women in the Ontario civil service. The numbers of women at senior levels increased through the late 1980s and early 1990s due to employment equity legislation (Collier 1997). In 1992, about 47 percent of the provincial public service was female (ibid.). Increased representation in the ranks of assistant deputy ministers and deputy ministers occurred at the same time as two main bureaucratic bodies advocated for women's issues within government; the Ontario Women's Directorate (OWD) and the Ontario Advisory Council on the Status of Women were significant femocratic units that arguably reached their peak levels of influence during the Rae years (ibid.). Funding for the OWD increased from $19 million in 1989-90 to a high of $24 million in 1991-92 and 1992-93 (Ontario 1993). Funding dropped slightly in the final two years of the NDP mandate to $23 million – a development that corresponded to a cooling of the relationship with the women's movement and tighter fiscal pressures on the government (Ontario 1995). Collier (1997) notes that, although funding for the advisory council also fell, the unit was not eliminated.

Research that compares anti-violence and child care policy in Ontario and British Columbia also reports that significant advances were made during the Rae years (Collier 2005, 2006). Collier (2006) notes that the Ontario NDP increased funding for sexual assault and assault prevention and women's shelters between 1990 and 1992 and reports that no cuts were made to anti-violence programs during the subsequent recession. She concludes that informal links between women's movement organizations and the Rae government helped improve access to decision makers – resulting, at least temporarily, in a more state-focused movement (Collier 2005). Not all of these connections were close and cordial, however, since relations between the Ontario Association of Interval and Transition Houses (the largest shelter coalition in the province) and the NDP government were strained (ibid.).

Some policy accomplishments of the NDP government were applauded by feminist groups, although they were far from unanimous in their support of the regime. Two of the Rae government's major platform commitments, public child care and pay equity legislation, were the subject of subsequent analyses that raised critical questions about both policy development and policy outcomes. Writing in 1997, Sue Findlay described her experiences as a consultant to the Pay Equity Commission. She noted that while pay equity legislation was a condition imposed by the NDP for signing an accord with the Liberals in the mid-1980s, the most significant component of that policy initiative, proxy comparison of predominantly male and female jobs, was not implemented until three years into the NDP's own mandate (Findlay 1997).

Paralleling this view, Tom Walkom has argued that Rae-era pay equity laws were watered down significantly. Extended deadlines for compliance and decisions to exclude approximately 420,000 Ontario nurses and child care workers from the purview of the legislation offered two pieces of evidence in support of this perspective. In Walkom's words, "Traditional NDP allies were outraged" when the minister of labour scaled back the original 1991 pay equity legislation (Walkom 1994, 214). George Ehring and Wayne Roberts made the same observation, claiming, "Women activists are fed up with the NDP government for its failure to follow through with announcements it had made" (Ehring and Roberts 1993, 318). The same authors pointed to constitutional tensions that resulted from Premier Rae's support for the Charlottetown Accord – a deal that was vigorously opposed by the National Action Committee on the Status of Women.

Lois Harder's study of child care policy concluded that, because the Rae government was sympathetic to moderate feminist perspectives, the overlap between government and movement positions effectively narrowed the consultation process (Harder 1993). Given that the government was on the same side as many of the advocates, other views, including those to the left of the cabinet, had minimal impact. Findlay (1997) describes a similar scenario and, ultimately, a process of co-optation that occurred among feminists situated in the bureaucracy, the cabinet, and high-profile women's organizations. Many of the latter believed the government had not accomplished enough – particularly during the final two years of its mandate, when the overwhelming focus was on fiscal restraint rather than social justice. Several ministers I interviewed referred to this slowing of progressive policy change as a disappointing part of their cabinet experience, one they did not want to repeat.

According to Sandra Burt and Elizabeth Lorenzin, the combined effects of a poor economic climate and political inexperience led the government away from its pre-election commitments to women and women's movement objectives. Ministers in the Rae government "saw themselves as spokespeople for responsible government – and this meant avoiding single issue groups like the ones they helped found" (Burt and Lorenzin 1997, 226). The same study argues that women in the Rae government failed to maintain links to the feminist community, which in turn made it possible for women's movement policy priorities to be eclipsed by a culture of fiscal restraint. My own interviews with NDP cabinet ministers point towards a distinct gender division in cabinet on the importance of fiscal restraint versus social issues, with women generally more concerned than men about the latter (Byrne 1997). Overall, female cabinet ministers said their male colleagues adopted fiscal priorities long before they did, but, by 1995, the entire Rae government, in their view, had been converted to fiscal conservatism.

If a party comes to power with feminist principles, and the leader appoints significant numbers of women to cabinet, then we conclude that such a regime can exert an important impact on public policy. What about the nature of legislative institutions? If more powerful women sit in the parliamentary front bench, is the tenor of debate changed in any way?

**Did NDP Women Change the Tenor of Debate?**

In interviews, every NDP minister referred without prompting to the male culture of the Ontario legislature. Each spoke at length about how, whenever a woman minister rose to speak, the ambient noise in the chamber rose suddenly. Male opposition MPPs often commented on the clothing worn by female ministers. Many of the women in cabinet were unaccustomed to the angry, argumentative, and inflamed rhetoric of parliamentary debate, and one said she would have preferred a public opportunity to "really explain the issue," rather than engaging in a heated legislative debate in which the facts of the matter at hand were seldom, if ever, revealed (interview with Elaine Ziemba, minister of citizenship, 1996).

Marion Boyd, in her role as minister responsible for women's issues, initiated a legislative debate on the tenor question in 1992. In a co-authored article published one year later, she defined the problem as follows: "Besides verbal attacks and manipulation of tone, other forms of behavior clearly discriminate but are harder to quantify. This behavior comprises a range of efforts to humiliate and intimidate members, usually women, as they fill their elected roles in the House. Non-verbal tactics included significantly increasing the volume – that is, more heckling, coughing and hissing when a woman rises to speak, introducing a wall of sound before she has even started her words, blowing kisses across the floor of the House, and mocking the higher-pitched voices of female members" (Boyd et al. 1992-93). Boyd's report did not make any legislative headway at Queen's Park, even though some opposition party members agreed with her position and co-authored a summary document with her. Yet, changing the tenor of legislative debate was simply not a Rae government priority. Moreover, a number of MPPs from other parties considered the Boyd report to be too strident. One female Conservative agreed that language used in the legislature was inappropriate but claimed that the problem was more a general climate of personal attack rather than an atmosphere that specifically alienated women.

While the tenor of legislative debate remained unchanged, women ministers found creative and untraditional ways to discuss public policy outside cabinet. Family obligations meant a number of them were unavailable for the round of social engagements enjoyed by their male colleagues, including those where informal conversations could take place. Women ministers indicated that they did try to get together socially, and for a time there was a women's caucus – but few cabinet members were able to attend. Instead, some women cabinet ministers got together in the washroom, and developed signals indicating it was time to meet one another, to discuss upcoming issues on the agenda. These external meetings sometimes happened by coincidence, including an occasion when the minister of consumer and commercial relations and the minister of economic development and trade were at the same hair salon at the same time and accomplished quite a lot at their serendipitous session. Interview data suggest the sheer numbers of women at the NDP cabinet table increased their ability – and their comfort level – to create the kinds of informal networking opportunities that male legislators had long enjoyed.

Interviews conducted with ministers in the subsequent Conservative government revealed quite different patterns. Tory women acknowledged that they were missing out on crucial opportunities and, on the rare occasions when they did manage to get a group together, that their socializing was met with suspicion by men in the same cabinet. As one Conservative minister noted, "We tried to have a women's caucus – it made the men paranoid. It was a social night. We had to be careful; the guys thought something was going on. We were extra supportive of each other, though; we always knew what was going on with each other's lives" (interview with former Conservative cabinet minister, 2006).

Stronger informal networks and heightened personal comfort levels, however, cannot by themselves alter legislative institutions. They might have some influence, though, on decision-making styles, including the opportunity to apply what women learned from feminist collectives in the authoritative and hierarchical realm of government. Frances Lankin, who held many portfolios after 1990, maintained that it was "hard to run a ministry like the Ministry of Health with a 17.4 billion dollar budget and huge issues of major public controversy and public interest, and get through that on a day-to-day basis, and be a consensus builder at the same time. There just isn't time. The pressures are to get through stuff" (interview with Lankin, 1996). Her reflections suggest that the organizational distance between smaller advocacy or service groups, on one side, and ministerial leadership, on the other, was so large as to render impossible a translation of decision-making styles. This conclusion is supported in other work, including Caroline Andrew's discussion in Chapter 2 of this volume. In addition, Blackmore (1993) notes that feminist leaders are expected to lead in feminist ways by using shared and communal decision-making styles, but, at the same time, they are also expected to be agents of change. New Democratic women ministers came face to face with the limitations of government and governing. That is, most had to make a difficult shift from advocate to minister and learned it was simply not possible to accomplish everything they had dreamed of doing as part of the government.

The high proportion of women at the NDP cabinet table had a subtle and temporary impact on the institutions of government in Ontario. Given the nature of parliamentary government, a new majority government offered the opportunity to alter the culture and decision-making style of the cabinet in order to better reflect the principles of the party in power. Women ministers noted their ability to raise feminist issues and analysis at the table.

They also pointed out that while their male colleagues were supportive of the policy issues that brought many of the females in cabinet into public life, NDP men, for the most part, did not comprehend the implicit sexism of legislative institutions. Several women ministers also noted that, over time, their male colleagues became more sympathetic to the issues that the women consistently raised.

Bob Rae's Ontario NDP government was path-breaking on many levels, since it represented the first time in power for these women and their party. During the five years from 1990 to 1995, the government's accomplishments were not inconsiderable, but, had the NDP won a second term, the wisdom of accumulated experience might have permitted cabinet women in particular to secure more policy and institutional changes.

From the perspective of opening doors for women in politics, the Ontario case demonstrates that if parties sympathetic to a women's movement agenda have more women running and winning, then voters will see progressive feminist policy action. What is less clear, however, is which parts of that causal chain are necessary, rather than merely sufficient. Were Ontario NDP activists well advised to focus on internal party rule changes that nominated more women and on guidelines that ensured that those nominations occurred in winnable seats? Or was the crucial piece of the puzzle the fact that activists pursued policy resolutions at party conventions that brought issues raised by the women's movement into the NDP policy book?

### Are Doors Opening Wider in Ontario?

More than a decade after the Rae government left Queen's Park, these questions remain significant. Women and political pressure groups continue their efforts to change the composition of the Ontario legislature – both by increasing the numbers of women MPPs and by advocating electoral system change.

Under pressure from multi-partisan organizations, particularly Equal Voice, all three Ontario party leaders committed themselves in 2006 to nominating more women candidates for the 2007 election (Legislative Assembly of Ontario 2006). Their historic statement included a promise by Premier Dalton McGuinty to nominate women candidates in half the provincial seats not held by the Liberals. In his words, "The party I lead ... is committed to attracting and welcoming more women candidates. The percentage of women in our caucus has risen from 6% in 1985, to 13% in 1995, to 24% today. What's more, almost one third of our cabinet ministers are women. So we've made progress, but we have much work left to do. To that end, our party is striving to seek out and nominate capable women in half of the ridings that we do not currently represent in this legislature. It's just one more step, but it's a step forward" (McGuinty, quoted in ibid.). Conservative opposition leader John Tory pledged that 30 percent of Tory candidates would be women, while NDP leader Howard Hampton said half of his party's nominees would be female.

In the 2007 Ontario election, all three parties ran more women: the NDP ran forty-two women candidates (up from thirty-four in 2003), the Liberals ran thirty-eight (up from twenty-three), and the Conservatives ran twenty-four (up from twenty-one). The overall proportion of nominated women candidates was 32.4 percent – a record high, and up from 25.2 percent in 2003 (G.P. Murray Research 2007). Potentially, the legislature could have moved from one-quarter women to one-third. However, five of the twenty-one incumbent female MPPs did not seek re-election, which reduced the incumbency edge referred to in Tremblay's discussion of Quebec (in Chapter 4) by about 25 percent. The election results demonstrated an improvement in numbers of women elected – but not a dramatic one. With twenty-nine women MPPs in place, the percentage of women in the legislature rose to 27 percent. All but one of the incumbent women members won re-election.

Beyond running more women, Ontario New Democrats have long argued that increasing the numbers of female MPPs requires province-wide electoral reform. Speaking in 2006, party leader Howard Hampton maintained that internal rule changes could only go so far: "Too many obstacles are placed in the paths of women in politics ... When we look around the world, we notice that those jurisdictions that have proportional representation elect far more women. It doesn't matter if you look at Europe, Australia or New Zealand, where you have proportional representation you have more women elected" (Howard Hampton quoted in Legislative Assembly of Ontario 2006).

Pressure from within and outside Queen's Park to examine electoral reform led the Liberals to create a Citizens' Assembly on Democratic Reform in March 2006 (see website, Ontario, Democratic Renewal Secretariat). The Assembly proposed a system that would combine locally elected with at-large MPPs in a 129-seat legislature. The stated rationale for introducing proportionally selected members was two-fold: first, to bring new perspectives into the legislature; and second, to "include more women and other citizens currently underrepresented in the legislature ... a Mixed Member Proportional system is more likely than Ontario's current system to increase the participation of women and other underrepresented citizens in the legislature" (Ontario 2007).

The proposal for electoral reform was soundly defeated in a fall 2007 referendum: 63 percent of voters who participated endorsed the existing system, while 37 percent supported change (Elections Ontario 2007). Media reports suggested the referendum failed because an ineffective education campaign failed to convince Ontarians to reform their 215-year-old system (CBC 2007). According to a June 2007 poll by Environics, some 70 percent of Ontarians were unaware of the referendum (Environics 2007). It seems fair to conclude that while a new system may have resulted in increased numbers of women in the provincial legislature, the reform proposal was not rejected for that reason. Few observers expect another Ontario referendum on electoral reform in the near future. In the absence of electoral reform, as Tremblay notes in Chapter 4, provincial party commitment to opening more doors for women has proven effective.

## Conclusion

Does opening the doors for women's participation make a difference to public policy? When we examine the Ontario experience of 1990 and the years that followed, it becomes clear that nominating, electing, and appointing significant numbers of women to the provincial cabinet contributed to significant policy innovations by the Rae government. In spite of disappointments expressed by women's movement activists and others, many important accomplishments of the era still stand – including groundbreaking midwifery programs and public health insurance coverage of elective abortions.

In the election of 1995, provincial parties fielded as many women candidates as in 1990, but far fewer were elected because the victorious Conservatives nominated the fewest women. The policy implications of the Mike Harris victory in 1995 are beyond the scope of this chapter, but it is notable that his government severely reduced social assistance payments, imposed major jurisdictional and fiscal changes on the province's cities and school boards, and eliminated the Ontario Advisory Council on the Status of Women.

Coming out of the Conservative years, the willingness of the McGuinty government to place a referendum proposal on electoral reform before the people of Ontario – especially one that so explicitly focused on increasing women's representation – signalled a clear shift in direction. The statements by all three provincial party leaders in spring 2006 also indicated a commitment to political equality. Women, therefore, find the doors to participation more open than during the Harris years; McGuinty's cabinet is one-third female, which remains below the figure reached during the Rae years but above the Conservative level.

### Notes

1 In 1990, 18 percent of Liberal candidates and 14 percent of Conservative candidates were female, according to data from Elections Ontario.

2 The initial opera site was, instead, used for a housing development. A new ballet and opera house opened elsewhere in Toronto in 2006, after the Ontario Liberals returned to office and renewed their funding commitment.

### References

Arscott, Jane, and Linda Trimble, eds. 1997. *In the Presence of Women: Representation in Canadian Governments*. Toronto: Harcourt Brace and Company.

Bashevkin, Sylvia. 1993. *Toeing the Lines: Women and Party Politics in English Canada.* 2nd ed. Toronto: Oxford University Press.
Blackmore, Jill, and Jane Kenway. 1993. *Gender Matters in Education Administration and Policy: A Feminist Introduction.* London: Falmer Press.
Boyd, Marion, Sean Conway, Greg Sorbara, and Barbara Sullivan. 1992-93. "Roundtable: Conduct of Members in the Ontario Legislature." *Canadian Parliamentary Review* 15, 4: 29-34.
Burt, Sandra, and Elizabeth Lorenzin. 1997. "Taking the Women's Movement to Queen's Park: Women's Interests and the New Democratic Government of Ontario." In *In the Presence of Women: Representation in Canadian Government,* ed. J. Arscott and L. Trimble, 202-27. Toronto: Harcourt and Brace.
Byrne, Lesley. 1997. "Feminists in Power: Women Cabinet Ministers in the New Democratic Party (NDP) Government of Ontario, 1990-1995." *Policy Studies Journal* 25, 4: 601-12.
*Canadian Parliamentary Guide.* 1995, 1996, 1997, 1998-99, 2000, 2001, 2002. Scarborough, ON: Gale Canada.
CBC (Canadian Broadcasting Corporation). 2007. "Ontario Rejects Electoral Reform in Referendum." CBC.ca, 11 October. http://www.cbc.ca/canada/ontariovotes2007/story/2007/10/10/mmp-referendum.html?ref=rss.
Childs, Sara, and Mona Lena Krook. 2006. "Should Feminists Give Up on Critical Mass? A Contingent Yes." *Politics and Gender* 2, 4: 491-530.
Collier, Cheryl. 1997. "Judging Women's Political Success in the 1990s." In *The Government and Politics of Ontario,* ed. Graham White, 268-83. 5th ed. Toronto: University of Toronto Press.
–. 2005. "Do Strong Women's Movements Get Results? Measuring the Impact of the Child Care and Anti-Violence Movements in Ontario 1970-2000." Paper presented at the annual meeting of the Canadian Political Science Association, London, ON, 2-4 June 2005.
–. 2006. "Above Retrenchment? Anti-Violence Policy in Ontario and British Columbia in Neo-Liberal Times." Paper presented at the annual meeting of the Canadian Political Science Association, Toronto, 1-2 June 2006.
Dahlerup, Drude. 1988. "From a Small to a Large Minority: Women in Scandinavian Politics." *Scandinavian Political Studies* 11, 4: 275-99.
Dunn, Christopher. 1996. *Provinces: Canadian Provincial Politics.* Peterborough: Broadview Press.
Ehring, George, and Wayne Roberts. 1993. *Giving Away a Miracle: Lost Dreams, Broken Promises and the Ontario NDP.* Oakville: Mosaic Press.
Elections Ontario. 1999. "1999 General Election, Election Summary." http://www.elections.on.ca/en-CA/Tools/PastResults.htm.
–. 2003. "2003 General Election, Election Summary." http://www.elections.on.ca/en-CA/Tools/PastResults.htm.
–. 2007. "Statistical Results," 2007 Referendum. http://www.elections.on.ca.
Environics. 2007. "Ontario Voters Divided about New Electoral System." http://erg.environics.net/media_room/default.asp?aID=637.
Findlay, Sue, 1997. "Institutionalizing Feminist Politics: Learning from the Struggles for Equal Pay in Ontario." In *Women and the Canadian Welfare State: Challenges and Change,* ed. Patricia M. Evans and Gerda R. Wekerle, 310-29. Toronto: University of Toronto Press.
G.P. Murray Research. 2007. *Women MPPs at Queen's Park 1981 through 2007.* Equal Voice. http://www.equalvoice.ca.
Gray, Charlotte. 1991. "Yes, 11 Ministers!" *Chatelaine* 64, 1 (January): 21-23, 86-88.
Grey, Sandra. 2006. "The 'New World'? Substantive Representation of Women in New Zealand." In *Representing Women in Parliament: A Comparative Study,* ed. Marian Sawer, Manon Tremblay, and Linda Trimble, 134-51. London: Routledge.
Harder, Lois. 1993. "The Trouble with Democracy: Child Care Reform in Ontario and the Politics of Participation." In *And Still We Rise: Feminist Political Mobilization in Contemporary Canada,* ed. Linda E. Carty, 243-78. Toronto: Women's Press.
Legislative Assembly of Ontario. 2006. *Debates* (Hansard), 14 June. http://www.ontla.on.ca/web/house-proceedings/house_current.do.

Ontario. 1993. "Budget 1993." Toronto: Ontario Ministry of Finance.
–. 1994. Office of the Minister Responsible for Women's Issues, "Progress and Promise: The Ontario NDP Government's Accomplishments on Women's Issues." Toronto: Government of Ontario.
–. 1995. "Ontario Budget Plan." Toronto: Ontario Ministry of Finance.
–. 2006. Democratic Renewal Secretariat website. http://www.democraticrenewal.gov.on.ca.
–. 2007. "The Recommendation of the Citizen's Assembly," 15 May, Citizens' Assembly on Electoral Reform. http://www.citizensassembly.gov.on.ca/en/the_recommendation/default.asp.
Ontario New Democratic Party. 1996. *Leadership That's Working: Policy Book*. Toronto: Ontario New Democratic Party.
Swers, Michelle. 2002. *The Difference Women Make: The Policy Impact of Women in Congress*. Chicago: University of Chicago Press.
Thomas, Sue. 1991. "The Impact of Women in State Legislative Policies." *Journal of Politics* 53, 3: 958-76.
Trimble, Linda. 1993. "A Few Good Women: Female Legislators in Alberta, 1972-1991." In *Standing on New Ground: Women in Alberta,* ed. Catherine Cavanaugh and Randi Warne, 87-118. Edmonton: University of Alberta Press.
Walkom, Thomas. 1994. *Rae Days*. Toronto: Key Porter.
Walks, Alan. 2004. "Suburbanization, the Vote and Changes in Federal and Provincial Political Representation and Influence between Inner Cities and Suburbs in Large Canadian Urban Regions, 1945-1999." *Urban Affairs Review* 39, 4: 411-40.
Welch, Susan. 1985. "Are Women More Liberal than Men in the U.S. Congress?" *Legislative Studies Quarterly* 10, 1: 125-34.
Young, Lisa. 2000. *Feminists and Party Politics*. Ann Arbor: University of Michigan Press.

# 7
# "Stage" versus "Actor" Barriers to Women's Federal Party Leadership

*Sylvia Bashevkin*

In recent decades, scholars and political activists alike have pondered the relative absence of women at the top levels of party organizations. Their widespread consensus on the real-world problem, captured in the phrase "why so few?" has inspired varied explanations for this pattern alongside diverse remedies for it (Stacey and Price 1981, ch. 1). Existing studies devote limited attention, however, to either organizational or parliamentary party leadership as a specific level of involvement, but they do offer useful insights that can be applied to this subject.

In asking whether doors are more open than they once were, and in proposing ways to widen the passageways, political scientists have focused on institutional characteristics that alternately help or hinder engagement. Much of this literature fits within a political opportunities approach to participation (see Gelb 1989). In *Women and Politics,* Vicky Randall (1987, 108) posited that left-wing organizations were substantially more open to women than right-wing organizations. Lisa Young's (2000) study of Canada and the United States examined relations between parties and second-wave feminism and suggested a positive relationship between close movement and party ties, on one side, and women's involvement, on the other. Casting the widest comparative net in this field, Ronald Inglehart and Pippa Norris (2003) analyzed World Values survey data from more than seventy countries and concluded that particular cultural values – notably social egalitarianism – enhanced female engagement.

Alongside this cluster of party ideology, party and movement relations, and attitudinal factors, researchers also devoted attention to a number of structural variables. Randall's (1987, 146) observation regarding the negative impact of political competitiveness, which concluded that "women do best where competition is least," was consistent with much of the literature on Canada and other countries (see Bashevkin 1985, 55; 1994, 150-51; Nelson and Chowdhury 1994; Trimble and Arscott 2003, 69). If applied to leadership selection contests, competitiveness arguments predict that parties holding power, or in a strong position to win it, would be less inviting towards women participants than those in a weaker political position.

Building on the work of Vallance (1984) and Norris (1985), Randall (1987) also drew a direct link between electoral rules, elite values, and women's recruitment. In her words, "Proportional representation party list systems coincide with comparatively high rates of female membership in national legislatures," particularly when party leaders are committed to increasing women's numbers (141). If applied to internal party votes, her observation suggested female candidates would be relatively welcome as leaders of parties with centralized selection systems and an active commitment to recruiting more women.[1]

Taken as a group, these studies offer the following response to the question of opportunities versus barriers as they affect top party posts: women candidates would likely be most welcome and most successful in socially egalitarian, left parties that enjoy cordial relations with women's movements; in parties in which competitive stakes are relatively low; and in parties where party leaders committed to increasing women's participation could employ central levers in their control towards this end. By way of contrast, they would probably be least welcome and least successful in non-egalitarian, right parties that have hostile relations with organized feminism; parties in which competitive stakes are comparatively high; and where party leaders are not committed to enhancing female engagement. Borrowing from theatrical terminology, it seems fair to characterize this literature as emphasizing a contextual, or "stage," interpretation of party engagement. That is, a combination of ideational and institutional circumstances shape elite participation in more or less conducive ways that parallel the manner in which lights and sets frame theatre performances for audiences.

Social psychological research offers a somewhat different response to the question, why so few? Instead of examining organizational and system-level factors, scholars in this stream have probed the attributes of individuals in order to understand patterns of party involvement. Much of this research has considered candidacy for legislative office, which is often a pathway to top party roles, and asked why some people seek party nominations while others do not. In her early study of state legislators in the United States, Jeane Kirkpatrick (1974) addressed the impact of conventional gender role norms, which, in her view, led relatively few women to develop the personal and occupational prerequisites – notably, strong ambition coupled with a high-income career in law or business – that men generally brought to their political careers. More than thirty years later, Jennifer Lawless and Richard Fox (2005) confirmed the continued presence of a gender gap in legislative ambition, despite significant changes in women's occupational and educational backgrounds. In their words, "Deeply embedded patterns of traditional gender socialization pervade U.S. society and continue to make politics a much less likely path for women than men" (ibid., 156).

Once again, concepts borrowed from the study of drama help to capture the emphasis in the social psychological literature on individual- or "actor"-level characteristics, as contrasted with systemic or "stage" drivers in institutional studies. The former cluster of variables reminds us that individual actors may, as agents, bring particular assets to the political stage that challenge prevailing ideational and structural limits. For example, as a confident lawyer with considerable financial assets, Margaret Thatcher, in her 1975 leadership campaign, arguably overcame the significant barriers posed by the right-of-centre values and reasonably strong competitive status of the British Conservative Party. At the same time, acknowledging the presence of a political stage and identifying its particular features remind us of the context in which participation occurs, which enables us to recognize that actors perform in environments that are variously welcoming or constraining.

The distinction between stages and actors raises a number of important questions. First, do women candidates thrive in the institutional circumstances that the literature portrays as most conducive to their success? Second, when compared with each other, do context-stage or individual-actor approaches better explain women's ability to capture party leadership positions? And third, is the Thatcher scenario typical; that is, do actor assets frequently override or even negate stage limitations?

This chapter addresses each query with reference to party leadership in Canada, which is one of the few democratic systems in which multiple women mounted credible campaigns for, and in some cases won, top posts in national parties between 1975 and 2006.[2] Beginning with Rosemary Brown's path-breaking campaign for the federal NDP leadership in 1975, women have contested federal Progressive Conservative (Flora MacDonald, 1976; Kim Campbell, 1993), New Democratic (Audrey McLaughlin, 1989; Alexa McDonough, 1995), Liberal (Sheila Copps, 1990 and 2003; Martha Hall Findlay, 2006), Alliance (Diane Ablonczy, 2002), and merged Conservative leadership races (Belinda Stronach, 2004). Of these ten campaigns, three were successful, notably those of McLaughlin, McDonough, and Campbell.

Since the races under consideration unfolded during a politically significant thirty-year period, they can be examined with reference to many important stage variables, including the ideological coloration of parties, the strength of women's movements, and relations between parties and organized feminism. At an individual level, the financial, occupational, and other personal characteristics of candidates could also be expected to vary over time, as Canadian women gained wider access to educational and employment opportunities (see Statistics Canada 2000, chs. 4 and 5).

Our focus on multiple women contenders breaks with the conventional emphasis in the leadership literature on males versus females – whether in parties, legislatures, or elsewhere (see Carroll and Fox 2006; Duerst-Lahti and Kelly 1995; Lawless and Fox 2005; O'Neill and Stewart 2006; Reingold 2000; Trimble and Arscott 2003). Rather than analyzing a series of political races, typically involving one female and multiple males, we examine federal leadership over time and across the political spectrum, focusing on parties that held seats in the House of Commons and fielded candidates in every region of Canada. In this way, we are able to assess systematically the structural and individual dynamics of participation at the apex of party organizations – where, we contend, women's involvement has the potential to be transformative in symbolic, substantive, and procedural ways.

This discussion opens with a brief review of the existing research on stage versus actor approaches, employs this framework in the core empirical section, and concludes that, while women have participated actively as federal leadership candidates since 1975, not one has yet won the top post in a competitive party. Given that female contenders were more successful in parties that were progressive, open to feminist interests, politically uncompetitive, and welcoming to women activists than in their mirror opposites, we report that stage arguments held up well. Actor claims proved somewhat less compelling, in part because individual-level variables did not systematically distinguish between cases; that is, many women candidates appeared confident, well financed, and not disadvantaged by occupational backgrounds outside law and business. Finally, actor attributes did not trump stage ones, since at least one leadership candidate (Belinda Stronach) lost, despite bringing considerable personal wealth and a business background to her 2004 campaign for the top position in a competitive right-wing party. The chapter concludes by exploring the significance of these findings for future research, and for efforts to increase women's participation in the highest party echelon.

One important caveat in this analysis concerns other obstacles facing elite-level female participants. They include discriminatory practices in parties, the higher average age of women versus men when first elected to public office, and greater family responsibilities (see Lawless and Fox 2005, 58-70). This project does not investigate any of these variables because the first is not amenable to direct measurement (since discriminatory practices are extremely difficult to calibrate) and none can be easily remedied (given that, in addition to their age and family responsibilities, individual candidates face party practices as fairly fixed circumstances), even if they are empirically demonstrated.

## Research Background

Comparative women and politics research offers a rich set of contextual propositions that can be applied to the study of party leadership. Randall's (1987) comprehensive study of democratic participation around the world considered both election to legislatures and party office holding. *Women and Politics: An International Perspective* reported that, although female representation declined "as one ascends the party hierarchy," left parties offered a more advantageous environment for political women than centre and right parties (108).

Young's (2000) study of relations between North American parties and women's movements also emphasized the ideational setting of political engagement. While acknowledging that "the difficulties faced by women building political careers inside the political parties" were considerable, *Feminists and Party Politics* suggested that left parties with close ties to organized feminism were more welcoming towards female activists than right-wing parties that had tense or hostile relations with women's movements (Young 2000, 169, 206).

Inglehart and Norris' (2003) quantitative study extended this focus on the role of political environment. Using data from more than seventy countries, it found social norms had "a powerful impact on political reality, since egalitarian values are significantly associated with women being successfully elected to office" (144). In *Rising Tide: Gender Equality and Cultural Change around the World,* Inglehart and Norris claimed that a receptive attitudinal climate was fundamental to increasing women's political engagement (ibid., 145-46). Their thesis indicated leadership candidates would benefit from running in parties with strong egalitarian cultures and during periods when pro-equality values enjoyed support in the general public.

Alongside research on party ideology, party relations with organized feminism, and the role of egalitarian values, this literature also probed the impact of macro-level institutional factors. Randall's book pointed towards a negative relationship between political competitiveness and women's participation (Randall 1987, 146). Her study noted that females were most numerous in less powerful echelons of public life, including local government. Barbara Nelson and Najma Chowdhury's (1994) edited collection considered forty-three international cases, relying on chapter authors to map the qualitative contours of representation in each. Their introductory chapter highlighted the impact of fraternalism in politics; it argued that "the male culture and ethos of formal politics ... is fashioned by male lifestyles and characterized by an aggressiveness and a competitiveness that are often viewed as male traits" (Chowdhury and Nelson 1994, 15-16). A number of chapters in their volume considered whether highly competitive political environments tended to exclude women, whereas lower-stakes ones were more inclusive. Writing about Canada, Bashevkin (1994, 150-51) reported an inverse relationship between a party's electoral success and women's presence in elite positions (see also Bashevkin 1985, ch. 4).

One ambiguity in this literature concerns the definition of political competitiveness. Trimble and Arscott (2003, 69), for example, concluded that female leaders in Canada were "typically pulled into the role to prop up ailing parties," but their study did not employ the concept of competitiveness in a consistent manner. Trimble and Arscott initially defined competitive party organizations as those "with elected representatives in the legislature during the woman's term as leader," and they included in that category organizations in which the female leader held her party's only seat (ibid., 73). They later described competitive parties as those "with at least a reasonable chance of winning, or retaining, office" (ibid., 76). Regardless of how the concept is defined, scholars have consistently viewed parties that held power or stood a strong change of winning office as less open to women than those in a weaker political position.

Finally, institutional treatments of female engagement have also considered interactions between electoral rules and party cultures. Randall's account of Scandinavia and other list proportional representation (PR) systems echoed the views of Vallance (1984), Norris (1985), and others in arguing that this particular electoral arrangement enhanced women's participation by encouraging "parties to devise slates of candidates who are representative of the main groups in society, including the two sexes, so as to maximize [party] electoral appeal" (Randall 1987, 140). In the absence of centralized control over legislative nominations, party elites in the United States and Canada could not directly influence women's participation in the same way. If applied to leadership candidacies, Randall's thesis suggested parties with both a relatively centralized selection system and a commitment to recruiting more women would provide more advantageous environments than those with decentralized schemes and no such commitment.

Taken as a whole, this literature characterizes the following environments as relatively welcoming towards female candidates: left parties, parties that have built positive ties with feminist groups, socially egalitarian parties, formations in a weak competitive position, and parties whose elite was committed to increasing women's participation and in control of central levers to use towards that end. Conversely, contexts that would be less inviting towards female candidates include right parties, parties whose relations with pro-equality movements were hostile, socially traditional parties, formations in a strong competitive position, and parties whose elite lacked commitment to increasing women's participation. We term the former group of circumstances a best-case stage scenario and the latter a worst-case one.

In contrast to this system-level literature, scholars who focus on the attributes of individual actors emphasize the degree to which men and women differ in the assets they bring to the political stage. Perhaps because this approach falls outside the prevailing institutionalist paradigm of North American party research, or because it is difficult to pursue at an empirical level, given the challenge of measuring individual politician's assets, the literature on actor attributes is relatively limited. Kirkpatrick's (1974) groundbreaking study of US state houses showed how female legislators often lacked the core background characteristics that benefited males in their political careers – notably strong ambition coupled with a high-income career in law or business. Lawless and Fox's (2005) research, undertaken decades later, revealed that even though more women had pursued higher education (including those who did so to build legal or business careers) during the intervening period and, thus, had entered what they termed the pipeline professions, prospective female candidates for public office still demonstrated far less political ambition than their male counterparts.

This stream of research trained a spotlight on a number of actor-level measures, including candidates' levels of ambition, occupational backgrounds, and ability to raise funds to pay for the costs of campaigning. If applied to party leadership races, the literature on individual attributes pointed towards strong ambition, generous financial resources, and work experience in the areas of law or business as more promising actor circumstances than low ambition, limited funds, and occupational backgrounds in other areas.

The next section examines federal party leadership outcomes in Canada with reference to these propositions.

## Empirical Discussion

Did left parties, parties that had built positive ties with feminist groups, socially egalitarian parties, formations in a weak competitive position, and parties whose elite was both committed to increasing women's participation and in control of central levers to use towards that end prove to be more welcoming towards female candidates than their mirror opposites? Table 7.1 provides a simplified overview of the Canadian data. Of the ten campaigns by women for top federal party jobs since 1975, 30 percent (3/10) took place in the NDP, which offered an institutional setting closest to our best stage scenario. Consistent with institutional expectations, two of the three NDP women candidates (McLaughlin and McDonough) won federal leadership, and they arguably benefited from both a hospitable values environment and low party competitiveness. Moreover, Rosemary Brown's pioneering run for federal leadership occurred in the NDP at a time when second-wave feminism was just beginning to challenge party organizations and channel activists towards mainstream engagement. It is notable that Brown was an immigrant to Canada from Jamaica, who grounded her arguments for social justice and equality in a set of personal experiences of both gender and racial discrimination.

By way of comparison, the federal Liberal organization presented less perfect institutional circumstances, in the sense that the party usually held a moderate ideological position and was, for most of the past century, Canada's "government party" (Whitaker 1977). The presence of a centrist and

*Table 7.1*

**Overview of women party leadership candidates, federal level only, 1975-2006**

| Name | Year | Party ideology | Party competitiveness | Outcome |
|---|---|---|---|---|
| Brown | 1975 | centre-left | no | lose |
| MacDonald | 1976 | centre-right | yes | lose |
| McLaughlin | 1989 | centre-left | no | win |
| Copps | 1990 | centre | yes | lose |
| Campbell | 1993 | centre-right | no | win |
| McDonough | 1995 | centre-left | no | win |
| Ablonczy | 2002 | right | no | lose |
| Copps | 2003 | centre | yes | lose |
| Stronach | 2004 | right | yes | lose |
| Findlay | 2006 | centre | yes | lose |

competitive party history was balanced, however, by reasonably cordial relations with organized feminism throughout the 1980s and by the existence of party rules designed to encourage women's participation (see Bashevkin 1993, 100). Three of the ten campaigns by women for federal leadership in Canada took place in the Liberal organization, which also hosted the first race featuring multiple women candidates (Carolyn Bennett, Martha Hall Findlay, and Hedy Fry in 2006, the first and third of whom dropped out before the convention vote). The fact that no Liberal convention elected a female to the top job suggests the party's ideational environment and highly competitive political stakes were less conducive to women candidates than circumstances prevailing during the same period in the NDP.

On the political right in Canada, the Progressive Conservative, merged Conservative, and Alliance parties can be arrayed in a left to right direction, with the PCs being the most inviting of the three from the perspective of supports for female engagement.[3] Four women, or 40 percent (4/10) of the total runs by female candidates for top positions, mounted campaigns between 1975 and 2006 for the leadership of these parties. Only one of the four campaigns was successful, that of Kim Campbell for the PC leadership in 1993; Campbell went on to serve briefly as Canada's first and, thus far, only female prime minister.

From an institutional perspective, the failure of successive Liberal contenders combined with Campbell's victory in the 1993 PC leadership race reinforces the importance of party competitiveness. Each of the men who defeated Sheila Copps in her 1990 and 2003 campaigns for the top Liberal post, Jean Chrétien and Paul Martin, subsequently won a general election and served as prime minister. Stéphane Dion, the winner of the 2006 Liberal leadership vote, was unable to do the same. Stephen Harper, who defeated Belinda Stronach for the merged Conservative top job in 2004, later became prime minister. In the PC party, by comparison, Kim Campbell's successful run took place when the Mulroney government had been in power for nine years, and when the party's and its incumbent leader's standing in public opinion polls were very weak (see Trimble and Arscott 2003, 83). As Campbell (1996, 263) herself acknowledged, party delegates in 1993 "were looking for a miracle worker to stop the Tories' slide into oblivion."

The relevance of both party climate and competitiveness is apparent when we consider Diane Ablonczy's third-place finish in the 2002 Alliance race. Right-of-centre voters tended to divide their support during that period between the Alliance and Conservative parties; this left the Alliance in a weak position and offered the governing Liberals a clear lead in public opinion polls (see Mackie 2000). The competitiveness thesis, in short, is overshadowed in Ablonczy's case by other contextual factors, notably the crucial partisan context in which she ran. Whether gauged with reference to right-wing party ideology, hostile relations between the Alliance and organized feminism, or the absence of any party commitment to women's engagement, the setting for Ablonczy's run was not congenial in any respect except low party competitiveness.

Leaving aside Ablonczy's Alliance candidacy and Brown's NDP run, which occurred at a very early point in women's movement engagement with the party system, political competitiveness looms large as an explanatory factor in the Canadian leadership context. Of the ten campaigns mounted by women, five took place in demonstrably weak parties and three of them were successful. All three candidates who won – McLaughlin, McDonough, and Campbell – led their parties in extremely unpropitious circumstances. The NDP seat count in the House of Commons dropped from forty-three to fourteen between 1989 and 2003, while the Conservatives reached their historic low of two MPs in 1993. Competitiveness arguments also highlight the obstacle posed by high stakes in the Liberal Party in 1990, 2003, and 2006, which in turn attracted prominent male candidates and made it hard for females to win, as well as the difficulties faced by MacDonald in 1976 and Stronach in 2004.

Turning to actor-level attributes, there is little support for the argument that female leadership candidates in Canada were constrained by limited personal ambition. Although both Brown and McLaughlin professed to be seeking the top NDP position because of the push from a larger network of women supporters, rather than from self-motivation, they shared the view that party power was a useful means towards a larger end (Brown 1989, 113, 150; McLaughlin 1992, 52, 55). In particular, the memoirs of Brown and Copps reveal not only sustained confidence in their own abilities but also a view that their leadership candidacies contributed in a meaningful way to Canadian politics (see Brown 1989; Copps 2004). It is notable that Copps contested party leadership on three occasions: in 1982, she ran for the top post in the Ontario Liberal party, and then in 1990 and 2003, she mounted campaigns for the federal Liberal leadership. A similar perspective permeates autobiographical writings by individuals who won their races (see Campbell 1996; McLaughlin 1992). If we adopt Lawless and Fox's (2005, 3) definition of ambition as "the desire to acquire and hold political power through electoral means," then women who contested top federal office in Canada did not appear deficient with respect to this attribute.

In terms of occupational experience, it is difficult to claim that women candidates as a group were disadvantaged by their lack of law and business careers. None of the three females (McLaughlin, McDonough, or Campbell) who won party leadership had built her major professional background in law or business. But the male candidates (Ed Broadbent, Joe Clark, and Stockwell Day) who defeated Rosemary Brown, Flora MacDonald, and Diane Ablonczy, respectively, also lacked this experience. As CEO of Magna International, a company founded by her father, Belinda Stronach was among Canada's most visible and well-paid business leaders when she declared her candidacy in 2004 for the merged Conservative leadership (see McDonald 2004). Yet, Stronach lost to an economist of relatively modest means, Stephen Harper. These patterns on the political left and right suggest Lawless and Fox's argument regarding occupation had limited traction in these parts of the Canadian political spectrum, where many successful male and female candidates came from education, social service, and political backgrounds.

In the Liberal Party, the absence of a law or business career arguably disadvantaged Sheila Copps (who had worked briefly as a journalist before entering public life) in her campaigns against Jean Chrétien and Paul Martin. Yet, given the highly competitive circumstances of the Liberal Party in 1990 and 2003 and the fact that Copps' political base was outside a major Canadian city, it is hard to link her losses to occupation alone. Moreover, since the victor in the 2006 Liberal leadership race (Dion) worked as a political science professor before he was elected to Parliament, while the leaders of other federal parties came from economics (Harper), political science (the NDP's Jack Layton), and trade union (the BQ's Gilles Duceppe) work, the occupational pipeline thesis may simply be irrelevant for both women and men in Canadian public life.

Aside from Kim Campbell, only one other female candidate during this period, Martha Hall Findlay, was a lawyer. Findlay had never held elective office when she declared her candidacy for the Liberal leadership, although she had run unsuccessfully against Stronach for a parliamentary seat. Parallel with Copps' case, Findlay's occupation did not seem central to her prospects, although it may have advantaged her somewhat in the Liberal milieu, just as the absence of a law or business background likely disadvantaged Copps. It is notable that both of the women who also declared their candidacies for the Liberal leadership in 2006, Carolyn Bennett and Hedy Fry, were high-profile physicians, from Toronto and Vancouver, respectively.

In terms of financial resources, there is little evidence that funding problems impeded left- or right-of-centre female candidates. As is shown in Table 7.2, women in those parts of the spectrum spent either as much or more money than men in the same contests. Belinda Stronach devoted enormous personal assets, reputedly in the millions of dollars, to her unsuccessful 2004 Conservative campaign (see Clark 2005). All three women who contested the NDP leadership spent roughly the same as or more than their male competitors. Flora MacDonald's campaign budget in 1976 was close to that of the eventual winner, Joe Clark, but was considerably less than that of other unsuccessful candidates, including Brian Mulroney, in the same race.

Financial assets seemed most problematic for Liberal candidate Sheila Copps, since her campaign budgets were significantly less than those of the top two candidates in 1990 and the top finisher in 2003. Copps (2004, 64) later noted that while Paul Martin spent $2.37 million and placed second in the 1990 campaign, she spent $800,000 and placed third. In the 2003 campaign, according to Copps (ibid., 186-87), "While Paul Martin had approximately two hundred paid employees on the ground, our total payroll could be counted on one hand."

Data on fundraising for the 2006 Liberal race indicated that the two initial front-runners, Michael Ignatieff and Bob Rae, enjoyed a significant early lead over other candidates, including the three women in the contest (see Clark 2006a). Tight party finance rules in 2006, especially as compared with the races in which Copps competed, meant money probably had only a minimal effect on the campaigns of Findlay and the two women who withdrew before the convention, Bennett and Fry.

Overall, then, actor-level variables do not distinguish in a systematic way between successful and unsuccessful leadership candidates. Since 1975, female contenders for top federal party posts generally projected high levels of personal confidence. If long-term backgrounds in business or law were highly relevant, then Stronach and Findlay should have been more successful than McLaughlin, McDonough, or Campbell. Outside the Liberal Party, financial assets were not useful predictors because female candidates generally raised as much or more money than their male competitors. It was only in the 1990 and 2003 Liberal races that occupation and financial assets were, perhaps, relevant.

Can actor attributes neutralize stage limitations? When she contested the merged Conservative Party leadership, Belinda Stronach was among the best-resourced candidates in the history of Canadian party politics, with

*Table 7.2*

**Campaign spending in federal party leadership races involving female candidates**

| Date | Party | Candidate (votes) | Campaign spending |
|---|---|---|---|
| 7 July 1975 | New Democratic | Ed Broadbent (948) | **<$15,000 |
| | | Rosemary Brown (658) | $13,147 |
| | | Lorne Nystrom | **<$15,000 |
| | | John Harney | **<$15,000 |
| | | Douglas Cambell | **<$15,000 |
| 22 February 1976 | Progressive Conservative | Joe Clark (1,187) | $168,353 |
| | | Claude Wagner (1,122) | $266,538 |
| | | Brian Mulroney | **$343,000-500,000 |
| | | Jack Horner | $278,383 |
| | | Flora MacDonald | $152,704 |
| | | Paul Hellyer | $287,788 |
| | | Sinclair Stevens | $294,106 |
| | | John Fraser | $116,107 |
| | | James Gillies | $192,847 |
| | | Patrick Nowlan | $58,635 |
| | | Heward Grafftey | $83,845 |
| | | Richard Quittenton | $9,336 |
| 2 December 1989 | New Democratic | Audrey McLaughlin (1,316) | $128,576 |
| | | Dave Barrett (1,072) | $113,987 |
| | | Steven Langdon | $52,462 |
| | | Simon de Jong | $42,517 |
| | | Howard McCurdy | $72,892 |
| | | Ian Waddell | $39,256 |
| | | Roger Lagassé | $11,892 |
| 23 June 1990 | Liberal | Jean Chrétien (2,652) | $2,446,036 |
| | | Paul Martin (1,176) | $2,371,690 |
| | | Sheila Copps (499) | $806,064 |
| | | Tom Wappel (267) | $143,186 |
| | | John Nunziata (64) | $166,076 |
| 13 June 1993 | Progressive Conservative | Kim Campbell (1,817) | $3,000,000 |
| | | Jean Charest (1,630) | $2,300,000 |
| | | Jim Edwards | $602,000 |
| | | Patrick Boyer | $197,000 |
| | | Garth Turner | $65,000 |
| 14 October 1995 | New Democratic | Alexa McDonough (566) | |
| | | Svend Robinson (655) | |
| | | Lorne Nystrom (545) | |
| 17 February 1996 | Bloc Québécois | Michel Gauthier (104) | |
| | | Francine Lalonde (51) | |

►

◄ *Table 7.2*

| Date | Party | Candidate (votes) | Campaign spending |
|---|---|---|---|
| 15 March 1997 | Bloc Québécois | Gilles Duceppe (25,561) | |
| | | Yves Duhaime (16,408) | |
| | | Rodrigue Biron (6,468) | |
| | | Francine Lalonde | |
| | | Daniel Turp | |
| | | Pierrette Venne | |
| 20 March 2002 | Alliance | Stephen Harper (48,561) | $374,131 |
| | | Stockwell Day (33,074) | $101,546 |
| | | Diane Ablonczy (3,370) | $23,867 |
| | | Grant Hill (3,223) | $3,924 |
| 14 November 2003 | Liberal | Paul Martin (3,242) | **$6,400,000-12,200,000 |
| | | Sheila Copps (211) | $340,000 |
| 20 March 2004 | Conservative | Stephen Harper (17,296) | $2,073,084 |
| | | Belinda Stronach (10,613) | $2,496,482 |
| | | Tony Clement (2,887) | $836,807 |
| 3 December 2006 | Liberal | Stéphane Dion (2,521) | $1,882,368 |
| | | Michael Ignatieff (2,084) | $2,316,028 |
| | | Bob Rae | $2,989,822 |
| | | Gerrard Kennedy | $1,425,086 |
| | | Ken Dryden | $650,266 |
| | | Scott Brison | $593,637 |
| | | Joe Volpe | $335,935 |
| | | Martha Hall Findlay | $422,958 |
| | | Carolyn Bennett | $254,864 |
| | | Hedy Fry | $194,779 |
| | | Maurizio Bevilacqua | $700,776 |

*Note:* Candidate names and vote numbers in parentheses are listed according to the order in which they finished on the final party ballot. Dollar figures for expenditures are reported for the year in which the vote occurred and are not adjusted for inflation. Estimated expenditures are indicated by a double asterisk.
*Sources: The Economist* (2003, 51); Clark (2006b, A10); Conservative Party of Canada (2004); Courtney (1993, 303, 315-17); Dawson (2003, A12); Dawson and Curry (2003, A5); Elections Canada website, financial reports; Geddes (2003, 20); Kom (2006, 1); Laschinger and Stevens (1992, 34-38).

significant levels of ambition, business prominence, and wealth. Her inability to marshal individual assets in such a way as to overcome institutional barriers posed by a competitive right-wing party suggests a negative answer to the question. Stronach's circumstances were not unique, however, since Brian Mulroney and other highly confident, well-resourced men from law and business all lost the 1976 PC leadership race to Joe Clark, who never obtained a law degree and raised considerably less money than his competitors (see Wearing 1988, 73).

**Conclusion**

This examination of federal party leadership in Canada offers multiple responses to the questions posed in the introductory chapter. First, the chronology presented in Table 7.1 reveals that the doors to participation at this level were more open in 1975 and the years that followed than they were before that date. Simply stated, leadership campaigns by women that were visible to media, public, and party audiences did not occur before the emergence of second-wave feminism.[4] This coincidence between elite engagement in parties and social movement mobilization was arguably clearest in Rosemary Brown's efforts to stake out an assertively feminist and socialist agenda for the NDP (see Brown 1989).

Second, empirical data shed critical light on efforts to widen real-world political passageways. One important finding is as follows: Not every female leadership candidate in a progressive or uncompetitive party succeeded, but, on the flip side, no woman who pursued right-wing or competitive party leadership won during this period. Since candidates who sought to head relatively weak parties on the left through centre-right were more likely to win than those who sought the top post in hard-right and competitive parties, we propose that efforts to increase women's elite-level participation need to consider more than individual attributes. Searching for plus-perfect candidates would appear to be a fairly fruitless exercise in competitive and right-wing parties, since the obstacles facing female candidates in those contexts appear to be related more to political stage than to individual actor characteristics.

A corollary observation follows from the relative ability of women candidates to win the leadership of uncompetitive formations. This pattern meant that parties led by women enjoyed limited electoral success and created an unfortunate association in public perceptions between women leaders and negative political outcomes. At the federal level in Canada, the circumstances associated with McLaughlin's and McDonough's leadership of the NDP and Campbell's term in the top PC post arguably created new obstacles for successive generations of female activists, thus posing the curious question of whether female engagement at the helm of uncompetitive parties was doing more to close than to open the passageways of engagement.

While they do not show that participation at the helm of weaker parties necessarily limits engagement, the results of this study suggest women and politics activists should pay closer attention to the consequences of uncompetitive party leadership. Just as older patterns in which women nominees were clustered in lost-cause legislative seats created an impression that female candidates could not win, the trend of women leading parties that were far from power has supported views that women at the top depress or weaken party fortunes.

The thesis that competitive parties are far from fertile territory for female candidates is confirmed in the case of the Bloc Québécois (BQ). The BQ was not examined in this chapter because, by fielding candidates in Quebec only, the party could not win power federally. Two women, Francine Lalonde and Pierrette Venne, ran and lost in 1997 to Gilles Duceppe, while Lalonde ran unsuccessfully in 1996 against Michel Gauthier. At the time, the BQ was a centre-left sovereignist formation that had a strong competitive position in its home base of Quebec.[5] Our analysis to this point suggests that the BQ's progressive ideological stance and reasonably close relations with organized feminism would benefit female candidates, but its competitive status would disadvantage them in a leadership race.

How did Canada become one of the only political systems (alongside New Zealand, considered in Chapter 10, and Bangladesh) in which multiple women won party leadership campaigns? This study points towards the very useful presence of uncompetitive parties on the left and centre-right. The NDP in particular provided a hospitable environment for Brown's historic run for federal leadership – an assertively socialist feminist campaign that marked the formal arrival of the second-wave women's movement on the political left and in the party system generally. The subsequent successful runs of McLaughlin and McDonough reinforce the view that the NDP's ideological placement, ties with organized feminism, egalitarian values, and commitment to improving women's representation created conducive conditions, as did distance from power at the federal level. On the centre-right, Campbell's selection as PC leader occurred when liberal feminist ideas were reasonably welcome in that part of the political spectrum and under weak competitive circumstances – the party was in decline after nearly a decade in office.

From a comparative perspective, the presence of less competitive parties in Canada may have also reduced the impact of such actor-level obstacles as occupational background and money. Both of these factors seemed significant to Copps' campaigns for the Liberal leadership, in which her contact networks and fundraising opportunities were vastly overshadowed by those of the leading candidates. By contrast, occupation and funding had limited resonance in less competitive party organizations, where law and business backgrounds combined with high fundraising capacity seemed far less de rigueur – for men and women.

If the Canadian circumstances that appeared to open opportunities to female leadership candidates could be exported, they would include the presence of uncompetitive parties, favourable relations between feminist movements and parties from the centre-left through centre-right, valuation of pre-leadership careers outside law and business, and low financial thresholds for political fundraising. Clearly, it is hard to imagine packaging these attributes for export, but, taken as a group, they help to explain the "why so many?" conundrum.

Do some variables loom in this study as possible brakes against women's participation? Our discussion suggests the decline of a vibrant, pan-Canadian organized feminism could severely limit future leadership bids at the federal level. In the absence of social movements that lobby for egalitarian values and for enhancing representation at all levels of public life, many of the stage factors that this study demonstrates were conducive to women's participation could either weaken or disappear.

As Ablonczy's 2002 run for the Alliance leadership reminds us, low party competitiveness is a far from sufficient condition for the victory of a woman candidate. Campaigning as a moderate in a hard- right formation dominated by social conservatives and other anti-feminist interests, Ablonczy was far less successful than would be expected, given the Alliance's weak competitive standing (see Simpson 2002). In the more progressive parts of the Canadian federal spectrum, however, pro-equality ideas resonated to a far greater degree: Kim Campbell regularly identified herself as a feminist, while Belinda Stronach publicly defended same-sex marriage as "an issue of rights and equality" before quitting the Conservative Party in early 2005 (see Campbell 1996; Galloway 2005). If feminist positions become more muted, or less securely entrenched, in the centre-left to centre-right terrain of the federal party system, in which they gained traction after 1975, then it is difficult to see how doors will open wider for women participants.

In terms of future research directions, this study opens up the question of success beyond leadership campaigns. Do candidates for top party positions exert transformative effects on their own organizations and, perhaps, the entire party system? Can leadership aspirants shape internal policies and practices, including those concerning participation in party organizations? For example, was women's 40 percent plus representation in the federal NDP caucus in 2007 attributable to feminist organizing in that party during the 1970s? In more general terms, how do we gauge the impact of individual leadership candidates, including those who lost a leadership race and those whose parties lost an election?

The media images of leadership candidates also deserve closer academic scrutiny. As Chapter 9 in this volume demonstrates, politicians are conscious of their framing by journalists. Yet, we know relatively little about how fairness or distortion characterizes media treatments of male and female candidates in different periods and different parties. Using the Everitt and Camp; Goodyear-Grant; and Gidengil, Everitt, and Banducci studies in this book as models, researchers can begin to probe media framing and public images as they affect party leadership.

In conclusion, decades after activists and scholars identified the problem, women remain under-represented in the highest echelons of democratic leadership in Canada. Propositions that suggest the higher the fewer and the more competitive the fewer (Bashevkin 1985) still resonate, but at this juncture we have a better understanding of the larger institutional and individual dynamics of women's engagement.

**Acknowledgments**
I am grateful to the Social Sciences and Humanities Research Council of Canada for its support of this project, and to Sarah Lamble for her research assistance. Helpful comments on earlier versions were offered by participants at the May 2006 Women and Political Leadership mini-conference at the University of Toronto and the July 2006 Canadian Studies conference at the Hebrew University of Jerusalem; by colleagues at February 2007 talks in New Zealand at the University of Auckland, Victoria University of Wellington, and the University of Otago; and by Cheryl Auger, Amy Nugent, Miriam Smith, and Joerg Wittenbrinck.

**Notes**

1 In contrast with Norris' (1985) earlier conclusion, Inglehart and Norris (2003) maintained that proportional, as opposed to single-member plurality (SMP), electoral systems did not measurably affect women's elite-level participation.

2 Credible campaigns are defined as those mounted with measurable visibility within the party, and with a reasonable chance of success. They do not include, for example, the campaigns of Mary Walker-Sawka, who won two out of more than twenty-two hundred votes cast in the 1967 federal Progressive Conservative (PC) leadership race, or of Bev Meslo, who won about 1 percent of the votes cast in the 2003 federal NDP contest. Major federal parties in this study do not encompass small formations on the political right or left or the Bloc Québécois, which only fields candidates in Quebec.

3 On mandated positions for women in the older PC organization, see Bashevkin 1993, 100. The Reform, Alliance, and merged Conservative parties included no such provisions: see Young 2006, 58-59, 61-62.

4 The first federal leadership campaign by a woman in Canada occurred in the Progressive Conservative Party in 1967, when Mary Walker-Sawka won 2 out of 2231 votes. See Canadawicki, "Electoral Firsts – Women."

5 In the 1993 federal elections, the BQ won official opposition status and, in 1997, maintained a firm hold on seats in Quebec. For further details of BQ leadership contests, see Parliament of Canada, "Leadership Conventions," Bloc Québécois.

**References**

Bashevkin, Sylvia B. 1985. *Toeing the Lines: Women and Party Politics in English Canada.* Toronto: University of Toronto Press.

–. 1993. *Toeing the Lines: Women and Party Politics in English Canada.* 2nd ed. Toronto: Oxford University Press.

–. 1994. "Building a Political Voice: Women's Participation and Policy Influence in Canada." In *Women and Politics Worldwide,* ed. Barbara J. Nelson and Najma Chowdhury, 143-60. New Haven: Yale University Press.

Brown, Rosemary. 1989. *Being Brown: A Very Public Life.* Toronto: Random House.

Campbell, Kim. 1996. *Time and Chance: The Political Memoirs of Canada's First Woman Prime Minister.* Toronto: Doubleday Canada.

Canadawiki. "Electoral Firsts – Women." Canadawiki. http://canadawiki.org/index.php/Electoral_Firsts#Women.

Carroll, Susan J., and Richard L. Fox, eds. 2006. *Gender and Elections: Shaping the Future of American Politics.* New York: Cambridge University Press.

Chowdhury, Najma, and Barbara J. Nelson. 1994. "Redefining Politics: Patterns of Women's Political Engagement from a Global Perspective." In *Women and Politics Worldwide,* ed. Barbara J. Nelson and Najma Chowdhury, 3-24, New Haven: Yale University Press.

Clark, Campbell. 2005. "Stronach Spent $4-million of Her Own on Race." *Globe and Mail,* 20 August, A4.

–. 2006a. "Rae, Ignatieff Have Big Financial Edge." *Globe and Mail,* 24 August, A1.

–. 2006b. "Ignatieff, Rae Well Ahead of Pack in Fund-Raising for Leadership Bids," *Globe and Mail,* 3 November, A10.

Conservative Party of Canada. 2004. "2004 Leadership Event." Conservative Party of Canada. http://www.conservative.ca/media/20050819-2004%20Leadership%20 Spending.pdf.

Copps, Sheila. 2004. *Worth Fighting For.* Toronto: McClelland and Stewart.

Courtney, John. 1993. *Do Conventions Matter? Choosing National Party Leaders in Canada.* Montreal and Kingston: McGill-Queen's University Press.

Dawson, Anne. 2003. "Martin's Big Backers." *Montreal Gazette,* 23 December, A12.

Dawson, Anne, and Bill Curry. 2003. "Companies Bet on Liberal Largesse: Corporate Canada Gave Five Times More to Grits than CA." *Calgary Herald,* 3 July, A5.

Duerst-Lahti, Georgia, and Rita Mae Kelly, eds. 1995. *Gender Power, Leadership and Governance.* Ann Arbor: University of Michigan Press.

*The Economist.* 2003. "The Americas: And Then There was One – The Canadian Succession." 26 July, 51.

Elections Canada. "Financial Reports." http://www.elections.ca/scripts/webpep/fin/summary_report.aspx.

Galloway, Gloria. 2005. "Harper's Use of Same-Sex Ads Questioned." *Globe and Mail,* 25 January, A4.

Geddes, John. 2003. "What Leadership Campaign?" *Maclean's,* 4 August, 20.

Gelb, Joyce. 1989. *Feminism and Politics: A Comparative Perspective.* Berkeley: University of California Press.

Inglehart, Ronald, and Pippa Norris. 2003. *Rising Tide: Gender Equality and Cultural Change around the World.* Cambridge: Cambridge University Press.

Kirkpatrick, Jeane J. 1974. *Political Woman.* New York: Basic Books.

Kom, Joel. 2006. "Ignatieff, Rae Dominate Leadership Funding Race." CanWest News, 25 August, 1.

Laschinger, John, and Geoffrey Stevens. 1992. "Secrets from the Back Room." *Maclean's,* 19 October, 34-38.

Lawless, Jennifer L., and Richard L. Fox. 2005. *It Takes a Candidate: Why Women Don't Run for Office.* Cambridge: Cambridge University Press.

Mackie, Richard. 2000. "Alliance Party Not Popular among Women." *Globe and Mail,* 6 October, A9.

McDonald, Marci. 2004. "Under the Influence." *Toronto Life* (June): 78-88.

McLaughlin, Audrey, with Rick Archbold. 1992. *A Woman's Place: My Life and Politics.* Toronto: Macfarlane, Walter, and Ross.

Nelson, Barbara J., and Najma Chowdhury, eds. 1994. *Women and Politics Worldwide.* New Haven: Yale University Press.

Norris, Pippa. 1985. "Women's Legislative Participation in Western Europe." In *Women and Politics in Western Europe,* ed. Sylvia Bashevkin, 71-89. London: Frank Cass..

O'Neill, Brenda, and David Stewart. "Comparing Male and Female Party Leaders in Canada." Paper presented at workshop on Women and Political Leadership, University of Toronto, May 2006.

Parliament of Canada. "Leadership Conventions." Bloc Québécois. Parliament of Canada. http://www2.parl.gc.ca/Parlinfo/Files/Party.aspx?Item=a639384e-e1a0-4169-83da-904925139b6a&Language=E&Section=LeadershipConvention.

Randall, Vicky. 1987. *Women and Politics: An International Perspective.* Basingstoke: Macmillan.

Reingold, Beth. 2000. *Representing Women: Sex, Gender and Legislative Behavior in Arizona and California.* Chapel Hill: University of North Carolina Press.

Simpson, Jeffrey. 2002. "Moderates among the Ideological Heathens." *Globe and Mail,* 8 March, A17.

Stacey, Margaret, and Marion Price. 1981. *Women, Power, and Politics.* London: Tavistock.

Statistics Canada. 2000. *Women in Canada, 2000: A Gender-Based Statistical Report.* Ottawa: Statistics Canada.

Trimble, Linda, and Jane Arscott. 2003. *Still Counting: Women in Politics across Canada.* Peterborough: Broadview.

Vallance, Elizabeth. 1984. "Women Candidates in the 1983 General Election." *Parliamentary Affairs* 37, 3: 301-9.
Wearing, Joseph. 1988. "The High Cost of High Tech: Financing the Modern Leadership Campaign." In *Party Democracy in Canada: The Politics of National Party Conventions,* ed. George Perlin, 72-83. Scarborough: Prentice-Hall.
Whitaker, Reginald. 1977. *The Government Party: Organizing and Financing the Liberal Party of Canada, 1930-58.* Toronto: University of Toronto Press.
Young, Lisa. 2000. *Feminists and Party Politics.* Vancouver: UBC Press.
–. 2006. "Women's Representation in the Canadian House of Commons." In *Representing Women in Parliament: A Comparative Study,* ed. Marian Sawer, Manon Tremblay, and Linda Trimble, 47-66. London: Routledge.

# 8
# One Is Not Like the Others: Allison Brewer's Leadership of the New Brunswick NDP

*Joanna Everitt and Michael Camp*

While women in Canada have steadily become more involved in positions of political leadership, their numbers at the elite level remain small and well below the 52 percent share that women hold in the general population. This situation is even more pronounced for particular groups of women such as lesbians. Few publicly identified or "out" lesbians have been willing to stand for public office, and, among those who have entered electoral politics, even fewer have won nominations and elections. Like other trail-blazing women, lesbians who have become their party's standard-bearer at the constituency level tend to come from socially progressive, yet politically uncompetitive, parties. As of the time of writing, only one declared lesbian, Libby Davies, has won a seat in the federal Parliament.[1] This background makes the experience of Allison Brewer, former leader of the New Democratic Party in New Brunswick, particularly interesting. As an out lesbian, Brewer became, for a short period of time, the highest-ranking homosexual politician in North America.[2] While she admittedly led a minor party in a small eastern Canadian province, she was the front-running candidate for most of her leadership race. This provides an unprecedented opportunity to explore the interplay of gender and sexual orientation in her leadership campaign, and, in particular, it offers an opportunity to explore how Brewer's campaign was covered by the media.

Although Brewer's leadership bid took place at a specific time and place, it revealed much about the challenges that lay ahead for gay women politicians. Moreover, her experiences shed light on the overall character of news reporting on individuals who do not fit the usual stereotype of the political person – someone who is male and heterosexual – and demonstrate how media coverage can create significant barriers to the full participation of individuals who are deemed atypical. Through an investigation of the Brewer case, it is possible to discern how lesbian politicians are constructed for the public at large and learn how public and media perceptions may affect lesbian engagement in the political process.

Since Brewer was relatively unknown when she announced her candidacy for the top NDP position, this chapter concentrates on newspaper stories published during the period in which the public was first introduced to her as a leadership candidate. As a starting point, the study focuses on the four-month period during which the first speculative stories appeared in New Brunswick's three major daily newspapers.[3] They covered Brewer's entrance to provincial politics, the declaration of her leadership candidacy, the convention victory, and the immediate aftermath. It was during the crucial period from late May to late September 2005 that Brewer's media identity was forged and public attitudes about her were entrenched.

We argue that media coverage during this period stereotyped Brewer in such a way that it was difficult for her to be perceived as a strong party leader – despite her winning the New Brunswick NDP leadership race. First of all, media accounts represented Brewer as a woman – a fact that, in itself, placed her outside the usual characteristics of a political leader (see Everitt and Gidengil 2003; Gidengil and Everitt 1999, 2000, 2003; see also Goodyear-Grant in this volume). Second, she was described as an advocate for reproductive choice and as a former director of Dr. Henry Morgentaler's abortion clinic in Fredericton, a role that was distinct from the traditional business or legal background of many politicians (see Bashevkin's discussion in Chapter 7 of this volume). The third conceptual frame highlighted by the media emphasized Brewer's sexual orientation: not only was she a woman who supported feminist causes, she was also a homosexual. We argue that by focusing on these frames and not others in the context of her decision to contest the leadership of an already weak opposition party, the media, in effect, pushed Brewer into the margins of political life and made it more difficult for her to present herself and to be seen by members of the public as a viable politician.

## Research Background

On the day after Brewer won the NDP leadership in September 2005, New Brunswick's largest circulation newspaper ran a front-page story with the headline "NDP Chooses Lesbian Activist as New Leader" (Kaufield 2005a). Above the fold was a photograph taken at the convention that showed Allison Brewer with a bright smile on her face. The news story could be seen as a benchmark of progress for declared homosexuals, since Brewer was the first openly lesbian woman in Canada to lead an established political party.

The attention paid to Brewer's sexual identity in post-convention news coverage was not unique. Libby Davies received similar headlines in 2001 when she revealed during a House of Commons debate that she was involved in a same-sex relationship.[4] The problem with this coverage in both cases was that the primary news emphasis was on Brewer's and Davies' sexual orientation, not their substantive accomplishments or beliefs. Allison Brewer was identified as both a lesbian and an "activist" – something new, something different. That was news.

Media coverage based on novelty is not surprising for pioneering women in politics. Decades earlier, the simple fact of being a female politician would have been sufficient to generate headlines (Robinson and Saint-Jean 1991, 1995). Yet, studies show that contemporary female politicians and party leaders continue to receive different coverage than their male colleagues (Everitt and Gidengil 2003; Gidengil and Everitt 2003; Gingras 1995; Ross and Sreberny 2000; Sampert and Trimble 2003). First, they often receive less coverage than male politicians (Everitt 2003; Gidengil and Everitt 2003; Kahn and Goldenberg 1991; Sampert and Trimble 2003; Scharrer 2002). Second, media accounts of political women tend to focus on stereotypically gendered character traits and policy preferences (Kahn 1996); give disproportionate attention to appearance, family background, and marital status (Robinson and Saint-Jean 1991; Ross and Sreberny 2000); and over-emphasize behaviours that conflict with traditional norms as to what constitutes appropriate female behaviour (Everitt and Gidengil 2003; Gidengil and Everitt 1999, 2000). Studies repeatedly show that women still stand out in the political realm, although their status may have been upgraded from "very rare" to "significant minority" or "not the average."

Even as more women become active in mainstream politics, that domain remains almost exclusively heterosexual. Openly homosexual politicians, be they women or men, are few and far between (Riggle and Tadlock 1999).[5] One serious challenge facing research about lesbian and gay politicians in Canada is the lack of data on the number of openly homosexual politicians holding public office. Quite simply, no verifiable figures are available.[6] Scholars in the United States have the advantage of information collected by two non-governmental organizations, the Gay and Lesbian Victory Fund and the National Association of Gay and Lesbian Elected Officials (Golebiowska 2002, 590). These two groups keep records about gay politicians at the US national, state, and even municipal levels. While numbers are increasing, homosexuals remain highly under-represented in that political system (Golebiowska 2002, 591). Estimates of the gay population in society in general are as high as 10 percent, yet, the number of openly homosexual politicians elected to public office in the United States does not even approach 1 percent (ibid.). The proportion of openly declared lesbian and gay politicians is slightly higher in Canada, where they make up 1.6 percent of the members of the House of Commons. There is some suggestion that in the United States, there are more lesbians and gay men elected to state and local office than at national levels, but no comparable statistics are available for Canada.[7]

As with any minority breaking into a previously restricted area of public life, lesbians and gay men have discovered that media stories, especially at the outset of their careers, focus on the fact that they are the "first" or "one of the very few" to arrive on the scene. While gay men have made significant progress in becoming accepted players on the Canadian political scene, lesbians remain such a tiny minority that they continue to be newsworthy for their sexual identity alone.[8] Homosexual politicians are already the exceptions to the rule, and, in politic,s lesbians are more rare than gay men.

Little research addresses the media coverage of openly lesbian, gay, bisexual, or transgendered (LGBT) politicians in Canada. Political scientists in the United States have devoted more attention to this subject, but their studies remain in the early stages. Evidence gathered thus far supports the view that media portrayals of LGBT politicians are considerably different than those of their heterosexual counterparts (Golebiowska 2002).

Paralleling this situation, no specific literature exists on the political experiences of openly gay women in Canadian or American politics. Researchers tend to assume homosexuals of both genders encounter roughly the same challenges when they enter public life and can, therefore, be analyzed as a single category of people. This view, however, is difficult to sustain. Lesbians are less visible, less understood, and less known to the public than gay men. Lesbians tend to be the invisible members of the gay population, though they are roughly equal in number to gay men. Furthermore, as noted above, lesbians are even more under-represented in the political domain than are gay men, and their position as a double minority – as women and lesbians – within this world likely makes their experiences very different from those of gay men.

Although lesbians and gay men have long played a significant role in the political process, they have remained for the most part "in the closet" because it was a political liability (if not political suicide) to reveal one's sexual orientation (Rayside 1998). More LGBT politicians over the years have felt sufficiently empowered to declare their identities to the public – although most keep their orientation hidden until after they have won office at least once. Given that the number of openly homosexual politicians in Canada remains small, it is not surprising that very little academic research has explained their experiences, let alone the ways they have been portrayed in the media (ibid.).

In 2001, Libby Davies became the first identified lesbian to sit in the Canadian House of Commons. As the NDP member for Vancouver East, she was first elected in 1997 and then re-elected in 2000, 2004, and 2006. Before the 2006 campaign, her official parliamentary website offered the following information: "She lives with her partner, Kimberly Elliot." Davies' political reputation was firmly established before she announced in a parliamentary debate on same-sex marriage in 2001 that she was in a relationship with Elliot. Yet, even though Davies was already a known quantity, a flurry of headline stories appeared in newspapers across the country when she revealed that she was involved in a same-sex relationship. Furthermore, the language of the initial coverage after her disclosure in the House of Commons was that Davies "admitted" (O'Neil 2001b) to being in a lesbian relationship; stories described her partner as a "gal pal" and "an active rabble-rouser on homelessness, racism, feminism, East Timor" and other issues (McGregor 2001). Journalists went on to report that Davies had previously been involved in a heterosexual relationship (O'Neil 2001a, 2001b; Saskatoon *Star Phoenix* 2001).

Little attention was given to the substantive content of Davies' parliamentary speech about a private member's bill on same-sex marriage. This coverage parallels that accorded to political women in general: attention is generally directed towards the individual's family and marital status, behaviour that conflicts with traditional gender role expectations, and actions that portray her as politically deviant. Lesbians face an even larger challenge because they do not conform to either the sexual orientation (heterosexual) or gender (male) norms of politics.

In a 2005 interview with the *Seattle Gay News,* Libby Davies said she was proud to be publicly identified as lesbian, even though other male and female politicians found it wiser to remain in the closet. In her words, "There are others, but they are not out. For one reason or another, they are not open about it" (Raketty 2005). Canadian attitudes towards lesbians and gay men have clearly softened in recent years, but a politician's decision to declare his or her homosexuality still carries considerable risk.

The timing of these disclosures sometimes lessens the impact of stereotypic assumptions, if the public has had an opportunity to learn about the candidate's characteristics without the shadow of a homosexual schema (Golebiowska 2002, 593). This may explain why Davies' sexual orientation is now seldom noted in media coverage unless the story focuses on such issues as same-sex marriage, hate crimes against gays and lesbians, and offensive statements by other MPs. Davies' extensive political experience prior to the public declaration of her sexual orientation paralleled the path taken by another NDP parliamentarian from British Columbia, Svend Robinson, and meant she was not framed simply as a lesbian. She was already known as a politician. On the other hand, when individuals declare their orientation before establishing a firm public image, sexuality becomes a core part of their political identity.

Existing research suggests that openly lesbian and gay candidates are seen as less politically viable than either heterosexual or rumoured-to-be-homosexual candidates (Herrick and Thomas 2001, 103; Tadlock and Gordon

2003, 9). Questions of viability are complicated by the nature of the communities in which candidates seek office. Libby Davies' constituency is located in downtown Vancouver, which is a large cosmopolitan city in which diverse lifestyles are more widely accepted than elsewhere. As suggested by Louise Carbert's discussion in Chapter 5, candidates running for office in less urban and more traditional parts of the country, such as Allison Brewer in New Brunswick, likely face a less welcoming public.

As Gidengil, Everitt, and Banducci argue in Chapter 10 of this volume, public impressions are important to a candidate's electoral success. It is thus imperative that lesbians and gays convey information that will permit them to transcend stereotypical impressions based solely on their sexuality. Golebiowska and Thomsen thus recommend that homosexual candidates delay announcing their orientation until after voters can collect other, attribute-based information: "In other words, if the candidate's sexual orientation is known from the beginning, it may color the perceiver's interpretation of individuating information that is subsequently learned about the candidate ... To the extent that the electorate harbors anti-lesbian and anti-gay prejudice, this suggests that candidates should generally enjoy more public support when their sexual orientation is learned later, rather than earlier, in their campaigns" (Golebiowska and Thomsen 1999). Until recently, most LGBT candidates in Canada have followed this advice and put off coming out; among MPs, only Bill Siksay announced he was gay before his first election. Other first-time candidates who have run as identified gays or lesbians have not been successful.[9] However, as more individuals announce their sexual orientation before seeking political office, the option of not divulging this information becomes less possible, as well as less common.

Research about stereotyping suggests impressions based on categorical information are quickly and easily formed; once in place, they are difficult to change (Fiske et al. 1987, 403). Studies show that gay and lesbian candidates often receive this type of low-information coverage to such a degree that stories often cancel out other attributes possessed by individuals (Golebiowska 2002, 599). Several gay male candidates told Golebiowska that the major challenge of their campaign was fighting the perception that they were "single-issue" politicians whose only concern was promoting homosexual rights and other matters of specific interest to the gay community.

As Golebiowska (2002) points out, stereotypes of lesbian candidates may be even more challenging and more of a barrier than those faced by gay men: "Because lesbians who are open about their sexual orientation are campaigning under the banner of memberships in two stereotyped groups that are traditionally at a disadvantage in electoral politics (women and homosexuals), stereotypes associated with their sexual orientation might interact with stereotypes associated with their gender in ways that cannot be anticipated on the basis of examining the electoral experiences of openly gay candidates alone" (605). This chapter explores Allison Brewer's bid to lead the New Brunswick NDP as a case study that stands at the intersection between a politician's gender and sexual orientation, on one side, and the manner in which she is presented by the media, on the other.

### Case Background and Methodology

Reporters followed the 2005 NDP leadership campaign with an interest that was in proportion to the party's significance in New Brunswick politics. The NDP had, to that point, not elected more than two MLAs at one time to the provincial legislature; this peak occurred during a three-year period in the mid-1980s. Like the provincial Progressive Conservatives, the New Brunswick NDP was wiped out by the 1987 wall-to-wall victory of Frank McKenna's Liberals. In the aftermath of the 1987 election, George Little, who had served as NDP leader since 1980, resigned and was replaced in June 1988 by Elizabeth Weir, the first female party leader in New Brunswick. [10]

In 1991, Weir won a provincial seat in Saint John by a slim margin; she managed not only to retain that constituency but also to increase her support base in three subsequent provincial elections, earning a reputation as one of the most effective opposition MLAs in the New Brunswick legislature. Weir's personal popularity failed to translate into broad support for the provincial party, however, and she remained the sole NDP MLA throughout her time as leader. In the fall of 2004, when Weir announced her resignation as NDP leader, pundits questioned whether the party would survive the next election. As a result, most coverage of the 2005 provincial NDP leadership campaign focused on Weir herself and ignored the individuals running to succeed her.

The party was slow to organize a leadership convention, but it eventually set a nomination deadline for 23 June 2005. Since only one candidate, Allison Brewer, had announced her intention to seek the leadership by that time, the party (with Brewer's consent) extended the deadline to 12 July. This extension permitted additional candidates to enter the race, ensuring more of a horserace in what was admittedly not a highly competitive party in terms of proximity to power. New Democrats hoped an actual leadership race would attract more public attention to their party, which was, parallel to Bashevkin's argument in Chapter 7, relatively open to women participants because the power stakes remained low. By the time the new deadline arrived, two other candidates had joined the field. Pam Coates was a well-known anti-poverty activist in Saint John and Oscar Doucette was a labourer from New Brunswick's North Shore. On 25 September 2005, the New Brunswick NDP held its first leadership convention in almost eighteen years. Brewer won the leadership on the first ballot with 62 percent of the vote.

To understand how Brewer's candidacy as an openly lesbian woman with a non-traditional political background was covered by the New Brunswick press, we focus on all of the stories printed about the NDP leadership campaign in the province's three daily newspapers between 14 May 2005, when Brewer announced she was considering a run for the NDP leadership, and the end of September 2005, after Brewer had won the leadership. This information was compiled using a journalistic search engine called Canadian Newspapers FULLTEXT (FP Informart) and included a total of twenty-one stories about the leadership campaign.

From this database, we created a list of all the descriptive words or phrases that were used to identify the candidates, their past accomplishments, and their political goals or ambitions. These included terms such as "lesbian," "feminist," and "reproductive-choice advocate," as well as phrases such as "worked in an abortion clinic" and "former civil servant." Each of these words describes particular attributes of party leadership candidates, and for Brewer in particular they may lend themselves to the formation of a stereotype; however, the terms are not, by themselves, stereotypical descriptions.

**Empirical Findings**

Allison Brewer, the first candidate to enter the race, received the most coverage of the three candidates and was generally perceived as the front-runner. Brewer was an out lesbian who had been actively involved in promoting gay rights. She was also the founder and director of the Morgentaler abortion clinic in Fredericton and a single mother of three children. She had also worked as a journalist and as a provincial government employee, and she had received a Governor General's Award in commemoration of the Persons Case. Despite these various accomplishments, it was her identity as a lesbian and as an abortion rights activist that became the main focus of media attention (see Table 8.1).

Each of the conceptual frames used in news stories about Brewer pushed her towards the political margins, even though her campaign platform focused on strengthening schools, hospitals, and other social services, and on building the party base in francophone areas of New Brunswick – where the NDP was historically weak.[11] Brewer's campaign website highlighted her experience in government and in the Public Service Alliance. However, as Table 8.1 shows, these messages and identities were lost in a sea of other information, which revealed the media's interest in Brewer's personal background as a woman, her orientation as a lesbian (28 percent), her background as a pro-choice crusader (24 percent), her history as a social and political activist (27 percent), and her responsibilities as the single mother of a disabled child (4 percent). The latter descriptions, often used in combination, created a political persona drawn almost entirely from stereotypical conceptions. And while the word "lesbian" itself is a powerful label, it becomes even more

*Table 8.1*

**Descriptors used in coverage of New Brunswick NDP leadership candidates**

| Brewer | | Coates | | Doucet | |
|---|---|---|---|---|---|
| Media reference | Times used | Media reference | Times used | Media reference | Times used |
| Sexual orientation | 22 (28%) | Anti-poverty activist | 5 (23%) | Former NDP candidate | 5 (22%) |
| Human and disability rights activist | 21 (27%) | Organizer of a poor people's conference | 4 (18%) | Involved in fight over expropriated land | 4 (17%) |
| Abortion activist | 19 (24%) | Community activist | 3 (14%) | Kent Homes worker | 3 (13%) |
| Political rookie | 5 (6%) | Former NDP candidate | 3 (14%) | President of local NDP | 3 (13%) |
| Persons Award winner | 4 (5%) | President of a national anti-poverty organization | 3 (14%) | Involved in fishing, forest industries | 3 (13%) |
| Mother of 3 | 3 (4%) | Presented brief to UN | 2 (9%) | Conservation council of NB | 2 (9%) |
| Life-long supporter of the NDP | 2 (3%) | Founder of a Saint John food bank | 1 (5%) | Former smallbusiness owner | 1 (4%) |
| Government advisor | 1 (1%) | Studied social justice and leadership development | 1 (5%) | Parish council/ parish choir | 1 (4%) |
| Journalist | 1 (1%) | | | Class 4 fishing captain | 1 (4%) |
| *Total* | 78 | | 22 | | 23 |

forceful when used in conjunction with the terms "feminist" or "abortion activist."

Given the obvious news value of the word "lesbian," it is striking that it was used so sparingly in coverage of the New Brunswick race. Brewer's work on behalf of lesbians and gays was frequently presented in a nuanced way and was often referred to as human rights and social rights activism. Brewer's sexual orientation was stated explicitly in only three of the eighteen articles, and it was not until the day after the NDP convention that the *Telegraph-Journal* identified her as a lesbian (Kaufield 2005a).

However, once Brewer won the leadership, reporters apparently felt they could discuss the implications of her sexuality more explicitly. The Fredericton *Daily Gleaner* was the most circumspect of the three provincial papers. Its post-convention headline read: "Brewer Claims NDP Victory: Teary-Eyed Weir Calls It a Day as Leader." Yet, the article's opening sentence clearly drew attention to Brewer's sexual orientation: "New Brunswick's first openly gay political party leader is vowing to lead a stronger New Democratic Party into the next election, with an ambitious goal of winning a majority government" (Hagerman 2005b). The Moncton *Times-Transcript* drew attention to Brewer's history of gay rights activism in the headline: "N.B. NDP Chooses New Party Leader: Allison Brewer Vows to Build Up Party Support, Fight for Gay Rights in N.B." (Moszynski and *Times-Transcript* staff 2005). This headline conveyed the impression that Brewer's primary concern was gay rights.

The Saint John *Telegraph-Journal* went the farthest, running its story under the headline "NDP Chooses Lesbian Activist as New Leader: Allison Brewer Wins Easily on the First Ballot." The body of the article read as follows: "New Brunswick New Democrats have chosen an openly gay social activist and founder of the province's Morgentaler abortion clinic as their new leader. With a convincing first ballot victory at the NDP leadership convention, Allison Brewer, 51, made history Sunday, becoming New Brunswick's first openly gay party leader. While Ms. Brewer acknowledged her win is 'an historic day for the lesbian and gay community,' she said she's not a single-issue candidate and vowed to lead her party to a majority government" (Kaufield 2005a). Later that same week, an article appeared in the *Telegraph-Journal* under the title "Does Sexual Orientation Matter for N.B. Voters? Opinions Differ about Intriguing Question Posed by Choice of Province's First Openly Gay Party Leader." The text of the article was as follows: "Can a self-described lesbian activist, a unilingual anglophone and founder of the controversial Morgentaler abortion clinic win the public acceptance needed to breathe new life into the NDP in this province? Ms. Brewer made history on Sunday by becoming the first openly gay party leader in this province. The question is, what will voters think? Do New Brunswick voters care about the sexual orientation of their politicians? Will Ms. Brewer's past connection to the highly charged abortion issue cost her and her party support" (Kaufield 2005b)?

Some members of the public were quick to react to this coverage and criticized the narrow way in which the paper was framing Allison Brewer. As one letter to the editor noted: "I think the headline on the front page on Monday (Sept. 26) – 'NDP chooses lesbian activist as new leader' – lacked a certain amount of decency. The new elected leader of the New Democratic Party, Allison Brewer, should not have been described according to her sexual orientation since we naturally don't mention sexual orientation when it comes to heterosexuals" (LeBlanc 2005). Another reader wrote to complain about the lesbian activist label, and the narrow coverage that ensues from this categorization: "I was shaking my head over the attempt to shackle Allison Brewer with labels right out of the gate ... Those of us who closely watched the leadership race unfold have learned her passions extend across several issues (as the article itself later alluded to) and her commitment to our party's many policies cannot be pigeonholed into one area of focus ... To imply that she can be defined simply as a 'lesbian activist' is to do her a great disservice" (Hackett 2005). A third letter of complaint posed the following question to the newspaper's editor: "If she was obese or skinny, would you have used those words instead of lesbian?" (Von Weiler 2005). The obvious answer, of course, is no. Unlike racial minorities and people who are at polar extremes on the weight scale, gays and lesbians are still identified in the media by the characteristic that makes them different from the majority of the population, their sexuality.

At first glance, the treatment of Brewer's lesbian orientation as a front-page story one day and as meriting less prominence on other occasions seems difficult to explain. Yet, closer study suggests reporters were uncomfortable with female homosexuality in New Brunswick in 2005. From this perspective, media references to Brewer's interest in human and social rights functioned as a surrogate for her sexuality and meant that it was not necessary to repeat the terms "lesbian" or "homosexual" in every story and headline.

Brewer's background as a social activist also presented a challenge to the stereotypes of traditional party leaders. Her NDP predecessor, Elizabeth Weir, worked as a lawyer, taught industrial relations and employment law courses for several years at the University of New Brunswick, and served as the executive director of the New Brunswick NDP before becoming party leader. By contrast, Brewer came from a civil service background, where she had worked on issues related to women, seniors, and people with disabilities and was known primarily for her activist work. This background, particularly her involvement in the pro-choice movement (notably the creation of the controversial Morgentaler abortion clinic in Fredericton) meant reporters focused more attention on this aspect of Brewer's identity than on others.

As is reported in Table 8.1, media accounts regularly referred to Brewer's background as an abortion activist and worker in an abortion clinic (24 percent), while her civil service employment with the New Brunswick and Nunavut governments was seldom mentioned (1 percent). Similarly, they mentioned Brewer's human rights and, to a lesser extent, disability rights campaigning (27 percent), but they ignored her involvement with the NDP (3 percent) and trade unions (0 percent).

By drawing attention to her advocacy work, published narratives characterized Brewer as an "outspoken" campaigner or "activist" – as if support for clear policy goals placed her at the extreme end of political discourse. This coverage may have led voters to wonder how any politician who was actively engaged with one or more human rights issues could have any time for, or interest in, such matters as the economy, health care, or the environment. It also glossed over the fact that Brewer's leadership bid was not visibly supported by members of the province's gay and lesbian communities and that the other candidates for the New Brunswick NDP leadership also supported gay marriage. Since only Brewer was referred to as an advocate or activist on that issue, the implication was that she had a personal stake in it, while the others did not.

Brewer, however, was not the only candidate to be labelled an activist. Pam Coates – the second woman to enter the race – was described primarily as an anti-poverty activist: she had worked in a community kitchen, served as president of the National Anti-Poverty Organization, and organized a regional poverty conference in 1996. Although Coates received substantially less coverage than Brewer during the leadership campaign, her descriptors in the press were overwhelmingly (almost 70 percent) about social activism. Given that reporters referred less to her than to Brewer, Coates' media presentation was slightly more balanced because it mentioned that she had run in the past as an NDP candidate (14 percent), presented a brief to the United Nations Social and Cultural Council in Geneva (9 percent), and studied social justice and leadership (5 percent). Nonetheless, as in the case of Brewer, repeated use of the term "activist" placed Coates outside the political mainstream because it emphasized unconventional and confrontational approaches to changing government policy, rather than traditional insider strategies.

Oscar Doucet, the third and only male candidate in the race, was spared the activist label. In six newspaper stories published before the NDP convention, he was described as having a background in local politics, fishing, forestry, business, and the church and a commitment to auto insurance reform and environmental energy initiatives (O'Kane 2005; Hagerman 2005a). Doucet was presented as a worker in a modular home factory and former owner of a small business who had a wide spectrum of policy objectives. He had been an activist in his youth, notably on the issue of land expropriation for a provincial park; however, his media descriptors hardly mentioned this involvement. Compared with Brewer and Coates, Doucet's press portrayal allowed him to express a much greater range of policy interests. As a man, a factory worker, and a small business owner, Doucet came closer to traditional concepts of a political candidate, especially in a party that saw itself as a vehicle for workers and progressive members of the middle class.

**Post-Convention Coverage**

After the NDP convention was over, the party's new leader was essentially ignored by New Brunswick newspapers until the provincial election twelve months later. Given that she did not have a seat in the legislature, Brewer's first year as leader was virtually invisible to members of the public and offered little opportunity to develop an alternative public profile to that created during her leadership bid. The lack of coverage of Brewer contrasts with that accorded to former leaders of the New Brunswick NDP. George Little, who held the same post during the 1980s, was described in a 2005 editorial in the *Telegraph-Journal* as "a charming well-read man with the gift of the gab" who was sought out "on every opportunity" to discuss the issues of the day (Davies 2005).

Elizabeth Weir, Brewer's immediate predecessor, also commented on a wide range of issues, possibly because her background and style resembled those of male party leaders. As Phillip Lee notes, "Weir was an imposing figure, both politically and personally. Standing six feet tall, she towered over [Liberal leader Frank] McKenna physically and was his intellectual equal ... she stormed into the hallways of the Legislature before she had a seat, establishing herself as McKenna's most persistent and effective critic" (Lee 2001, 213).[12]

Brewer presented a far less imposing public persona than Weir, and her interests were so sharply and narrowly defined by the media that she found it hard to stake out mainstream political space. Brewer was fully conscious of this portrayal and its implications; she tried to address the problem early on by assuring reporters that there was more to her political agenda than promoting reproductive choice or gay rights. On the day she declared her candidacy, Brewer told a news conference, "I'm not a two-issue person. I've worked for people with disabilities, I've been strong in my union, I've worked on issues of violence against women in the feminist movement, and in my job. Once people start talking about the things I do beyond these two issues, I don't think it will be a problem" (Mclean 2005). Brewer repeated that view at the NDP convention, arguing that although her election as leader would be a victory for the gay and lesbian community, her agenda as party leader would extend to all the issues facing New Brunswick. Yet, as Elizabeth Goodyear-Grant suggests in Chapter 9 of this volume, female politicians face many challenges in controlling their media coverage; in Brewer's case, she was unable to persuade journalists that she had something worthy to say on other topics of the day.

During the provincial election campaign in the summer of 2006, Brewer's share of media references was only one-third that of the other party leaders, Bernard Lord of the Conservatives and Shawn Graham of the Liberals. As she herself noted at the beginning of the campaign, "We have a really, really hard time making our presence felt ... We don't get the media attention we deserve and without that, it's really hard to capture the imagination of the public" (Morris 2006). Although the NDP fared poorly and Brewer lost her bid to win a seat, this limited coverage was not entirely attributable to the party's weak fortunes. In 2003, NDP leader Elizabeth Weir was referred to in half of the election stories that discussed Lord and almost three-quarters of those that addressed Graham, which represented a far larger proportion of attention than Brewer attracted three years later.

While there is some evidence that the media relied less on stereotypical framing and categorical descriptions of Brewer during the 2006 election, these direct or encoded references to her sexual orientation or activism were never completely eliminated (see Everitt and Camp 2007). Furthermore, although the range of issues she was allowed to address was broadened in the election coverage (services for families, unemployment, rising insurance costs, public health, and environmental protection), most of the references to her were at the end of long articles about the other two party leaders, reflecting traditional patterns of media coverage for female politicians.

In November 2006, Brewer announced that she was unable to continue as an unpaid party leader, and she resigned from the top post in the New Brunswick NDP.

## Discussion

Differences between the coverage of Allison Brewer and other candidates in the 2005 New Brunswick NDP leadership race highlight the distinctive conceptual frames used to understand and assess politicians. Given the limited press attention devoted to the race overall, and relatively low levels of public knowledge about the three leadership candidates, we conclude that frequent newspaper references to Brewer's human rights and reproductive choice activism directly shaped assessments of her qualifications and issue priorities. Media coverage of Brewer – both in the leadership campaign period and later, during the 2006 New Brunswick provincial election campaign – tended to refer to her in ways that implied she was a radical feminist whose views were inconsistent with mainstream public norms in the province.

To date, the NDP has arguably been the most ideologically welcoming of the Canadian mainstream parties to lesbian and gay candidates, as it has been to Aboriginal, racial minority, and women candidates (see Bashevkin's contribution, Chapter 7, in this volume).[13] The federal NDP caucus in 2006 included the only lesbian MP and two of the four out gay MPs then holding seats in the House of Commons. The NDP has also fielded more lesbian candidates for federal office than other parties. Therefore, within the political spectrum, the New Democratic Party would seem to offer some of the most congenial spaces in Canada for a leader such as Allison Brewer.

It is important to recall, however, that of the four openly homosexual federal candidates who won in 2006 all but one was already elected before making a public announcement about sexual orientation. Allison Brewer chose to be open about her sexuality from the outset, and she may represent a newer generation of politicians who are proud to be what they are from the starting point. She also took a risk by participating in a provincial party that stood little chance of electoral success. These circumstances meant she encountered the type of low information media coverage that framed her as different but provided little opportunity to transcend the boundaries of an assigned outsider-activist stereotype.

Brewer's experiences suggest that any level of commitment to homosexual rights by candidates like her will tend to evoke the term "activist," a descriptor that can offend the sensibilities of the general public, particularly in areas outside Canada's largest cities. It would seem that declared lesbians are by definition "activists" – perhaps with the corollary proposition that their very existence in full view of the public remains a radical political statement.

Little evidence exists that the media framing of New Brunswick's NDP leader was constructed with malice, as part of an attempt to harm her personally or politically. Indeed, before Allison Brewer's election as NDP leader, the provincial media were careful to use coded language in their reports, referring to her as a human rights activist rather than as an out lesbian. Still, it was apparent that her news profile was constructed with a stereotypical view of lesbians and crafted by the news values of mainstream journalism, which train a spotlight on "deviant" individuals and events that occur outside the realm of the ordinary.

This kind of coverage may not intentionally damage the aspirations of political candidates, but it does little to reveal, or even accurately reflect, their viability as political players. Once Brewer was presented in the lesbian activist frame, few news stories probed her substance as a politician – her beliefs and plans on a full spectrum of important issues, including those that fall outside the presumed interests of a "lesbian activist." Newspaper coverage of Allison Brewer's leadership campaign provided a ready-made message to readers that this candidate was different; in effect, her sexual orientation was merged with her political orientation. Rural and small town New Brunswick voters were presented with a marginal politician who clearly spoke for "them," not "us." However, we would argue that the narrow framing of Brewer's political identity would have harmed her even in the most metropolitan of settings, as one- or two-issue candidates are seldom viewed as viable politicians. As a result, Allison Brewer was made to seem not like other leaders in Canadian politics.

## Notes

1 One other successful lesbian politician is Kathleen Wynne, Liberal MPP for the Toronto constituency of Don Valley West and minister of education in the McGuinty government.

2 André Boisclair subsequently became leader of the Parti Québécois, serving between 15 November 2005 and 8 May 2007. He resigned after his party did poorly in the spring 2007 election.

3 The three major daily newspapers in New Brunswick are the *Telegraph-Journal,* based in Saint John; the *Daily Gleaner,* based in Fredericton; and the *Times-Transcript,* based in Moncton. All three papers are owned by Brunswick News, which is controlled by the Irving family.

4 In response to Davies' announcement, the *Vancouver Sun* ran the headline "Davies Admits Gay Relationship: Vancouver MP Is First Woman in House to Declare Same-Sex Partner" (O'Neil, 2001b). The *National Post* headline said "B.C. MP First to Declare She Is in a Lesbian Relationship" (*National Post* 2001). The *Ottawa Citizen* headline said "B.C. Politician Is First Female MP to Reveal Same-Sex Partnership" (O'Neil 2001a).

5 Among the out gay, bisexual, lesbian, or transgendered (GBLT) politicians who have been elected at the federal level in Canada are Scott Brison (Liberal), Libby Davies (NDP), Réal Ménard (Bloc Québécois), Svend Robinson (NDP), Bill Siksay (NDP), and Mario Silva (Liberal). Two senators, Laurier LaPierre (retired) and Nancy Ruth, are also openly gay.

6 Incomplete data can be found on the Wikipedia and Saskatchewan Resources for Sexual Diversity websites.

7 No openly homosexual members presently hold seats in the US Senate. Of the 424 members of the US House of Representatives, two were openly homosexual in 2007, including one lesbian, Democrat Tammy Baldwin from Wisconsin. Homosexual representation at the state level in the United States was .4 percent (34/7461).

8 In Canada the first openly homosexual MP was Svend Robinson, who served as an NDP MP from 1988 to 2004. In 2003, Nova Scotia Liberal MP Scott Brison became the first openly gay man in the federal cabinet, where he served as the minister for public works and government services. Although both Robinson and Brison sought major party leadership at the federal level, the first openly gay man to win such a position in North America was André Boisclair, who served as Parti Québécois leader in from 2005 to 2007.

9 Federal New Democrats who ran initially and unsuccessfully as out candidates include Betty Baxter (Vancouver Centre, BC, 1993), Jennifer Howard (Brandon-Souris, MB, 1997), Matthew McLaughlin (Verdun–Saint-Henri–Saint-Paul–Pointe Saint-Charles, QC, in 2000 and 2003 by-election and Jean-Le Ber, QC, 2006), Cindy Moriarty (Carleton-Gloucester, ON, 1993), Peg Norman (St. John's South-Mount Pearl, NL, 2006), and Mary Woo Sims (Port Moody-Westwood-Port Coquitlam, BC, 2006). Both Woo and Norman were open for years about their sexual orientation, and both were described as "activists" on social issues, human rights, reproductive choice, and same-sex marriage. Former Winnipeg mayor Glen Murray ran unsuccessfully for the federal Liberals in the Charleswood St. James-Assiniboia riding in Manitoba in 2004.

10 Weir went into the convention as the only candidate but was challenged at the last minute by Mona Beaulieu, who was nominated from the floor as a protest against Weir's association with urban academics in Fredericton and Saint John, who were accused of having too much influence over party policy. Of the ninety-five votes cast, Weir won fifty and Beaulieu won forty-five.

11 While former NDP leader Elizabeth Weir was bilingual, she failed to increase the party's support base in northern francophone regions of New Brunswick. In most cases, NDP candidates in these regions did not receive enough of the popular vote (15 percent) to receive a reimbursement of their election expenses.

12 Even though Weir was an important New Brunswick political figure, she, too, experienced media stories that focused more on her appearance and personality traits than did accounts of male party leaders in the province. See Everitt 2003, 93.

13 It should be noted that Quebec nationalist parties were also quite open to gays and lesbians, as is reflected in the number of Bloc Québécois MPs (Réal Menard and Raymond Gravel), Parti Québécois MNAs (André Boisclair, André Boulerice, Sylvain Gaudreault, and Agnes Maltais), and party leaders (André Boisclair for the PQ) from these backgrounds.

**References**

Davies, Carl. 2005. "Time for NDP to Revive 'The Waffle': Provincial Party Finds Itself in a Leadership Race with Little Momentum." New Brunswick *Telegraph-Journal,* 22 August.

Everitt, Joanna. 2003. "Media in the Maritimes: Do Female Candidates Face a Bias?" *Atlantis* 27, 2 (Spring-Summer): 90-98.

Everitt, Joanna, and Elisabeth Gidengil. 2003. "Tough Talk: How Television News Covers Male and Female Leaders of Canadian Political Parties." In *Women and Electoral Politics in Canada,* ed. Manon Tremblay and Linda Trimble, 194-210. Toronto: Oxford University Press.

Everitt, Joanna, and Michael Camp. 2007. "Changing the Game Changes the Frame: The Media's Use of Lesbian Stereotypes in Leadership Versus Election Campaigns." Paper presented at the annual meeting of the Canadian Communications Association, Saskatoon, Saskatchewan, May 2007.

Fiske, Susan, Steven Neuberg, Ann Beattie, and Sandra Milberg. 1987. "Category-Based and Attribute-Based Reactions to Others: Some Informational Conditions of Stereotyping and Individuating Processes." *Journal of Experimental Social Psychology* 23, 5: 399-427.

Gidengil, Elisabeth, and Joanna Everitt. 1999. "Metaphors and Misrepresentation: Gendered Mediation in News Coverage of the 1993 Canadian Leaders' Debates." *Press/Politics* 4, 1: 48-65.

–. 2000. "Filtering the Female: Television News Coverage of the 1993 Canadian Leaders' Debates." *Women and Politics* 21, 4: 105-31.

–. 2003. "Conventional Coverage/Unconventional Politicians: Gender and Media Coverage of Canadian Leaders' Debates, 1993, 1997, 2000." *Canadian Journal of Political Science* 36, 3: 559-77.

Gingras, François-Pierre. 1995. "Daily Male Delivery: Women and Politics in the Daily Newspapers." In *Gender and Politics in Contemporary Canada,* ed. François-Pierre Gingras, 191-207. Toronto: Oxford University Press.

Golebiowska, Ewa. 2002. "Political Implications of Group Stereotypes: Campaign Experiences of Openly Gay Political Candidates." *Journal of Applied Social Psychology* 32, 3: 590-607.

Golebiowska, E., and C. Thomsen. 1999. "Group Stereotypes and Evaluations of Individuals: The Case of Gay and Lesbian Political Candidates." In *Gays and Lesbians in the Democratic Process,* ed. Ellen Riggle and Barry Tadlock, 192-219. New York: Columbia University Press.

Hackett, David. 2005. Letter to the editor, *Telegraph-Journal,* 28 September.

Hagerman, Shannon. 2005a. "Three People Running for Party's Top Spot: Allison Brewer; Pam Coates; Oscar Doucet." *Daily Gleaner,* 23 September 23: A3.

–. 2005b. "Brewer Claims NDP Victory: Teary-Eyed Weir Calls It a day as Leader." *Daily Gleaner,* 26 September.

Herrick, Rebekah, and Sue Thomas. 2001. "Gays and Lesbians in Local Races: A Study of Electoral Viability." *Journal of Homosexuality* 42, 1: 103-27.

Kahn, Kim Fridkin. 1996. *The Political Consequences of Being a Woman.* New York: Columbia University Press.

Kahn, Kim Fridkin, and Edie N. Goldenberg. 1991. "Women Candidates in the News: An Examination of Gender Differences in US Senate Campaign Coverage." *Public Opinion Quarterly* 55, 2: 180-99.

Kaufield, Kathy. 2005a. "NDP Chooses Lesbian Activist as New Leader: Allison Brewer Wins Easily on the First Ballot." *Telegraph-Journal,* 26 September.

Kaufield, Kathy. 2005b. "Does Sexual Orientation Matter for N.B. Voters? Opinions Differ about Intriguing Question Posed by Choice of Province's First Openly Gay Party Leader." *Telegraph-Journal,* 28 September.
LeBlanc, Alcide. 2005. Letter to the editor. *Telegraph-Journal,* 28 September.
Lee, Phillip. 2001. *Frank: The Life and Politics of Frank McKenna.* Fredericton: Goose Lane Editions.
McGregor, Glen. 2001. "Writer Gets Big Bucks to Put Words in Martin's Mouth." *Ottawa Citizen,* 4 November 4, A13.
McLean, Everton. 2005. "Brewer Enters Race for NDP Leadership." *Telegraph-Journal,* 25 May.
Morris Chris. 2006. "Break the Mould, NDP Leader Urges." *Daily Gleaner,* 19 August, A4.
Moszynski, Mary, and *Times-Transcript* staff. 2005. "N.B. NDP Chooses New Party Leader: Allison Brewer Vows to Build Up Party Support, Fight for Gay Rights in N.B." *Times-Transcript,* 26 September.
*National Post.* 2001. "B.C. MP First to Declare She Is in a Lesbian Relationship." 30 October, A2.
O'Kane, Joel. 2005. "Three Enter Race for NDP's Top Job." *Daily Gleaner,* 14 July, A3.
O'Neil Peter. 2001a. "B.C. Politician Is First Female MP to Reveal Same-Sex Partnership." *Ottawa Citizen,* 30 October, A1.
–. 2001b. "Davies Admits Gay Relationship: Vancouver MP is First Woman in House to Declare Same-Sex Partnership." *Vancouver Sun,* 30 October, B1.
Raketty, Robert. 2005. "An Interview with MP Libby Davies, New Democratic Party House Leader." *Seattle Gay News,* 1 July, s. 1. http://www.sgn.org/sgnnews26/page2.cfm.
Rayside, David. 1998. *On the Fringe: Gays and Lesbians in Politics.* Ithaca: Cornell University Press.
Riggle, Ellen, and Barry Tadlock. 1999. "Gays and Lesbians in the Democratic Process: Past, Present and Future." In *Gays and Lesbians in the Democratic Process,* ed. Ellen Riggle and Barry Tadlock, 1-21. New York: Columbia University Press.
Robinson, Gertrude, and Armande Saint-Jean. 1991. "Women Politicians and Their Media Coverage: A Generational Analysis." In *Women in Canadian Politics: Towards Equity in Representation,* ed. Kathy Megyery, 127-69. Vol. 6, Research Studies for the Royal Commission on Electoral Reform and Party Financing. Toronto: Dundurn Press.
–. 1995. "The Portrayal of Women Politicians in the Media: Political Implications." In *Gender and Politics in Contemporary Canada,* ed. François-Pierre Gingras, 176-90. Toronto: Oxford University Press.
Ross, Karen, and Annabelle Sreberny. 2000. "Women in the House: Media Representation of British Politicians." In *Gender, Politics and Communication,* ed. Annabelle Sreberny and Liesbet van Zoonen, 79-99. Cresskill: Hampton Press.
Sampert, Shannon, and Linda Trimble. 2003. "'Wham, Bam, No Thank You Ma'am': Gender and the Game Frame in National Newspaper Coverage of Election 2000." In *Women and Electoral Politics in Canada,* ed. Manon Tremblay and Linda Trimble, 21-26. Toronto: Oxford University Press.
Saskatchewan Resources for Sexual Diversity. "Perceptions: The First Twenty-Two Years, 1983-2004 – An Index to the Canadian Gay and Lesbian Newsmagazine Compiled by Alex Spence." http://library2.usask.ca/srsd/perceptions/1875.html.
Saskatoon *Star Phoenix.* 2001. "MP Davies Declares Same-Sex Relationship." 30 October, A9.
Scharrer, Erica. 2002. "An 'Improbable Leap': A Content Analysis of Newspaper Coverage of Hillary Clinton's Transition from First Lady to Senate Candidate." *Journalism Studies* 3, 3: 393-406.
Tadlock, B., and A. Gordon. 2003. "Political Evaluations of Lesbian and Gay Candidates: The Impact of Stereotypic Biases in Press Coverage." Paper presented at the annual meeting of the American Political Science Association, Philadelphia, August.
Von Weiler, Joost. 2005. Letter to the editor. *Telegraph-Journal,* 28 September.
Wikipedia. "LGBT Politicans from Canada." http://en.wikipedia.org/wiki/Category:LGBT_politicians_from_Canada.

# Part 4
# Media and Public Images

# 9

# Crafting a Public Image: Women MPs and the Dynamics of Media Coverage

*Elizabeth Goodyear-Grant*

Is leadership a masculine concept that impedes women's political representation? Scholars who study leader attributes, particularly from a gender perspective as they are presented in news reports, generally answer in the affirmative. News is a predominantly masculine narrative that privileges men and masculinity, a point that is underscored by Everitt and Camp in the preceding chapter. While women politicians' gendered experiences of media have become less negative over time – presumably lessening obstacles to women's political participation – this chapter presents unequivocal evidence, based on a series of interviews with Canadian members of Parliament, that media portrayals continue to generate unique challenges for women office-seekers. Plainly stated, women face an uneven playing field in the media, which in turn contributes to their continued political underrepresentation and to the repercussions that are laid out compellingly in Bashevkin's introduction to this volume.

Among the chief concerns for women candidates is how to position themselves in order to obtain fair, balanced, or positive news coverage. Using data gathered in interviews with Canadian MPs, this chapter demonstrates that women legislators experience news coverage in distinctly gendered ways. Male and female MPs have different expectations of how the media will cover them, which in turn produce divergent self-presentation styles. By focusing on how women politicians try to frame themselves for reporters, including efforts to minimize what they regard as harmful coverage, this chapter shows that politicians' relationships with the media are symbiotic, dynamic, and context-dependent.

Women participate in their own mediation, the process whereby real-world speech and behaviours are selectively chosen and interpreted for presentation in news stories. Often, women's participation in their mediation involves self-censorship of speech, dress, and behaviour in order to discourage journalists from focusing on their gendered identities. In some cases, women politicians avoid events or behaviours because they fear negative coverage that might exploit particularly damaging gender-role stereotypes; this self-censorship follows from the reality that women's speech, appearance, and behaviour tend to be selectively presented, or misrepresented, in news, a pattern found in other Anglo-American systems as well as in South Africa (see Fox 1997; Jamieson 1995; Niven and Zilber 2001; Ross 2002; Ross and Sreberny 2000).

Few scholars have examined how women politicians understand their mediation and what strategies they adopt to navigate news coverage (for exceptions, see Bystrom and Miller 1999; Bystrom et al. 2004; Ross 2002; Ross and Sreberny 2000). A blind spot in the literature, parallel with the scarcity of work on gender and political leadership more generally, has resulted. Given that few citizens have first-hand knowledge of politicians, news organizations are important political actors connecting ordinary citizens with the political sphere. Therefore, how politicians perceive their treatment in the media environment is crucial to understanding this field.

Research shows that news media not only play an important macro-level role in contemporary politics but also that they matter to the decision making of individual citizens (Iyengar and Kinder 1987). Political decisions, including how people vote and evaluate political candidates, are reached on the basis of personas that are reflected through media. In the next chapter of this volume, Gidengil, Everitt, and Banducci challenge prevailing assumptions that voters use gender stereotypes to attribute traits to individual candidates. They do agree, however, that the selective presentation of female candidates in media stories can raise doubts about women's viability or suitability for leadership positions, thereby contributing to women's chronic under-representation in politics at all levels.

This chapter concludes with a pessimistic prognosis. Available options for tackling the gendered mediation of women politicians – such as media regulation and increasing the number of women journalists – offer limited prospects for altering established modes of coverage, at least in the short- to medium-term. Gendered mediation is a function primarily of collectively held stereotypes about gender and about political leadership, both of which are resistant to change. Pragmatically speaking, women (and their male allies) must continue to embrace every opportunity to challenge prevailing norms and stereotypes, and political parties at both the national and constituency levels must continue and extend efforts to inform and prepare female (and male) candidates for dealing with a fraught media environment.

## Methodology

This chapter presents the results of twenty-seven semi-structured interviews conducted in 2005 with current and former Canadian MPs. My method of targeting interviewees combined theoretical or purposeful sampling with "snowball" or convenience techniques (Warren 2001). With theoretical sampling, "the interviewer seeks out respondents who seem likely to epitomize the analytic criteria in which he or she is interested" (ibid., 87). All MPs possess the primary criteria of being federal-level politicians who have fought an election campaign and, therefore, have experience dealing with a variety of news media. Since all MPs were possible interviewees, the most important task, then, was to decide which types of MPs to target. My primary goal was to obtain interviews with MPs of both sexes from all three political parties that fielded candidates across the country, namely the Liberal, Conservative, and New Democratic parties. To a lesser extent, I also targeted MPs by region, experience in federal politics, age, and visible minority status. Ultimately, the objective was to ensure the participation of MPs with diverse characteristics, since "the philosophy of responsive interviewing suggests that reality is complex; to accurately portray that complexity, you need to gather contradictory or overlapping perceptions and nuanced understandings that different individuals hold" (Rubin and Rubin 2004, 67). In other words, my general selection strategy was to target MPs so that comparison and control were built into the sample (King, Keohane, and Verba 1994).

A priori research designs provide good frameworks, but qualitative interviewing often poses sampling challenges because of time and access limitations. In this study, gatekeeping was a general obstacle, particularly for Liberal MPs who were government members at the time. Telephone and email communications with MPs were never direct; instead, my interview requests were routed through administrative staff. I used a combination of contact methods, always combining phone calls with follow-up emails, and, in most cases, repeated contact was necessary in order to receive responses from MPs or their staff. Many of the MPs I contacted never responded to the requests for interviews, and many others denied access, usually because of overburdened schedules. While my approach was to target MPs according to specific primary (sex and party) and secondary (region, age, experience, and minority status) criteria, the reality was that I interviewed whoever agreed to participate. As it turns out, I had more success securing interviews through MPs' own personal recommendations – that is, when one MP I had interviewed personally requested a fellow MP (usually a member of the same party) to also grant me an interview. This style of participant recruitment is known as the snowball or convenience method.

Of the twenty-seven interviewees, several had served as cabinet ministers and one – Kim Campbell – as prime minister. The sample included eighteen women and nine men, which permitted direct comparison of men's and women's experiences of mediation. Among the interviewees, nine were Liberals (in government at the time), twelve were Conservatives, and six were

New Democrats. Kim Campbell is counted as a government member because she served on that side of the House of Commons during her time in federal politics. My sample thus includes ten government and seventeen opposition MPs (eleven of the twelve Conservatives plus six New Democrats).

Interviews were conducted in a semi-structured style. A list of broad topics or questions (see appendix at end of chapter) was used to guide, though not determine, the course of the interviews. This style provided room for each interview to vary, including in terms of the order of questions or specific follow-up queries. Many participants raised issues that I had not considered previously, and these issues in turn became a focal point of those interviews. Ultimately, I aimed to give interviewees an opportunity to choose their own topics of discussion, since the issues that respondents chose to talk about often revealed a great deal about their media experiences.

Six of the twenty-seven interviewees agreed to be identified in this research.[1] Among the twenty-one who chose to remain anonymous, seventeen agreed to include any part of their comments in this chapter, while the other four indicated through the course of the interview what could or could not be reported. It is noteworthy that of the eighteen women interviewed, only two (Kim Campbell and Alexa McDonough) agreed to be identified in this research. By contrast, nearly half of the men interviewed (4/9) said they could be identified, which suggests that women politicians may be more guarded than their male counterparts, possibly because of negative media experiences.

Interviewees were informed that this research project focused on media coverage of elections and politicians. To avoid priming interviewees towards certain topics or positions, no specific mention was made of the treatment of women versus the treatment of men. If, by the end of their interviews, MPs had not mentioned any type of gender issue, they were asked a specific question about the presence of stereotypes or biases in Canadian televised news. Of the eighteen female interviewees, twelve spoke spontaneously about how being a woman had influenced their news coverage, while the other six did not. When asked at the end of their respective interviews whether gender played a role in their news coverage, all six women responded affirmatively, and most gave short examples of how being a woman had either hindered or helped their coverage.

## Perspectives on Media Presentation

Like their Australian, British, and South African counterparts (Ross 2002; Ross and Sreberny 2000), Canadian politicians distinguished among different media formats. Former prime minister Kim Campbell was unequivocal in her preference for print and radio over television, arguing, "TV is difficult, because they take a five-second sound bite and end up presenting none of your points and often you are presented out of context" (personal interview,

Kim Campbell, 22 September 2005). Campbell was sensitive to misrepresentation issues; in her view, Liberal leader Jean Chrétien "was repeatedly let off the hook with off-the-cuff comments and blunders." She stated explicitly, "this is a gender thing." Echoing several women MPs at Westminster (see Ross 2002), Campbell maintained that "radio is the best of all, because you can talk and get your points out, and people can hear the tone, pitch, and variety in your voice, but without the distraction of the visuals." Campbell spoke in detail about the fast pace and visual focus of TV, which, in her view, drew voters' attention away from the sometimes-complex messages of politicians.

Campbell's reasons for preferring print and radio over television included a view that "this may be an age thing." Gender was therefore not the only factor affecting her preferred media format. Campbell's preference for print and radio as an "age thing" contrasted with the views of Conservative MP Rahim Jaffer. Jaffer's preferred news coverage was television; in his words, "TV is key ... A second best is a print story with a picture accompanying it, preferably in colour" (personal interview, Rahim Jaffer, 21 February 2005). Thirty-three years of age at the time of our interview, Jaffer was one of the youngest MPs in the House of Commons.[2] He grew up in the era of personalized, candidate-centred politics (Wattenberg 1995) and felt comfortable with the visual media. Moreover, his comments about print media expressed a clear preference for visual content, since he said a print story must have a picture to accompany it and, ideally, a picture in colour.[3]

Other MPs tended to share Jaffer's perspective. One Conservative woman believed local or, less often, national television news coverage of her participation in Question Period was "by far" the best way for constituents to see her. Subscribing to the view that "there's no such thing as bad publicity," she aimed to be very visible to the public and especially to voters in her district. When this same sentiment was expressed by British and Australian legislators, Ross and Sreberny (2000) concluded that, "in an era of presentation politics and an apathetic polity, many women feel their constituents only believe they are actually doing their job and representing their interests when they see them 'live' on television" (86).

In short, conversations with Canadian MPs revealed a generational dimension to media format preferences. Some older interviewees, notably former NDP leader Ed Broadbent, observed that, back when newspapers had more reporters in Ottawa, journalists could develop clear areas of expertise (personal interview with Ed Broadbent, 24 February 2005). Past difficulties with different media formats also played a role in politicians' preferences. Believing that she faced critical coverage of her physical appearance as well as misrepresentation in television coverage, Kim Campbell preferred the medium of radio interviews. In her view, this format offered more time for articulating complex points.

Regardless of media format, women MPs raised the common theme that reporters focused on their physical appearance and personal life. Former NDP leader Alexa McDonough recalled a story in the *Ottawa Citizen* during her early years in Ottawa (personal interview, Alexa McDonough, 25 February 2005).[4] After an aide called excitedly to tell her about page-one coverage, McDonough opened the paper to see a large photo of herself above the headline, "Alexa McDonough, Call Your Dry-Cleaner" (*Ottawa Citizen* 1998). The main point of this front-page column was that she had worn the same dress to two different events in the same week.[5]

Although McDonough was angered at the time, she saw over the years that this type of coverage was "par for the course." Comments about her appearance and that of other women MPs were made with sufficient frequency that they could not be ignored. For McDonough, the amount of writing about women's physical appearance was not matched by similar coverage of men in the House of Commons. Referring explicitly to the *Ottawa Citizen* story, she wondered how many male MPs did *not* wear the same suit twice in one week. "Could you imagine a story," she asked, "with the following headline: 'Jean Chrétien Wears Same Suit Twice in One Week'? No man has ten suits, and no one expects him to, but a woman is supposed to have a closet full of clothes."

Ross and Sreberny's (2000, 87) study of women MPs in Britain reported similar findings. They quote Labour member Dawn Primarolo, who said: "I don't know whether it is deliberate or it's so ingrained, but a woman's appearance is always commented on. That never happens to male politicians, ever, unless they have made a particular point about their style, but then they are presented as extreme, exceptions that prove the rule. Women are never the right age. We're too young, we're too old. We're too thin, we're too fat. We wear too much make-up, we don't wear enough. We're too flashy in our dress, we don't take enough care. There isn't a thing we can do that's right." Frustration over the attention reporters paid to physical appearances was therefore not peculiar to women politicians in Ottawa.

Female MPs interviewed for this study believed journalists were intrusive in their treatment of women's personal lives. One argued that the fact that many women in the House of Commons were divorced or single was disproportionately prominent in news coverage. In her view, print outlets were particularly likely to mention the divorced or single-mother status of female MPs. This view is confirmed by a number of empirical analyses conducted outside Canada (see, for example, Bystrom, Robertson, and Banwart 2001; Kahn 1992, 1996; Kahn and Goldberg 1991; Muir 2005; Robertson et al. 2002). As Carmen Lawrence, the first female premier of an Australian state, noted, "When I became Premier, all this stuff came out, [using my] first name, wanting images of me shown in domestic situations and references to my family and all that stuff that comes out with women ... you rarely see a man described as Joe Bloggs, 54, father of three" (Ross 2002, 87).

Given the attention paid to their personal lives, many women politicians retreat from media scrutiny. Kim Campbell noted that endeavouring to keep their "love lives" out of the public eye followed from a realistic sense that this type of coverage can harm women's careers – even if parallel coverage of bachelorhood and single fatherhood can glorify men's lives. Alexa McDonough said she made concerted efforts throughout her political career to keep her personal life out of the public spotlight, including shielding her children from media scrutiny.[6] McDonough was concerned that her status as a divorcee could – and would – be used in a negative way, particularly if members of the general public absorbed ideas from the media and elsewhere that her leadership and policy abilities were questionable because she was divorced.

Women politicians outside Canada share the view that care must be taken to shield one's personal life from media scrutiny (see van Zoonen 1998, 2000a, 2000b, 2005, 2006). Legislators as diverse as German chancellor Angela Merkel, Finnish prime minister Tarja Halonen, US senator Hillary Clinton, and Dutch Green leader Femke Halsema have all become "reticent about opening up their private personae to the scrutiny of the media and public" (van Zoonen 2006, 297). Shielding partners and spouses from media attention is important for two reasons: first, few are willing to jeopardize the privacy and security of their families, particularly their children, by exposing them to media scrutiny; and second, keeping family members out of the picture helps discourage the use of traditional "wife" and "mother" designations in media coverage.

As Chapter 8 by Everitt and Camp in this volume demonstrates, Canadian women politicians have additional reasons to be concerned about news framings of "unconventional" aspects of their personal lives. If they are unmarried or unattached, or if they are not regarded as "feminine" in the stereotypical sense of the term, then questions about their sexual orientation tend to follow. Journalists have hinted about lesbianism in their coverage of a number of federal MPs, including Audrey McLaughlin, Sheila Copps, and Deborah Grey (see Sharpe 1994, 31-32). In the United States, innuendos about Clinton-era attorney general Janet Reno were so frequent that Reno told a number of reporters, "I am just an awkward old maid with a very great affection for men" (Reno, as quoted in Jamieson 1995, 73). Analysts can debate the wisdom of replying to such rumours, particularly in the candid manner employed by Reno, but the fact remains that female politicians often believe they need to present themselves explicitly as heterosexuals.

Not all the women I interviewed were critical of media interest in women's private lives. One Liberal MP, for example, believed that women politicians sometimes invited this sort of commentary. Referring specifically to Belinda Stronach's decision to cross the floor to join the Liberal cabinet in 2005, she said too much coverage of this story focused on the reaction of Stronach's ex-companion in the Conservative caucus (Peter MacKay) and all the "jilted lover garbage." Yet, in her view, Stronach should have expected this kind of attention because she had engaged in an "office romance"; for women to be taken seriously, according to this interviewee, they needed to keep their personal and private lives separate. This MP maintained it was foolish to expect reporters to turn down headline-grabbing information, since news is a business, and political gossip sells.

No male interviewees had much to say about their families or personal lives. One of the two male MPs who mentioned this dimension was Gurmant Grewal, a Conservative MP from British Columbia. Grewal spoke in some detail about the fact that his wife, Nina Grewal, also held a seat in the Commons. He noted with some pride that they were the first married couple to serve as MPs at the same time, and that they had received considerable media attention as a result. The second interviewee mentioned family in the context of his wife's view that party events were boring and that, as a result, she did not usually accompany him to "official events." Clearly, men and women in Parliament perceived media scrutiny of their personal lives differently. Women cited endless pitfalls, while men revealed little concern, let alone pressure, for strategic self-presentation. Kim Campbell seemed particularly troubled by this obvious double standard; in her words, "look at Trudeau, for example, whose love life was a mess. It didn't hurt him. Quite the opposite – media and the public thought he was dashing and sexy."

### Quality and Quantity of Coverage

Paralleling Gidengil, Everitt, and Banducci's findings in the next chapter, interviewees revealed that party connections played an important role in distinguishing among MPs. Conservative and NDP members on the opposition benches criticized reporters for focusing too much on the Liberals, who were in power at the time. New Democrats claimed it was particularly hard for them to attract attention, although Ed Broadbent saw it as "appropriate for media to pay more attention to government." Six of the eighteen women interviewees mentioned party or region before gender as a factor in their coverage, which reminds us of the variety of factors that shape press accounts.

Several women politicians mentioned reporters' lack of knowledge about them; one, for example, claimed that, unless you are a "high profile" candidate (for instance, a veteran MP or cabinet minister), you tend to be ignored. In her experience, journalists did not take the time to "do their research," since they asked questions about children of childless candidates. This may result from a history of women candidates running in unwinnable seats, which leads journalists to expect female nominees will lose on election day. Experience is also a factor in this case: women have only entered federal campaigns in large numbers since the 1980s, which makes them less familiar as a group to journalists than their male colleagues.

Do reporters treat political women as seriously as they do male politicians? Alexa McDonough recalled that when she first came to Ottawa in 1995, and throughout the 1997 federal election campaign, she was routinely addressed by journalists as "Audrey." Audrey McLaughlin was McDonough's predecessor as federal NDP leader; both were social workers, had two children, were divorced, and shared the initials "A. Mc." However, McDonough insisted this treatment did not befall men in politics. During the 1980s, she pointed out, several men named John served as MPs, including John Turner, John Crosbie, and Jean Chrétien, but reporters did not confuse them. Many men named Bill and Mike participated in Canadian politics, shared the same professional background, and had the same number of children but were not mixed up with each other.

McDonough claimed that women such as herself and McLaughlin were "interchangeable" in the minds of reporters, and her view draws on cognitive psychology research on "outgroup homogeneity bias" (see Mullen and Hu 1989). This perspective leads individuals to perceive members of other groups as more alike or "interchangeable," in McDonough's words, than members of their own group. The dynamic at play renders members of marginalized groups, such as women in politics, homogeneous and essentialized. McDonough admitted that, other than wearing a name tag to press conferences and media scrums, she could do little to avoid being confused with McLaughlin. She often asked an assistant to introduce her to journalists at formal events, including press conferences and speeches, but could not use the same strategy when a journalist "puts a microphone in your face."

Kim Campbell linked reporters' lack of knowledge to their assumptions about women politicians. In her view, journalists implied that she slept her way to the top because they found it difficult to grasp that women could achieve success through "intelligence, political know-how, and hard work." She noted that reporters repeatedly called her a "rookie," even though she was one of the most experienced politicians to become prime minister: Campbell had held a variety of federal cabinet portfolios, including national defence and justice, as well as positions at all three levels of government, before becoming Conservative leader. By way of comparison, Pierre Trudeau had one year of cabinet experience before becoming prime minister, while Brian Mulroney and Joe Clark had none. Campbell's point, ultimately, was that "the media could have called me a moron or an idiot, which is a matter of opinion, but the facts just did not support the use of the adjective 'rookie' to describe me." When asked how she dealt with this aspect of her coverage, Campbell replied that, while a politician can do a lot to cultivate favourable coverage during non-election periods, "there is little a politician ... can do about damage control" in the midst of a campaign.

Other women interviewees, including four who had attended campaign schools earlier in their careers, were more optimistic about their ability to influence coverage during a campaign. The four women said this training had markedly improved their media skills. The fact that three of them were Liberals may indicate a greater commitment of resources to that activity by one party than by others. One woman who participated in campaign training after her first nomination as a Liberal candidate said running a campaign and, in particular, dealing with reporters are "not intuitive," since both require public speaking and networking skills. No male MPs mentioned campaign schools or other forms of campaign and media training.

The comments about campaigns by both men and women MPs suggested that many were more concerned with the quantity rather than the quality of media coverage. Some had learned, for example, that campaign events had to be timed for maximum visibility so that nightly television stories were based on morning or early afternoon appearances. Less high-profile appearances in hospitals or seniors' homes could take place at the end of the day and receive local newspaper coverage.

Marked gender divides can be discerned in the ways MPs assessed Question Period in the House of Commons. Of the twenty interviewees (eleven women, nine men) who mentioned Question Period in response to a question about news between elections, women tended to focus on their dislike of these sessions – including ways they had found to avoid them by retreating to caucus lounges.[7] This is not to say that all women politicians were uncomfortable with the raucous atmosphere of Question Period. Some excelled and possibly revelled in this environment – as did many male MPs. Former Liberal MP and cabinet member Sheila Copps, for example, was a member of the so-called Rat Pack that vigorously criticized the Mulroney Conservatives during their first term in office.[8] Copps seemed comfortable with adversarial politics (see Copps 1986 and 2004); she grew up in a political household, which likely prepared her for combative debates from an early point in her personal background (see Lawless and Fox 2005).[9]

Among interviewees, only one man, former NDP leader Ed Broadbent, expressed dissatisfaction with the tone of Question Period. Other male MPs focused their comments on their use of Question Period to attract news coverage. This was particularly the case for Conservative Rahim Jaffer, who spoke at length about his adversarial talents in "going over the top, getting theatrical in QP" as part of a three-man "hit squad" that attacked the governing Liberals.

When asked for their thoughts about how reporters covered Question Period, women tended to explain the dynamics of coverage with reference to the rowdiness of the sessions. No female MP shared Jaffer's comfort with the conflictual style of Question Period. In fact, even Jaffer recognized this gender angle, since during his interview he mentioned "hit squad" attacks on Judy Sgro, the minister of immigration, that were presented in reports as "all-male aggressors harass woman in the House who is just trying to work on social issues." Jaffer noted that the Conservative caucus worked right away to "re-tool" the Question Period strategy so that, the next day, all of the party's questions were assigned to women. From then on, Jaffer said, the Conservatives tended to assign women caucus members to "go after" women ministers in the government.

This story sheds light on how gendered norms can challenge and constrain men. Jaffer's comments, as well as changes to the Conservative Party's Question Period strategy, show how men's attacks on women politicians can backfire because they breach norms of "gentlemanly" conduct. Research in this area in the United States identifies a common tactic for male politicians: avoiding direct attacks on women (see Kahn 1993). As Kahn's analysis of campaign commercials reveals, men are less likely to run candidate-centred attack ads when their rivals are women because they do not want to be seen as "beating up on" women (ibid., 491). At the same time, the fact that male politicians often avoid direct attacks on or verbal arguments with their female rivals may further trivialize women politicians. While none of my interviewees framed the issue in such terms, the unavoidable implication is that women politicians may be seen as lacking the mettle to defend themselves in a way that entails verbally sparring with their male counterparts. Put plainly, the suggestion is that women politicians are weak or timid.

How do media accounts frame conflicts between women in politics? Five of the eighteen female MPs noted their purposeful avoidance of situations that could be portrayed as "cat-fights." Alexa McDonough recalled that as a member of the Nova Scotia legislature and leader of the Nova Scotia NDP, she was invited to join the provincial delegation to the Charlottetown constitutional discussions. Although leaders of the Canadian women's movement under the umbrella of the National Action Committee on the Status of Women (NAC) mobilized against the accord that came out of those talks, McDonough supported the deal. She chose not to participate in a televised debate, however, with NAC president Judy Rebick.[10] McDonough found the situation regrettable because a debate would have drawn public visibility to the Charlottetown Accord, to NAC, and to individual political women, including Rebick and McDonough.

## Relations with Reporters

Sharp differences existed between men and women, as well as among women, in the extent to which MPs built personal relationships with journalists. Except for Ed Broadbent, every male legislator I interviewed talked about efforts to forge ties with reporters. Stockwell Day spoke at length about his experiences in the Alberta provincial legislature, where friendly relations with local reporters produced favourable media coverage (personal interview, Stockwell Day, 24 February 2005).[11] Day noted that these relations extended beyond the workplace, since MLAs and reporters often socialized together at charity functions, party events, and so on.

Women politicians with provincial experience maintained that relations with the media were more cordial at that level. Alexa McDonough, for example, claimed she never felt uncomfortable or marginalized by Nova Scotia journalists during her provincial career; in fact, MLAs and reporters shared a sense of intimacy and of working towards the "same goals." Kim Campbell believed the "Ottawa press pack" was tightly knit and often caught up in a political "who's who game" that excluded her and many other women. Campbell maintained that, outside Ottawa, regional "reporters do not focus exclusively on national politics, and they would listen to my policies on the wheat trade, for example." She argued that regional reporters cared about issues affecting their area – such as the wheat trade in the Prairies – while members of the Ottawa press corps were narrowly preoccupied with partisan politics and gossip.

Conservative politicians from western Canada viewed the challenge of winning favourable media coverage in Ottawa as particularly difficult. Stockwell Day said that as a westerner, leader of the Canadian Alliance, and purported "right-wing nut-job" and "Christian fundamentalist," getting Ottawa journalists to "warm up" to him was far from easy. Rahim Jaffer shared the view that bias against westerners and politicians on the right was a reality, but he said the trick was to bring journalists into "your fold." He organized frequent social events where politicians and journalists met for drinks or dinner.

No female MPs talked about cultivating personal relationships with journalists; nor did they mention participating in events, receptions, or dinners with members of the press. When asked about ties with reporters, women tended to be either negative or ambivalent. Comments along the former lines emphasized the conflictual nature of journalist-politician relations. One Liberal woman referred to the parliamentary press corps as a "shark tank," while another characterized it as having a "barracuda mentality" because of reporters' reliance on questions that aimed "straight for the jugular." McDonough was less harsh than these respondents; she was struck most by how "impersonal" relations were between MPs and Ottawa journalists. McDonough believed the latter were doing their jobs, trying to sell their stories to editors and readers. These views contrasted with more negative ones expressed by two Liberal women who, unlike McDonough in either Halifax or Ottawa, sat on the government side. Government MPs, whether men or women, may find themselves disproportionately on the defensive with reporters, while opposition MPs seem inclined to appreciate whatever coverage they receive.

Female MPs voiced particularly intriguing views of women journalists. Two interviewees spontaneously mentioned this subject. McDonough said that at several points over the years she had felt supported by women journalists. She and a Liberal MP singled out Julie Van Dusen, who became the CBC's Middle East bureau chief after serving in Ottawa. The Liberal MP saw Van Dusen as the best reporter in Ottawa, one who was willing to tell male journalists to "back off" or "get real" when a "sexist" question was posed. This Liberal remarked that in the midst of a media scrum on a rough day, a shared sense of fairness among women made a world of difference.

When I asked the other sixteen female MPs about their experiences with women journalists, most recalled incidents in which the latter had been sensitive or supportive, either in person or in their reporting. A minority viewed male and female journalists as indistinguishable. Kim Campbell pointed out that not only were women journalists expected to conform to standard journalistic modes of writing, which tend to be adversarial and masculine in style, but also that "women are not making the editorial decisions" in media organizations. As Chambers, Steiner, and Fleming (2004) demonstrate in their book on this subject, the absence of women in senior decision-making positions in the news industry is not peculiar to Canada.

One bright spot in female MPs' relations with the media was the reality that members of rare species tend to attract attention. Parallel to Ross and Sreberny's (2000) findings in Britain, several Canadian women commented on how the relative novelty of female politicians increased their media visibility and shaped the content of coverage in a positive way. One Liberal noted (with what might be called a slightly tongue-in-cheek tone) that she had greatly benefited from "all the fuss" about women in politics. This interviewee was a backbencher who believed she would have received less media coverage if she had been a male backbench MP. In short, women politicians' relations with journalists are multi-faceted and do have favourable dimensions. As van Zoonen reminds us, there exist "opportunities that the personalization of political culture produce for female politicians" (2006, 289).

In cases in which enhanced visibility follows from women's minority status in legislatures, it is understandable that politicians will view this situation as advantageous. Prospects for re-election can improve with more coverage; one can imagine scenarios in which women politicians might decide to strategically, and subtly, draw attention to gender as a marker of difference so as to attract press attention. It is important to bear in mind that the primary goal of many woman politicians, like their male colleagues, is re-election, not revolutionary change in the political system or the journalism profession. Put differently, it is important to interpret the statements of interviewees in light of their chosen priorities and goals. Many women I met expressed serious dissatisfaction with biased media coverage; at the same time, they recognized the positive aspects of their outsider status. As Everitt and Camp's discussion in the preceding chapter reminds us, multiple markers of difference can be used to marginalize and discredit "outsider" women like Allison Brewer, thus neutralizing any advantage that might have accrued from greater press attention.

## Discussion

News coverage helps to shape how voters in a democracy perceive political figures (a topic taken up in greater detail by Gidengil, Everitt, and Banducci in Chapter 10), but the news is also the most unpredictable form of political communication for politicians. Stated simply, MPs exert little to no control over how information is presented and interpreted. Public figures may try to predict how audiences will react to their self-presentations – including their style, speech, ideas, interpersonal manner, and gestures – but they also need to anticipate how newsmakers will portray these same characteristics to the public. Moreover, they must do all this while maintaining the appearance of spontaneity, which is one of the key ingredients in a successful presentation of self (Goffman 1959).

This chapter has examined how Canadian MPs understand the coverage of political news and, further, how they tailor presentations of self in light of these perspectives. Both men and women viewed press coverage as a distortion of reality, notably one that focuses on or even exploits stereotypes. Many Canadian women MPs mentioned gender stereotypes as a defining feature of their coverage. One man, former Alliance leader Stockwell Day, reported stereotypical coverage of his religious beliefs ("Fundamental Day" and "right-wing nut-job," for example). Given that the comparative literature reveals similar findings, we know dissatisfaction of this type is hardly unique to Canadian politicians (see Ross 2002; Ross and Sreberny 2000).

In our interview conversation, Kim Campbell took this analysis one step further. She viewed stereotyping as a widespread problem that is not necessarily a function of media coverage. In her words, it is difficult for women "to act in a naturally feminine way given that politics is defined by men. Disempowered people never know what it is like to be themselves in politics. Women CEOs have the same problems ... Women leaders have to hold back and cannot be their true selves, because their true selves do not mesh with the definition of leadership. What is the professional and psychological price of holding back?" The phrase "psychological price" refers to the personal cost to women politicians of adopting a neutered or masculine public face. Campbell believed this practice was harmful because "you forget to be true to yourself."

Former NDP leader Audrey McLaughlin offered a similar perspective in her autobiography: "The danger in all this is that you will lose track of who you really are, that your public persona will no longer reflect your private self" (1992, 204). Amid debates about whether voters use stereotypes to ascribe traits or policy positions to women candidates or whether "acting tough" harms or helps women at the polls – questions that Gidengil and her colleagues address in the next chapter – we may have overlooked another important issue: How does the adoption of neutered or masculine political personas affect women politicians personally? This is a consequential question, since women's individual decisions to enter or remain in political office are highly personal considerations.

In the end, it is clear that the Canadian women MPs understood media coverage in ways that resembled those of their counterparts in Australia, the United Kingdom, South Africa, and the United States. Ultimately, if generalizations are to be made, my analysis suggests the following: first, female political leaders *do* confront disadvantages in their media presentations; and second, these disadvantages hold clear consequences for their chances of winning and retaining elected office.

Gendered mediation affects not only women who hold public office but also those who are considering entering public life – since it may discourage *potential* women candidates. Factors that lead women to avoid politics – such as awareness of the negative coverage they are likely to encounter – exacerbate the demonstrated supply-side problems in the recruitment of women politicians (see Lawless and Fox 2005; Norris and Lovenduski 1995). Stated bluntly, despite an increasingly large pool of highly qualified potential female candidates, disproportionately fewer women seek political office compared to men. Women's expectations about gendered mediation may be one explanation for this pattern. Given the manner in which female politicians tend to be covered, some women with solid leadership credentials will avoid political careers, their avoidance based, in part, on a conscious desire to steer clear of negative media and public scrutiny. Therefore, the nature of news media coverage is relevant not only to the current generation of legislators but also to the future supply of women politicians.

The second question we collectively address in this volume is simple: What can be done? What strategies can be adopted to eliminate barriers to women's representation in politics? The menu for reform is extensive: from formal government-mandated policy prescriptions – such as quotas – that could alter political party nomination procedures to less formal changes in societal attitudes. In the case of the press coverage of politicians, policy-mandated reform is tricky terrain because media regulation is a contentious issue in any democracy, whether Canada or elsewhere. Most newspapers, the Canadian Broadcasting Corporation, the Canadian Broadcast Standards Council, and the Canadian Association of Broadcasters have already adopted guidelines on sex-role portrayal to encourage gender-neutral reporting (see Canadian Broadcasting Corporation 1998). Beyond these voluntary measures, it is not clear what policy solutions can be adopted.

Another possible remedy for gendered mediation is to increase the number of women journalists. If journalism as a profession were more gender-balanced, the argument goes, we would see more equitable coverage of men and women politicians. A concerted effort to hire and promote more women journalists is viewed as desirable and, in fact, the experiences of some of my interviewees speak to this potential.

In the main, however, prescriptive options are unlikely to work. First, rank-and-file journalists in traditional news organizations have relatively little control over their assignments, and, in television news, rank-and-file reporters rarely write their own copy. In order for women to have substantial influence on coverage, they need to occupy decision-making positions in the profession. Unfortunately, "the higher, the fewer" rule (Bashevkin 1993) tends to hold in news organizations as it does in political organizations: women journalists are disproportionately clustered at the lower levels of the news profession. For example, Robinson (2005, 43) found that while 55 percent of reporters for Canadian dailies were women in 1995, only 8 percent of "star" reporters, 4 percent of desk heads, and 2 percent of editors-in-chief were female. The distribution of women in decision-making positions for television news was very similar (ibid., 57).

Second, the extent to which individual women journalists can challenge patterns of gendered mediation depends not only on their feminist consciousness but also on their willingness to act on these perspectives. Women journalists are seldom *able* to act in such a way as to produce gender-neutral reportage. The masculine narrative that pervades political news functions at a systemic level. Two meta-level factors in particular govern how news is produced: the sociology of the journalism profession and the political economy of the media system. Stated simply, the organization and practice of reporting limits the influence of a journalist's gender. As in other work environments, "organizations with male-dominated power structures and political climates may promote social interactions in which female employees are expected to act and perform much like their male counterparts, perhaps to avoid exclusion or gain promotion" (Rodgers and Thorson 2003, 662).

One of the core themes that connects research on women in politics in this volume and in the wider literature is a focus on collectively held, deeply ingrained gender-role stereotypes. This dimension of the problem should be the real target for reform. Stereotypes not only establish expectations about individuals based on their group membership, they also have a prescriptive element because they tell people what types of behaviours are *appropriate* for a particular group. Stereotypes help explain why news content tends to be gendered. Indeed, counter-stereotypical behaviour – such as a woman leader attacking a political rival – is newsworthy because it is unexpected and dramatic. As Gidengil, Everitt, and Banducci point out in the next chapter, this explains why women's aggressive behaviour tends to be exaggerated in news coverage; moreover, it helps us understand why female politicians often see the culturally constituted stereotypes in which they are presented to the public as straightjackets.

Unfortunately, stereotypes are hard to change at both the aggregate and individual levels. At the aggregate level, stereotypes are part of our collective culture. At the individual level, as Festinger (1957) noted five decades ago, people tend to resist new information that contradicts their existing knowledge and beliefs. Until our collectively held beliefs are more accepting of the notion that women belong in the political world, and that their private and public lives are not necessarily more in tension than those of men, women politicians' gendered experience of media and of politics will persist.

This is a bleak prognosis. However, my conclusion does not mean that women politicians are powerless, nor does it mean that they see themselves as powerless. In particular, media training initiatives seem to help, and this underlines the fact that parties need to take some responsibility for ensuring that female candidates and legislators have access to the necessary resources, financial and otherwise, for making the most of their public personas.

In the end, media organizations and their employees are important political actors who are difficult to regulate and impossible to ignore. Changing the collectively held assumptions of journalists about who is and is not suited for public office takes a great deal of time. In the meantime, women politicians, their male allies, and their political parties need to work collaboratively to better navigate the precarious media terrain discussed in this chapter. At the same time, the cause of equality in Canadian public life would benefit from these groups taking every opportunity to challenge prevailing masculine norms about the traits and behaviours of the archetypical politician.

**Appendix: Topic Guide Used for Interviews with Federal Politicians**

The following list of topics and questions guided my interviews. This list was sent to interviewees approximately a week before our meetings.

- Place of News Media in the Political Career of a Member of Parliament (MP)
- Relationships between MPs and Individual Journalists
- Perceptions of Different Types of News Media (Print, Television, and Radio)
  *Are there differences in coverage?*
  *Which types of news coverage are more valuable or sought after?*
- News Media in Campaigns and Elections
  *What role does news coverage play in getting elected?*
  *How do MPs and candidates attain positive news coverage?*
  *In what ways have you been satisfied or dissatisfied with your coverage? with the coverage of MPs, candidates, and elections in general?*

- News Media in Non-Election Periods
  *How is news coverage different (if at all) in non-election periods?*
  *How would you characterize your news coverage or that of other members in the House of Commons?*
  *Is favourable coverage important in non-election periods? If so, what efforts can MPs make to attain favourable coverage?*

- Challenges
  *What are some of the challenges MPs face in becoming visible in the Canadian news media?*
  *What challenges do they face in attaining positive news visibility?*

**Notes**

1 The six respondents who gave permission to be identified were Ed Broadbent, Kim Campbell, Stockwell Day, Gurmant Grewal, Rahim Jaffer, and Alexa McDonough.

2 In fact, Jaffer was first elected in 1997 "at the tender age of 25," as the biography on his website notes.

3 Jaffer did not mention radio media at all during the interview, perhaps because of a brief scandal in 2001 involving one of his parliamentary assistants who impersonated him on the radio. The explanation offered following the incident was that, because Jaffer had been double-booked, his assistant Matthew Johnston stepped in to take the MP's place on a Vancouver radio program. Jaffer initially lied and said he had done the interview himself but later admitted that his assistant had done the interview. See *National Post* 2001.

4 McDonough resigned as NDP leader in 2003 and was succeeded by former Toronto city councillor Jack Layton. McDonough is currently an NDP MP.

5 Although McDonough believed the piece was a news story, it was a political gossip column called What the Gargoyle Heard.

6 McDonough makes this point again in *Why Women Run* (1999), a National Film Board documentary on her 1997 effort to win the federal constituency of Halifax against two-time Liberal incumbent Mary Clancy.

7 Each party has a lounge, featuring telephones, computers, and food and beverage services, with direct access to the House of Commons. Stockwell Day explained to me that many MPs come in and out of their party's lounge through the course of a typical day in the House. They also use the lounges to meet with people and have messengers who carry notes in and out because access to each lounge is restricted to caucus members only.

8 The Rat Pack was the nickname given to a group of highly visible Liberal opposition MPs during the mid-1980s. Its members included Don Boudria, Brian Tobin, Sheila Copps, and John Nunziata, who were known for their sharp, sustained attacks against the Mulroney government.

9 Members of the Copps family were very prominent in Hamilton-area politics: Sheila's father, Victor, was an influential mayor of Hamilton from 1962 to 1976, and her mother, Geraldine, was a Hamilton city councillor (1985-2000). Copps Coliseum, Hamilton's primary sports and entertainment centre, is named after Victor Copps.

10 As Nadeau discusses in Chapter 3 of this volume, NAC had a highly conflictual relationship with the Mulroney government. The umbrella organization opposed the Charlottetown Accord on a number of grounds, including the view that this deal weakened the federal government and would result in a loss of national standards for social programs and policies of importance to women. In addition, feminist critics maintained that the negotiations that produced the accord offered little room for women to participate.

11 Day was a Conservative MLA in the Alberta provincial legislature from 1986 to 2000 and became Alberta's treasurer, the equivalent of finance minister, in 1997.

**References**

Bashevkin, Sylvia. 1993. *Toeing the Lines: Women and Party Politics in English Canada*. 2nd ed. Toronto: Oxford University Press.

Bystrom, Dianne, and J.L. Miller. 1999. "Gendered Communication Styles and Strategies in Campaign 1996: The Videostyles of Women and Men Candidates." In *The Electronic*

*Election: Perspectives on the 1996 Campaign Communication*, ed. L.L. Kaid and D.G. Bystrom, 293-302. Mahwah: Lawrence Erlbaum Associates.

Bystrom, Dianne, Mary Christine Banwart, Lynda Lee Kaid, and Terry Robertson. 2004. *Gender and Candidate Communication: VideoStyle, WebStyle, and NewsStyle*. New York: Routledge.

Bystrom, Dianne, T. Robertson, and M.C. Banwart. 2001. "Framing the Fight: An Analysis of Media Coverage of Female and Male Candidates in Primary Races for Governor and U.S. Senate in 2000." *American Behavioural Scientist* 44, 12: 1999-2013.

Canadian Broadcasting Corporation. 1998. *Gender Guidelines*. Ottawa: Canadian Broadcasting Corporation.

Chambers, Deborah, Linda Steiner, and Carole Fleming. 2004. *Women and Journalism*. London and New York: Routledge.

Copps, Sheila. 1986. *Nobody's Baby: A Survival Guide to Politics*. Toronto: Deneau.

–. 2004. *Worth Fighting For*. Toronto: McClelland and Stewart.

Festinger, Leon. 1957. *A Theory of Cognitive Dissonance*. Stanford: Stanford University Press.

Fox, Richard Logan. 1997. *Gender Dynamics in Congressional Elections*. Thousand Oaks: Sage.

Goffman, Erving. 1959. *The Presentation of Self in Everyday Life*. Garden City: Doubleday.

Iyengar, Shanto, and Donald Kinder. 1987. *News that Matters: Television and American Opinion*. Chicago: University of Chicago Press.

Jamieson, Kathleen Hall. 1995. *Beyond the Double Bind: Women and Leadership*. New York: Oxford University Press.

Kahn, Kim Fridkin. 1992. "Does Being Male Help? An Investigation of the Effects of Candidate Gender and Campaign Coverage on Evaluations of US Senate Candidates." *Journal of Politics* 54, 2: 497-517.

–. 1993. "Gender Differences in Campaign Messages: The Political Advertisements of Men and Women Candidates for U.S. Senate." *Political Research Quarterly* 46, 3: 481-502.

–. 1996. *The Political Consequences of Being a Woman*. New York: Columbia University Press.

Kahn, Kim Fridkin, and Edie N. Goldenberg. 1991. "Women Candidates in the News: An Examination of Gender Differences in US Senate Campaign Coverage." *Public Opinion Quarterly* 55, 2: 180-99.

King, Gary, Robert O. Keohane, and Sidney Verba. 1994. *Designing Social Inquiry: Scientific Inference in Qualitative Research*. Princeton: Princeton University Press.

Lawless, Jennifer L., and Richard L. Fox. 2005. *It Takes a Candidate: Why Women Don't Run for Office*. New York: Cambridge University Press.

McLaughlin, Audrey. 1992. *A Woman's Place: My Life and Politics*. Toronto: Macfarlane Walter and Ross.

Muir, Kathie. 2005. "Political Cares: Gendered Reporting of Work and Family Issues in Relation to Australian Politicians." *Australian Feminist Studies* 20, 46: 77-90.

Mullen, B., and L. Hu. 1989. "Perceptions of Ingroup and Outgroup Variability: A Meta-Analytic Integration." *Basic and Applied Social Psychology* 10, 3: 233-52.

*National Post*. 2001. "The Great Rahim Jaffer Phone-in Hoax." 21 March.

Niven, David, and Jeremy Zilber. 2001. "How Does She Have Time for Kids and Congress? Views on Gender and Media Coverage from House Offices." *Women and Politics* 23, 1-2: 147-65.

Norris, Pippa, and Joni Lovenduski. 1995. *Political Recruitment: Gender, Race, and Class in the British Parliament*. Cambridge: Cambridge University Press.

*Ottawa Citizen*. 1998. "Alexa McDonough, Call Your Dry-Cleaner." 3 October.

Robertson, Terry, Allison Conley, Kamila Scymcznska, and Ansley Thompson. 2002. "Gender and the Media: An Investigation of Gender, Media, and Politics in the 2000 Election." *New Jersey Journal of Communication* 10, 1: 104-17.

Robinson, Gertrude J. 2005. *Gender, Journalism, and Equity: Canadian, US, and European Perspectives*. Cresskill: Hampton Press.

Rodgers, Shelly, and Esther Thorson. 2003. "A Socialization Perspective on Male and Female Reporting." *Journal of Communication* 53, 4: 658-75.

Ross, Karen. 2002. *Women, Politics, Media: Uneasy Relations in Comparative Perspective.* Cresskill: Hampton Press.

Ross, Karen, and Annabelle Sreberny. 2000. "Women in the House: Media Representations of British Politicians." In *Gender, Politics and Communication,* ed. A. Sreberny and L. van Zoonen, 79-100. Cresskill: Hampton Press.

Rubin, Irene S., and Herbert J. Rubin. 2004. *Qualitative Interviewing: The Art of Hearing Data.* 2nd ed. Thousand Oaks: Sage.

Sharpe, Sydney. 1994. *The Gilded Ghetto: Women and Political Power in Canada.* Toronto: HarperCollins.

van Zoonen, Liesbet. 1998. "'Finally I Have My Mother Back': Politicians and Their Families in Popular Culture." *Press/Politics* 3, 1: 48-64.

–. 2000a. "Broken Hearts, Broken Dreams? Politicians and Their Families in Popular Culture." In *Gender, Politics and Communication,* ed. Annabelle Sreberny and Liesbet van Zoonen, 101-20. Cresskill: Hampton Press.

–. 2000b. "The Personalization of Politics: Opportunities for Women." *International Journal for Politics and Psychology* 9, 3-4: 19-35.

–. 2005. *Entertaining the Citizen: When Politics and Popular Culture Converge.* Oxford: Rowman and Littlefield.

–. 2006. "The Personal, the Political and the Popular: A Woman's Guide to Celebrity Politics." *European Journal of Cultural Studies* 9, 3: 287-301.

Warren, Carol A.B. 2001. "Qualitative Interviewing." In *Handbook of Interview Research: Content and Method,* ed. Jaber F. Gubrium and James A. Holstein, 83-102. Thousand Oaks: Sage.

Wattenberg, Martin P. 1995. *The Rise of Candidate-Centered Politics.* Cambridge: Harvard University Press.

# 10
# Do Voters Stereotype Female Party Leaders? Evidence from Canada and New Zealand

*Elisabeth Gidengil, Joanna Everitt, and Susan Banducci*

In the previous chapter, Elizabeth Goodyear-Grant highlighted the challenges that female politicians face as they attempt to craft positive public images. According to the literature on gender stereotyping, the optimal strategy for a woman aspiring to top political office is to project an image of toughness (Huddy and Terkildsen 1993b; Leeper 1991; Rosenwasser and Dean 1989; Rosenwasser and Seale 1988). However, this conclusion is based on experimental studies with hypothetical candidates. It is possible that this research has overstated the extent to which gender stereotyping occurs in actual election campaigns, when voters have many cues available to them other than the candidate's sex. If research on actual campaigns shows that voters do not gender stereotype female politicians, then women in public life may not need to adopt traditionally masculine qualities in order to succeed. Indeed, women candidates may pay a price for acting tough.

The limited number of elite women in Western democracies has hampered efforts to determine whether voters evaluate real-life female leaders on the basis of gender stereotypes. In 1993, a unique opportunity presented itself when, for the first time in Canada's history, two major federal political parties were led by women. The presence of Kim Campbell and Audrey McLaughlin, leading two very different political parties, the Progressive Conservative and New Democratic (NDP) parties, made it possible to examine the extent to which gender stereotyping occurred in the real world of electoral politics. In 1999, a similar situation arose in the New Zealand general election, when Helen Clark led the Labour Party and Jenny Shipley headed the National Party.

Comparing the 1993 Canadian and 1999 New Zealand experiences allows us to sort out the extent to which evaluations of female party leaders reflect gender stereotyping or other factors, notably party, political ideology, or standing in the polls. We focus mainly on "gender-trait stereotypes" (Huddy and Terkildsen 1993a).[1] These are personality traits that are ascribed to male and female candidates in experimental studies based solely on their sex. Consequently, they reflect widely held cultural assumptions about the nature of men and women (Williams and Best 1990). "Gender-belief stereotypes," on the other hand, are political beliefs or ideological positions that are imputed on the basis of sex alone.[2]

We also consider who stereotypes and when. Experimental studies indicate that gender stereotyping is most likely to occur when people lack other relevant information about the candidate. Accordingly, we examine whether voters who are less informed about politics are more prone to attribute stereotypical traits to party leaders and whether gender stereotyping is more common early in an election campaign, when voters may be less familiar with the leaders. In light of the literature on gendered-differentiated media coverage (Carroll and Schreiber 1997; Gidengil and Everitt 1999, 2000, 2003a; Robinson and Saint-Jean 1991; Ross 1995; Trimble 2005), we also ask whether exposure to television coverage is associated with stereotypical perceptions of party leaders that are based on gender. Finally, we examine whether voters' sex and gender role beliefs affect their propensity to engage in gender stereotyping.

## Gender-Trait Stereotyping

Numerous experimental studies report that participants attribute different personality traits to hypothetical candidates who are identical in every respect save their sex (Huddy 1994; Huddy and Terkildsen 1993a, 1993b; Leeper 1991; Rosenwasser and Dean 1989; Rosenwasser and Seale 1988). Male candidates are typically perceived as tough, aggressive, self-confident, and assertive, while their female counterparts are described as warm, compassionate, people-oriented, gentle, kind, passive, caring, and sensitive.[3] Female candidates are also seen as more moral, hard-working, and honest than their male counterparts (Huddy and Terkildsen 1993a, 1993b; Leeper 1991; Rosenwasser and Dean 1989).

These studies also suggest that respondents view traditional masculine traits as more important than traditional feminine ones for high political office (Huddy and Terkildsen 1993b; Rosenwasser and Dean 1989; Rosenwasser and Seale 1988). In almost every instance, female candidates who were seen as having masculine traits were evaluated more favourably than identical female candidates who projected feminine traits (Riggle et al. 1997). The implication seems clear: "A female candidate stereotyped as a typical feminine woman would almost certainly lose electoral support because she would be seen to lack typical male traits and expertise in policy areas thought most necessary for effective national leadership" (Huddy 1994, 177). However, these studies also find that female candidates can successfully portray themselves as possessing typically masculine traits without jeopardizing their warm, compassionate image. Participants in experimental studies infer that female candidates possess traditional feminine strengths even when they deliver a tough masculine message (Leeper 1991).

The usual conclusion drawn from this experimental literature is that women can only win public office if they project stereotypical masculine qualities. While the advice offered to political women has been to act tough, this counsel is disturbing. After all, one rationale for seeking greater legislative representation for women – as is discussed in the introduction to this volume – has been that women will bring something different to the political process. This is not likely to happen if women have to take on the same proverbial masculine qualities as their male counterparts in order to get elected.

Moreover, there are reasons to doubt whether experimental results hold in actual electoral settings, especially outside the United States, where most studies have been conducted. Matland (1994) suggests that variation in women's representation in public office could be related to cross-national differences in gender stereotyping, that the presence of large numbers of women in elective office may have socializing effects that lead women to be seen as the political equals of men. According to this view, the prevalence of gender stereotyping among US respondents may reflect the low number of women legislators in that country. It is also possible that militarization heightens the importance of stereotypical masculine traits in the United States (Duerst-Lahti and Kelly 1995).[4] Finally, most of the experimental evidence is based on evaluations of hypothetical state, local, and congressional candidates. It is not at all clear that the same patterns would hold for party leaders in parliamentary systems, especially given the salience of party labels in Westminster-style systems.

We also question the generalizability of existing findings in light of the design of the studies from which they are drawn. Experiments allow us to examine gender stereotyping under very tightly controlled conditions that are free of other factors that complicate research in real-life settings. This is their main strength and their main weakness. Participants in experiments are typically asked to evaluate a hypothetical candidate based on, say, a brief profile or a speech supposedly given by that individual. Some participants are told the candidate is a woman, while others are told the candidate is a man. Besides the candidate's sex, participants base their evaluations on identical information. If respondents perceive "Joan" as having different traits than "John," that variation must reflect the impact of the candidate's sex. Experimental studies thus provide an unequivocal basis for inferring gender-trait stereotyping.

However, the artificiality of the experimental setting may limit the applicability of these results to the real world. In an actual campaign, many varied cues are available to voters. The candidate's party may be an especially powerful factor that triggers partisan stereotypes (Dolan 2004; Hayes 2005;

Huddy and Capelos 2002; Rahn 1993). Indeed, Hayes (2005) argues that trait-based partisan stereotypes are so deeply engrained that candidates can be said to "own" particular traits in much the same way that their parties own particular issues. Imagine a female candidate running for a conservative party: her party label could lead voters to infer that she is less compassionate than her male opponent from a more progressive party. Given that voters in actual elections can draw on other cues, such as party label and issue position, to make inferences about candidates' personality traits, gender-trait stereotypes may be irrelevant to the evaluation of candidates.[5]

The few studies that have examined perceptions of real-life candidates suggest experimental studies may have overstated the extent of gender-trait stereotyping. Looking at all US House of Representatives elections from 1990 through 2000, Dolan (2004) found little evidence that voters either stereotyped female candidates as more liberal than their male counterparts or evaluated candidate competencies in gender stereotypic ways. She concluded that partisan stereotypes were more important than gender stereotypes and could offset or reinforce the latter, depending on the candidate's party affiliation. In the same vein, Koch (1999) concluded that variations in assessments of male and female candidates in the 1988, 1990, and 1992 US Senate elections probably owed more to sex differences in campaign messages and media coverage than to gender stereotyping (see also Alexander and Anderson 1993; Powell and Butterfield 1987; Sanbonmatsu 2002).

### Who Stereotypes and When

The experimental literature suggests that stereotyping may be more prevalent under some conditions than others. Most importantly, gender-trait stereotyping may be most common when information is sparse. Studies in controlled settings typically find that respondents are more likely to engage in stereotyping when they lack relevant background data (Wyer and Scrull 1986). For example, gender stereotyping of political candidates has proven to be more common for hypothetical challengers than for hypothetical incumbents (Kahn 1992) and for traits that are not mentioned in the hypothetical candidate's speech or profile (Leeper 1991; Sapiro 1981-82). Lack of information encourages people to draw inferences from cues that are readily available, and sex is one of the most easily accessible cues (Cutler 2002; McDermott 1997). People need only know that a candidate is female in order to draw on broader cultural stereotypes about her personality. If they think women in general are more compassionate than men, for example, they may label the female candidate as compassionate.

Given the relationship between scarce information and the propensity to resort to stereotypes, gender-trait stereotyping should be more prevalent for candidates who are new to the electoral scene than for those who are well known to voters. By the same token, gender-trait stereotyping should be more evident in the earlier than the later stages of an election campaign. As a campaign progresses, familiarity with the candidates increases, and voters form their own impressions instead of relying on stereotypes. However, stereotypes may create filters. Some voters will abandon a stereotype when it is inconsistent with new information (Fiske and Neuberg 1990), but those holding well-defined stereotypes may only perceive and process information that is consistent with preconceived beliefs.

If gender-trait stereotyping occurs in real-life elections, it is most likely to occur among less knowledgeable and less sophisticated voters who lack the expertise to use more informative cues, such as partisanship. Unsophisticated voters may simply be unaware of partisan stereotypes. Gender-trait stereotypes are largely the product of cultural norms,[6] but partisan stereotypes depend on cognitive processes and clearly require more cognitive sophistication. Gender-trait stereotypes require no information other than whether the candidate in question is a man or a woman. Studies of the relationship between education and gender-trait stereotyping lend support to this argument (see, for example, Huddy 1994).[7]

As Elizabeth Goodyear-Grant notes in Chapter 9 of this volume, media coverage can create gender-trait stereotypes in the minds of voters because, as Pippa Norris argues, "gendered news frames may combine and thereby reinforce a range of sex stereotypes" (Norris 1997a, 8). While Norris (1997b) found few traces of gender-trait stereotyping in media coverage of women leaders worldwide, other studies reported that female politicians were framed in stereotypical "feminine" ways (Carroll and Schreiber 1997; Robinson and Saint-Jean 1991; Ross 1995; Trimble 2005). As well, political reporting tends to reinforce traditional conceptions of politics as a male preserve by portraying election campaigns as battles or boxing matches (Gidengil and Everitt 1999, 2000, 2003a). This framing of politics as a masculine activity highlights women's minority status at elite levels of public life, and it may enhance the salience and accessibility of gender-trait stereotypes in the minds of voters. Accordingly, we may find that gender stereotyping among voters is positively related to their exposure to media coverage.

Does sex affect the attribution of personality traits? Some studies predict that women are more likely than men to base their judgments on gender stereotypes (Kahn 1994; Mills and Tyrrell 1983). This implies that women rate female candidates higher on stereotypical feminine traits and lower on stereotypical masculine traits than men and rate male candidates lower on "feminine" traits and higher on "masculine" ones. This view assumes that women's gender-role identity is heightened by their awareness of being a minority in politics (Swan and Wyer 1997). However, an opposing view suggests this same circumstance may make females more likely than males to rate women highly on both stereotypical feminine and stereotypical masculine traits out of a sense of gender solidarity. Neither perspective has been consistently demonstrated, even in an experimental setting, at an empirical level (for contrasting findings, see Huddy 1994; Kahn 1994; Lewis and Bierly 1990), and Sanbonmatsu (2001) concluded that sex was a weak predictor of gender stereotypes.

How do gender-role beliefs shape gender-trait stereotyping? In one of the few studies to examine the attribution of traits to real candidates, Alexander and Anderson (1993) found that individuals with egalitarian beliefs rated female challengers very positively on both stereotypical masculine and stereotypical feminine traits, perhaps because they were engaging in a form of "female boosterism." Conversely, traditional respondents ranked female challengers lower than their male counterparts on both sets of traits. The only group that engaged in gender-trait stereotyping was located between the egalitarian and traditional perspectives; these moderates gave male candidates more positive assessments on male traits than on female ones.

**Using Real-World Cases**

It is easy to criticize experimental research for the artificiality of the laboratory setting but much harder to sort out the effects of sex in a real-world setting. For example, how can scholars disentangle the impact of an individual's sex from all of the other possible sources of trait attributions? How can we determine whether the attribution of traits results from stereotypes or from conscious strategic decisions on the part of female politicians to emphasize particular "feminine" traits in a campaign? If a voter rates a woman leader as more compassionate, does this reflect gender stereotyping, her party label, or her issue positions? How would we know whether one leader really is more compassionate than another? If a female leader is rated as weaker than a male leader, does this imply gender stereotyping or, given Bashevkin's findings in Chapter 7, is it because her party is demonstrably weaker than his?

In this study, we simplify the task of disentangling gender effects from other potentially confounding factors by examining two real-world elections – the 1993 Canadian federal election and the 1999 New Zealand election – that enable us to approximate experimental conditions.[8] Both elections featured two female party leaders. These four women led parties with distinctly different positions on the ideological spectrum, with McLaughlin's NDP and Clark's Labour Party being clearly to the left of Campbell's Progressive Conservative Party and Shipley's National Party. The task of disentangling gender stereotypes is further simplified by the fact that, in both countries, male-led parties inhabited similar ideological space. In Canada, the NDP's closest rival was the centre-left Liberals led by Jean Chrétien, while, on the right, the Conservatives' closest rival was the Reform Party, led by Preston Manning. In New Zealand, ACT New Zealand, led by Richard Prebble, was to the right of the National Party, while Alliance, led by Jim

Anderton, was to the left of the Labour Party. New Zealand First, led by Winston Peters, was in the centre of the spectrum.[9]

While both Clark and Shipley led parties that were highly competitive and would likely form either the government or the official opposition, both McLaughlin and Campbell served in demonstrably weaker formations. In fact, both women were the ultimate "sacrificial lambs" in that they were chosen to lead political parties that were destined to go down to defeat (see Bashevkin's discussion in Chapter 7). In 1993, the NDP and Conservatives were likely to lose seats, and lose they did, quite spectacularly. This contrast between the two countries makes it possible to sort out whether attributions of leadership ability reflect the leader's sex or simply the standing of her party.

Finally, this comparison permits us to test the hypothesis that gender stereotyping is more likely to occur when women leaders are new on the political scene (see Koch 2002b). In 1999, both New Zealand female party leaders were established parts of the electoral landscape. Clark became the Labour Party leader following its defeat in the 1993 election, and party strategists featured her in their 1996 campaign strategy. By 1999, Clark was running for the second time and had been well known for more than five years. As leader of the National Party, Jenny Shipley had been prime minister throughout the previous year. In 1993 in Canada, by contrast, Kim Campbell had only been leader of the Progressive Conservative Party and prime minister for three months when the election was called; as she observed in her interview with Elizabeth Goodyear-Grant (see Chapter 9), however, she was no political rookie. Audrey McLaughlin had been NDP leader for a longer period of time, but this was her first campaign as party leader and her low-key debating style in the House of Commons had attracted little media attention.[10] Clearly, then, the two New Zealand women were more familiar to voters than the two Canadian women, especially McLaughlin.

Both the 1993 Canadian Election Study (CES) and the 1999 New Zealand Election Study (NZES) featured a rolling cross-sectional design that permits us to ask whether the attribution of gender traits diminished as the campaigns progressed.[11] Both surveys included questions on a set of four leader traits: compassion, trustworthiness, leadership ability, and arrogance. The two election studies thus offered researchers a unique opportunity to examine the relationship between the sex of leaders and the public attribution of personality traits.[12] Both studies also asked respondents to evaluate each leader's ability to speak for women. While this is not a personality trait per se, it does enable us to evaluate one of the key components of gender-belief stereotyping. In their experimental study, Huddy and Capelos (2002) found that when partisan cues were present, the impact of the candidate's sex on candidate evaluations was limited to the handling of issues of particular interest to women voters. We probe whether women politicians in real-world elections were ascribed a similar capacity to speak for women, regardless of their party label.

We proceed in two stages: first, we compare trait attributions for each leader; and second, we examine how each leader's trait ratings were affected by the respondents' sex, gender-role beliefs, knowledge of politics, level of educational attainment, and exposure to TV coverage of the campaign. For the campaign analyses, we also took into consideration whether the interviews took place early or late in the election campaigns.[13] Since trait attributions can reflect sociocultural and partisan loyalties, we controlled for both social background and party identification in this analysis. We also controlled for the possible effects of economic evaluations on the popularity (or lack thereof) of the party in power.

Given the smaller scale of the New Zealand campaign survey, the analysis of that country was restricted to the two top party leaders, Clark and Shipley, with sex, timing of interviews, and education serving as key explanatory variables. The New Zealand campaign analysis is also restricted to the random half-sample that was asked the trait questions. Our study of the 1993 Canadian election was restricted to people living outside Quebec. The emergence in 1993 of the separatist Bloc Québécois, combined with the fact that the Reform Party ran only token candidates in Quebec that year, meant the federal election unfolded very differently in Quebec than it did in the rest of Canada. The wording for all the survey items used in this chapter is provided in the appendix on page 187.

## Gender and Trait Attributions

Consistent with the literature in this field, we found the clearest evidence of stereotyping in views about the perceived ability of party leaders to speak for women. In Canada, both Campbell and McLaughlin ranked much higher on the ability to speak for women than did male party leaders (see Figure 10.1). Campbell was rated almost as highly as McLaughlin, which is notable since the Conservative leader did not make a single major campaign speech on such issues as child poverty, pay equity, child care, or violence against women. By contrast, McLaughlin sought throughout the campaign to distinguish herself from Campbell; she reminded voters that being a woman was the only thing that she and Campbell had in common. In McLaughlin's words, "We have one woman who stood up and supported the Gulf War, and one woman who stood up and spoke for peace. We have one woman who wanted to re-criminalize abortion and one woman who said, 'No, women have the right to choose'" (quoted in Kennedy 1993).

A similar pattern appeared in the New Zealand data, where Shipley on the right ranked only slightly behind Clark on the left for her perceived ability to speak for women (see Figure 10.2). During the 1999 campaign, Clark portrayed herself as understanding the plight of New Zealand families despite

*Figure 10.1*

**Mean trait ratings by leader (Canada campaign period)**

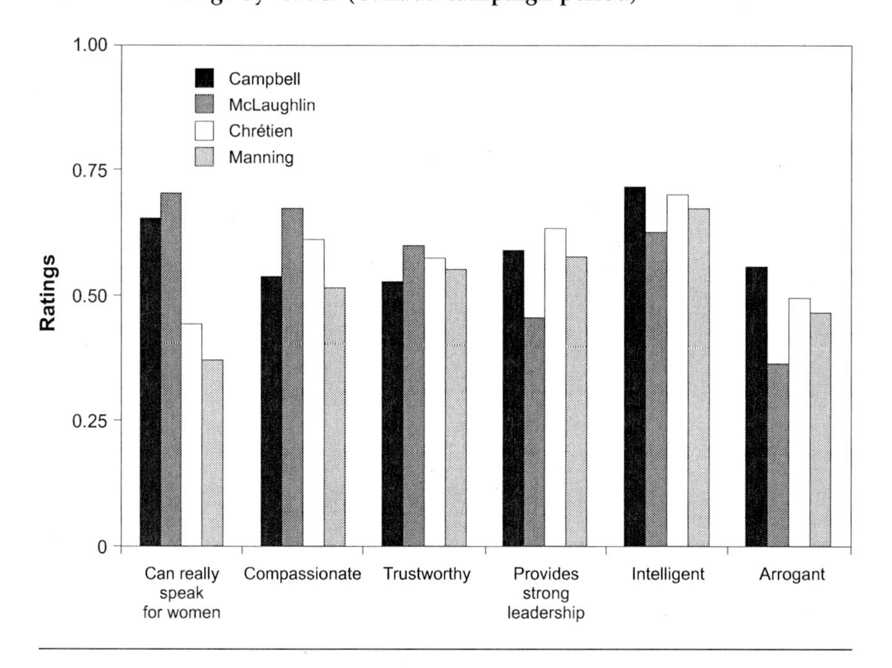


not having children herself, whereas Shipley focused on the issue of making families self-sufficient. In the post-election survey, voters distinguished more clearly between the two women than they had during the campaign (see Figure 10.3). Yet, both female leaders were rated more highly than male leaders for their perceived ability to speak for women. This perceived ability to speak for women, however, did not seem to compromise their perceived ability to speak for men (a question that was asked only in New Zealand), since Clark and Shipley were ranked similarly on both dimensions during the campaign (see Figure 10.2).[14]

We found little evidence of gender stereotyping in the attribution of the two "feminine" traits. In Canada, and especially in New Zealand, voters clearly perceived one woman to be more compassionate and trustworthy than the other. In both countries the attributions of compassion and trustworthiness followed partisan lines: the woman leading the left party was perceived to be more compassionate and trustworthy than the woman leading the right party. This pattern was starker when we compared the ratings of female and male party leaders. In Canada, Campbell was judged to be barely more compassionate and slightly less trustworthy than Manning, her rival on the right, while Chrétien, in the centre, was perceived to be a little

*Figure 10.2*

**Mean trait ratings by leader (New Zealand campaign period)**

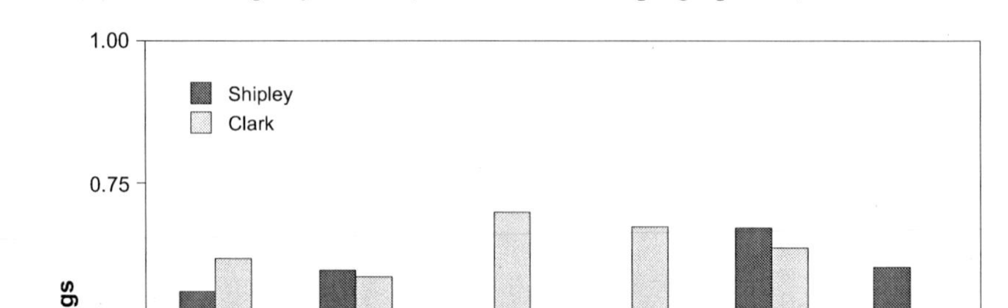


*Figure 10.3*

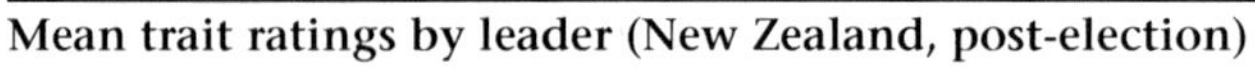

**Mean trait ratings by leader (New Zealand, post-election)**

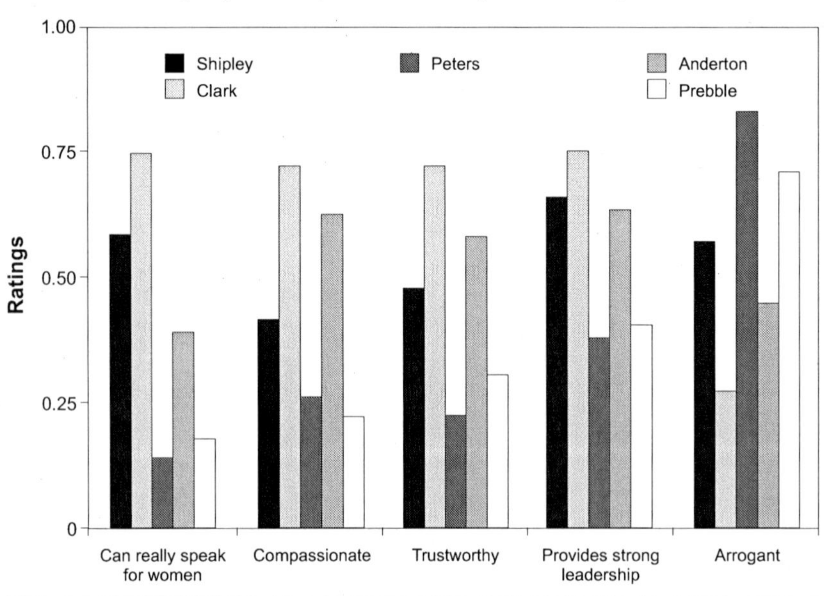

less trustworthy than McLaughlin and second to McLaughlin on perceived compassion. By the time the 1993 election took place, this differentiation by party had sharpened to the extent that, in the post-election survey, Manning and especially Campbell were perceived to be much less trustworthy than Chrétien and McLaughlin (see Figure 10.4).

In New Zealand, perceptions of Shipley's compassion and trustworthiness were more similar to those for Prebble than for Clark, and Anderton ranked second to Clark on both dimensions. Perceived differences between the two women were all the more interesting, given that Shipley tried to portray herself as a compassionate mother and, thus, distinguishable from the childless Clark. She opened her party's broadcast with the line, "I'm a politician, but I'm a mum as well," and her husband and children accompanied her on many campaign outings. However, Shipley's attempt to use motherhood as a cue for compassion did not seem to resonate with voters. Partisan schemas apparently trumped gender schemas in voters' minds (Conover and Feldman 1986; Dolan 2004; Hayes 2005; Huddy and Capelos 2002; Rahn 1993).

On the question of "masculine" traits, McLaughlin was rated markedly lower during the campaign for her perceived ability to provide strong leadership (see Figure 10.1), but Campbell tied with Manning on this trait and scored only slightly below Chrétien. A similar pattern held in Canada for

*Figure 10.4*

**Mean trait ratings by leader (Canada, post-election)**

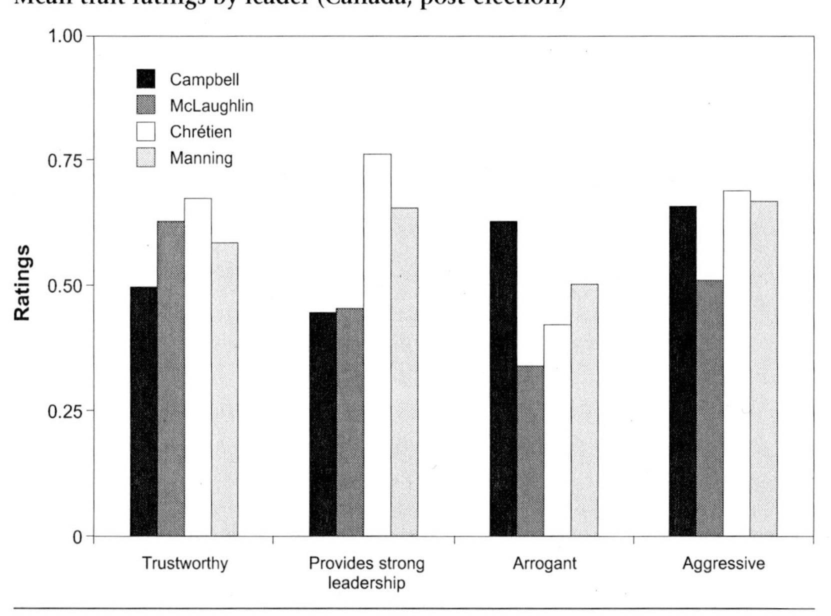

perceived intelligence (the question was not posed in New Zealand): although all four leaders fared relatively well on this dimension of competence, McLaughlin was ranked lowest. Her weak competence rankings could reflect gender stereotyping – since McLaughlin was less well known than Campbell, Manning, or Chrétien – but it could also be explained by her low-key, consensus-building style of leadership. After the election, both McLaughlin and Campbell received lower scores than their male counterparts for perceived leadership ability (see Figure 10.4). Rather than gender-trait stereotyping, this result may have followed from the stunning defeats of the women's parties in the 1993 elections.

Data from New Zealand underline the importance of party competitiveness in attributions of leadership ability, a pattern that echoes arguments in the Everitt and Camp and Bashevkin chapters in this volume. During the campaign, Shipley and Clark were rated similarly on perceived leadership ability (see Figure 10.2). These ratings likely reflected their status as leaders of the two major parties. Shipley was rated much higher on leadership ability, a stereotypical masculine trait, than on compassion and trustworthiness, two stereotypical feminine traits. Clark fared equally well on all three traits. Post-election ratings show that Shipley and Clark received the highest rankings on leadership ability, which paralleled their parties' competitive positions in the election results (see Figure 10.3).

Although arrogance is not generally considered to be a stereotypical feminine or masculine trait, research on non-political settings concludes that "competent assertiveness" (Butler and Geis 1990) by a woman elicits more negative responses than the same behaviour by a man. One meta-analysis of sixty-one studies of gender and leader evaluation argues that "women are negatively evaluated when they exhibit masculine leadership styles" (Eagly, Makhijani, and Klonsky 1992, 16), particularly if they occupy leadership roles that were traditionally held by men. Butler and Geis (1990) suggest that assertive women pay a price for violating gender stereotypes: in their words, "schema violation causes negative affect" (55).

Do these patterns hold for women who led political parties? In New Zealand in 1999, the answer was "no." Although Prime Minister Shipley was perceived as more arrogant than Opposition Leader Clark, she was seen as less arrogant than two of the three male party leaders (see Figure 10.3). In Canada in 1993, by contrast, Prime Minister Campbell was clearly considered the most arrogant of the four party leaders, both during and after the campaign. Tellingly, Manning and Chrétien were perceived to be just as aggressive as Campbell, yet they were considered to be much less arrogant. The implication is that aggressive behaviour on the part of a female leader elicits more negative reactions than does similar behaviour by a male leader. McLaughlin, meanwhile, was perceived to be the least aggressive of the four leaders, which probably reflected her low-key style of campaigning.

## How Do Information, Sex, and Gender-Role Beliefs Affect Attributions?

Aggregate results show little evidence of gender-trait stereotyping, though they do demonstrate gender-belief stereotyping in ascribing the ability of female party leaders to speak for women. Was gender-trait stereotyping more evident early in the campaigns, when voters were less familiar with party leaders? If so, this should be most evident for McLaughlin, the least known of the female leaders. However, there is nothing to suggest that respondents interviewed in the early weeks of the campaign were more likely to attribute stereotypical feminine traits to McLaughlin (see Table 10.1). On the contrary, voters actually came to see her as better able to speak for women and less arrogant as the campaign moved on.

Similarly, the New Zealand results offer little support for the low information thesis (see Table 10.2), since they reveal very few campaign effects. The only exception involved perceptions of Clark's leadership ability, which improved as the campaign progressed. This may reflect the fact that her party won the election and that she was therefore seen as running a strong campaign. Clark demonstrated that she was the equal of Shipley, the incumbent prime minister, during the debates. Meanwhile, media coverage of Shipley tended to focus on negative aspects of her public appearances (Harris 2000).

At first glance, the pattern of campaign effects for Campbell point towards gender-trait stereotyping: as the campaign progressed and their familiarity with Campbell presumably increased, voters were less likely to ascribe to her stereotypical feminine qualities, including compassion, trustworthiness, and the ability to speak for women. However, the fact that Campbell's ratings became more negative on every trait suggests that voters instead reappraised her personal qualities in light of a weak campaign, negative media coverage, and declining Conservative Party popularity.

The Canadian data also show that less informed respondents were more likely to perceive Campbell as compassionate, trustworthy, and able to speak for women. While this could mean they were relying on feminine stereotypes to make inferences about her personal qualities, the pattern fails to hold for attributions of arrogance and aggressiveness: well-informed respondents rated Campbell higher on both traits than did those who were poorly informed (see Table 10.3). Moreover, the pattern fails to hold for McLaughlin. Given that less-informed voters also rated Manning higher on both compassion and ability to speak for women than did well-informed voters, the only clear indication of possible gender-trait stereotyping relates to Campbell's perceived trustworthiness.[15] Canadian interviewees who were better informed were less likely to ascribe this stereotypical feminine trait to Campbell.

Indeed, for both Canada and New Zealand (see Table 10.4), we found little evidence that gender-trait stereotyping was associated with lack of

*Table 10.1*

**Determinants of trait attributions in Canada (campaign period)**

| | Sex | Day | Knowledge | Education | TV news | Sex roles | Constant | $R^2$ | *N* |
|---|---|---|---|---|---|---|---|---|---|
| *Compassionate* | | | | | | | | | |
| Campbell | -.01 (.01) | -.08 (.02)† | -.13 (.02)† | -.03 (.02) | -.00 (.02) | -.01 (.02) | .76 (.03)† | .07 | 1,906 |
| McLaughlin | -.01 (.01) | .02 (.02) | .02 (.02) | .08 (.02)† | .05 (.02)*** | -.01 (.02) | .48 (.03)† | .07 | 1,657 |
| Chrétien | -.04 (.01)*** | .03 (.02) | -.00 (.02) | .05 (.02)*** | .04 (.02)** | .02 (.02) | .41 (.03)† | .09 | 1,864 |
| Manning | -.02 (.02) | -.04 (.02) | -.06 (.03)** | -.05 (.02)*** | -.03 (.02) | .07 (.02)† | .62 (.04)† | .10 | 1,452 |
| *Trustworthy* | | | | | | | | | |
| Campbell | .05 (.01)† | -.05 (.02)† | -.08 (.02)† | -.02 (.02) | -.03 (.02) | -.05 (.02)† | .68 (.03)† | .12 | 1,920 |
| McLaughlin | .03 (.01)** | .01 (.02) | -.03 (.03) | .03 (.02) | .01 (.02) | .00 (.02) | .45 (.03)† | .08 | 1,686 |
| Chrétien | -.03 (.01)*** | .02 (.02) | -.04 (.02) | -.00 (.02) | .01 (.02) | .02 (.02) | .46 (.03)† | .09 | 1,950 |
| Manning | -.02 (.02) | -.03 (.02) | -.01 (.03) | .03 (.02) | -.01 (.02) | .08 (.02)† | .51 (.04)† | .12 | 1,517 |
| *Speaks for women* | | | | | | | | | |
| Campbell | -.04 (.01)*** | -.05 (.02)** | -.08 (.03)† | -.06 (.02)*** | -.02 (.02) | .01 (.02) | .87 (.03)† | .06 | 1,965 |
| McLaughlin | -.04 (.01)† | .05 (.02)*** | -.02 (.02) | -.01 (.02) | .03 (.02)* | -.02 (.02) | .66 (.03)† | .04 | 1,720 |
| Chrétien | -.06 (.01)† | .02 (.02) | -.03 (.02) | -.05 (.02)*** | .03 (.02)* | .03 (.02)* | .36 (.03)† | .12 | 1,782 |
| Manning | -.04 (.01)† | -.05 (.02)*** | -.09 (.03)*** | -.09 (.02)† | -.01 (.02) | .10 (.02)† | .47 (.04)† | .14 | 1,394 |

| | | | | | | | | | |
|---|---|---|---|---|---|---|---|---|---|
| *Strong leader* | | | | | | | | | |
| Campbell | .07 (.01)† | -.10 (.02)† | -.03 (.02) | .03 (.02) | .00 (.02) | -.05 (.02)*** | .71 (.03)† | .11 | 1,997 |
| McLaughlin | .04 (.01)*** | -.02 (.02) | -.14 (.03)† | -.04 (.02)** | -.04 (.02)*** | .01 (.02) | .55 (.04)† | .09 | 1,745 |
| Chrétien | -.02 (.01) | .05 (.02)*** | -.04 (.02)* | -.06 (.02)*** | .02 (.02) | .01 (.02) | .67 (.03)† | .07 | 2,002 |
| Manning | -.05 (.02)† | .00 (.02) | -.01 (.03) | .04 (.02)* | -.01 (.02) | .05 (.02)*** | .52 (.04)† | .10 | 1,568 |
| *Intelligent* | | | | | | | | | |
| Campbell | .06 (.01)† | -.06 (.02)† | -.03 (.02) | .11 (.02)† | .01 (.02) | -.04 (.02)** | .68 (.03)† | .08 | 2,049 |
| McLaughlin | .04 (.01)† | -.02 (.02) | -.04 (.02) | .07 (.02)† | -.02 (.02) | -.02 (.02) | .49 (.06)† | .06 | 1,762 |
| Chrétien | -.00 (.01) | -.01 (.02) | -.01 (.02) | .00 (.02) | .03 (.01)** | -.00 (.01) | .70 (.03)† | .03 | 2,035 |
| Manning | -.05 (.01)† | .01 (.02) | .06 (.03)** | .03 (.02) | -.00 (.02) | .02 (.02) | .62 (.04)† | .06 | 1,595 |
| *Arrogant* | | | | | | | | | |
| Campbell | -.01 (.02) | .14 (.02)† | .17 (.03)† | .06 (.02)*** | .03 (.02) | .03 (.02)* | .23 (.04)† | .08 | 2,026 |
| McLaughlin | -.04 (.02)*** | -.05 (.02)** | -.09 (.03)*** | -.10 (.02)† | -.00 (.02) | .07 (.02)† | .66 (.04)† | .06 | 1,732 |
| Chrétien | .02 (.02) | -.09 (.02)† | -.11 (.03)† | -.08 (.02)† | -.03 (.02) | .03 (.02) | .82 (.04)† | .08 | 2,008 |
| Manning | -.03 (.02) | -.03 (.03) | .02 (.04) | -.01 (.03) | -.02 (.02) | -.05 (.02)** | .56 (.04)† | .06 | 1,577 |

*Note:* The column entries are unstandardized ordinary least squares regression coefficients with standard errors shown in parentheses. Controls were included for age, region, religion, union membership, employment status, occupation, employment sector, ethnicity, party identification, and economic evaluations.

* $p < .10$ ** $p < .05$ *** $p < .01$ † $p < .001$

*Table 10.2*

**Determinants of trait attributions in New Zealand (campaign period)**

| | Sex | Day | Education | $R^2$ | N |
|---|---|---|---|---|---|
| *Compassionate* | | | | | |
| Shipley | 0.03 (.12) | -0.00 (.00) | -0.04 (.05) | 0.15 | 1,435 |
| Clark | 0.09 (.12) | 0.01 (.00) | 0.02 (.05) | 0.07 | 1,409 |
| *Trustworthy* | | | | | |
| Shipley | 0.19 (.12) | -0.00 (.00) | 0.03 (.05) | 0.26 | 1,435 |
| Clark | 0.23 (.12)* | 0.01 (.00) | 0.16 (.05)*** | 0.08 | 1,373 |
| *Speaks for women* | | | | | |
| Shipley | -0.03 (.12) | -0.00 (.00) | -0.16 (.05)*** | 0.19 | 1,389 |
| Clark | 0.03 (.12) | 0.01 (.00) | 0.06 (.05) | 0.08 | 1,394 |
| *Strong leadership* | | | | | |
| Shipley | 0.45 (.12)† | -0.00 (.00) | 0.00 (.05) | 0.16 | 1,455 |
| Clark | 0.21 (.12)* | 0.01 (.00)*** | 0.07 (.05) | 0.08 | 1,398 |
| *Arrogant* | | | | | |
| Shipley | -0.25 (.12)** | 0.00 (.00) | -0.01 (.05) | 0.14 | 1,449 |
| Clark | -0.24 (.11)** | -0.00 (.00) | -0.10 (.05) | 0.04 | 1,431 |
| *Speaks for men* | | | | | |
| Shipley | 0.27 (.12)** | -0.01 (.00) | -0.00 (.05) | 0.12 | 1,310 |
| Clark | 0.16 (.12) | 0.00 (.00) | -0.03 (.05) | 0.04 | 1,302 |

*Note:* The column entries are maximum likelihood estimates from logistic regression with standard errors shown in parentheses. Controls were included for age, education, ethnicity, party identification, and economic evaluations.
* $p < .10$ ** $p < .05$ *** $p < .01$ † $p < .001$

information. This was true whether we focused on the effects of the campaign or on measures of individual political sophistication, like information and education. Partisan schemas came into play more frequently than gender stereotypes, and they were more prevalent among the better informed. Moreover, differences among leaders pointed to the importance of their own personalities and their parties' competitive positions during and after the elections. Finally, media exposure was not linked to gender-trait stereotyping in either Canada or New Zealand.

Similarly, there is no support for the notion that women are more likely than men to base their judgments on gender stereotypes (Kahn 1994; Mills and Tyrrell 1983). To the extent that sex made a difference, women, more so than men, tended to rate the female leaders higher on both stereotypical feminine and stereotypical masculine traits. There are two striking findings, though. First, Canadian women gave both female leaders lower ratings than

*Table 10.3*

**Determinants of trait attributions in Canada (post-election)**

| | Sex | Knowledge | Education | TV News | Sex roles | Constant | $R^2$ | *N* |
|---|---|---|---|---|---|---|---|---|
| *Trustworthy* | | | | | | | | |
| Campbell | .02 (.01) | -.07 (.03)** | -.02 (.02) | .01 (.02) | -.02 (.02) | .55 (.04)† | .09 | 1,647 |
| McLaughlin | -.01 (.01) | .05 (.03) | .07 (.02)† | .04 (.02)*** | -.02 (.02) | .34 (.03)† | .12 | 1,515 |
| Chrétien | -.02 (.01)* | .06 (.03)** | -.03 (.02) | .01 (.02) | -.00 (.02) | .52 (.03)† | .13 | 1,689 |
| Manning | -.02 (.02) | .02 (.04) | -.01 (.02) | -.02 (.02) | .04 (.02)* | .48 (.04)† | .12 | 1,419 |
| *Strong leader* | | | | | | | | |
| Campbell | .04 (.01)*** | -.04 (.03) | .01 (.02) | -.01 (.02) | -.04 (.02)** | .48 (.04)† | .06 | 1,654 |
| McLaughlin | .04 (.01)*** | -.08 (.03)*** | -.05 (.02)** | .00 (.02) | .01 (.02) | .50 (.04)† | .06 | 1,529 |
| Chrétien | -.01 (.01) | .01 (.02) | -.05 (.02)*** | .00 (.01) | .01 (.01) | .73 (.03)† | .07 | 1,698 |
| Manning | -.03 (.02)** | .16 (.03)† | .05 (.02)** | -.05 (.02)*** | -.01 (.02) | .49 (.04)† | .10 | 1,467 |
| *Arrogant* | | | | | | | | |
| Campbell | -.01 (.02) | .08 (.04)** | .03 (.03) | .03 (.02) | .02 (.02) | .53 (.04)† | .03 | 1,664 |
| McLaughlin | -.01 (.02) | -.12 (.04)† | -.10 (.02)† | .00 (.02) | .02 (.02) | .57 (.04)† | .06 | 1,530 |
| Chrétien | .02 (.02) | -.12 (.04)† | -.12 (.02)† | .00 (.02) | .06 (.02)*** | .68 (.04)† | .08 | 1,710 |
| Manning | -.03 (.02) | .04 (.04) | -.03 (.03) | .04 (.02)* | -.02 (.02) | .56 (.05)† | .07 | 1,469 |
| *Aggressive* | | | | | | | | |
| Campbell | .06 (.01)† | .13 (.03)† | .05 (.02)** | -.00 (.02) | -.01 (.02) | .50 (.04)† | .04 | 1,666 |
| McLaughlin | -.01 (.02) | -.04 (.04) | -.06 (.02)*** | -.01 (.02) | .00 (.02) | .64 (.04)† | .05 | 1,536 |
| Chrétien | -.03 (.01)*** | .02 (.03) | -.14 (.02)† | .01 (.02) | .03 (.02)* | .80 (.03)† | .05 | 1,718 |
| Manning | -.08 (.02)† | .12 (.03)† | .00 (.02) | -.04 (.02)** | -.02 (.02) | .67 (.04)† | .04 | 1,481 |

*Note:* The column entries are unstandardized ordinary least squares regression coefficients with standard errors shown in parentheses. Controls were included for age, region, religion, union membership, employment status, occupation, employment sector, ethnicity, party identification, and economic evaluations.

* $p < .10$    ** $p < .05$    *** $p < .01$    † $p < .001$

*Table 10.4*

**Determinants of trait attributions in New Zealand (post-election)**

| | Sex | Education | Knowledge | TV news | Sex roles | $R^2$ | *N* |
|---|---|---|---|---|---|---|---|
| *Compassionate* | | | | | | | |
| Shipley | 0.03 (.01)*** | -0.01 (.00)* | -0.07 (.02)† | 0.02 (.02) | 0.03 (.02) | 0.22 | 4,072 |
| Clark | 0.02 (.01)** | 0.00 (.00) | -0.01 (.02) | 0.10 (.02)† | -0.03 (.01)** | 0.12 | 4,012 |
| Anderton | -0.01 (.01) | 0.01 (.00)** | 0.02 (.02) | 0.10 (.02)† | -0.04 (.02)** | 0.13 | 3,714 |
| Peters | -0.03 (.01)*** | -0.00 (.00) | 0.01 (.02) | 0.08 (.02)† | 0.04 (.02)** | 0.10 | 3,894 |
| Prebble | -0.00 (.01) | -0.01 (.00) | -0.08 (.02)† | 0.01 (.02) | 0.02 (.02) | 0.12 | 3,541 |
| *Trustworthy* | | | | | | | |
| Shipley | 0.03 (.01)*** | -0.00 (.00) | -0.00 (.02) | 0.00 (.02) | 0.00 (.02) | 0.29 | 4,194 |
| Clark | 0.04 (.01)*** | 0.01 (.00)*** | 0.02 (.02) | 0.01 (.01)† | -0.02 (.01)* | 0.14 | 3,966 |
| Anderton | -0.01 (.01) | -0.00 (.00) | -0.02 (.02) | 0.08 (.02)† | -0.06 (.02)† | 0.19 | 3,687 |
| Peters | -0.01 (.01) | -0.01 (.00)*** | -0.02 (.02) | 0.07 (.02)† | 0.03 (.02)** | 0.16 | 4,100 |
| Prebble | -0.02 (.01) | 0.02 (.00)† | -0.01 (.02) | 0.02 (.02) | 0.05 (.02)*** | 0.17 | 4,160 |
| *Speaks for women* | | | | | | | |
| Shipley | 0.00 (.01) | -0.01 (.00)** | -0.05 (.02)** | 0.01 (.02) | 0.01 (.02) | 0.16 | 3,815 |
| Clark | 0.02 (.01)** | -0.00 (.00) | -0.06 (.02)† | 0.10 (.02)† | -0.02 (.01) | 0.07 | 3,816 |
| Anderton | -0.05 (.01)† | -0.02 (.00)*** | -0.03 (.02) | 0.11 (.02)† | -0.00 (.02) | 0.16 | 3,232 |
| Peters | -0.03 (.01)† | -0.01 (.00)*** | -0.03 (.01)** | 0.05 (.01)† | 0.04 (.01)*** | 0.11 | 3,530 |
| Prebble | -0.03 (.01)*** | -0.01 (.00) | -0.04 (.02)*** | 0.03 (.01)* | 0.03 (.01)** | 0.07 | 3,149 |

| | | | | | | | | | | | | |
|---|---|---|---|---|---|---|---|---|---|---|---|---|
| *Strong leadership* | | | | | | | | | | | | |
| Shipley | 0.06 | (.01)† | 0.00 | (.00) | -0.01 | (.02) | -0.01 | (.02) | -0.05 | (.02)*** | 0.16 | 4,174 |
| Clark | 0.04 | (.01)† | 0.00 | (.00) | 0.01 | (.01) | 0.07 | (.01)† | -0.03 | (.01)** | 0.12 | 4,046 |
| Anderton | -0.00 | (.01) | 0.01 | (.00)** | 0.01 | (.02) | 0.08 | (.02)† | -0.01 | (.02) | 0.11 | 3,828 |
| Peters | -0.03 | (.01)† | 0.01 | (.00)* | 0.02 | (.02) | 0.05 | (.02)*** | 0.06 | (.02)*** | 0.07 | 4,031 |
| Prebble | -0.04 | (.01)*** | 0.04 | (.00)† | 0.10 | (.02)† | -0.00 | (.02) | 0.07 | (.02)† | 0.14 | 3,602 |
| *Arrogant* | | | | | | | | | | | | |
| Shipley | -0.04 | (.01)† | 0.01 | (.00) | 0.07 | (.02)*** | 0.10 | (.02)† | -0.02 | (.02) | 0.20 | 4,145 |
| Clark | -0.02 | (.01) | -0.01 | (.00) | -0.02 | (.02) | -0.03 | (.02)* | 0.05 | (.02)*** | 0.07 | 4,081 |
| Anderton | 0.00 | (.01) | 0.01 | (.01)** | 0.08 | (.02)† | -0.02 | (.02) | 0.08 | (.02)† | 0.13 | 3,867 |
| Peters | 0.02 | (.01)** | 0.01 | (.00)† | 0.01 | (.02) | -0.04 | (.02)** | -0.05 | (.01)† | 0.12 | 4,130 |
| Prebble | 0.00 | (.01) | 0.01 | (.00)* | 0.09 | (.02)† | 0.02 | (.02) | -0.03 | (.02)* | 0.10 | 3,800 |

*Note:* The column entries are unstandardized ordinary least squares regression coefficients with standard errors shown in parentheses. Controls were included for age, education, ethnicity, occupation, public employee, religion, party identification, and economic evaluations. Party leaders in the analysis are those from parties that had representation in the previous Parliament, with the exception of Peter Dunne, leader of the United Party.

* $p. < .10$ ** $p < .05$ *** $p < .0$ † $p < .001$

men did for their ability to speak for women. Second, women were more likely than men to consider Campbell aggressive. The reverse was true for the two male leaders.

Finally, traditionalists in both countries rated male leaders more positively on their ability to speak for women than did people with more egalitarian gender-role beliefs. In the case of Campbell and Clark, we also found some evidence that traditionalists tend to evaluate female leaders more negatively on both stereotypical masculine and stereotypical feminine traits.

## Discussion

Our results suggest that experimental studies have overstated the degree of gender-trait stereotyping that occurs in actual elections.[16] Analyses of the 1993 Canadian and 1999 New Zealand data show that leaders' own personalities, campaigns, and parties mattered more to the traits respondents attributed to them than did their sex. In short, trait attributions were more likely to be based on a leader's party label or the party's standing in the polls than on the sex of a party leader.

If gender-trait stereotyping did occur, it should have been most evident early in the election campaigns, when voters may have needed stereotypes to fill in gaps in their knowledge about the leaders. Little consistent evidence appeared in either the 1993 Canadian or the 1999 New Zealand data to support the view that gender-trait stereotyping occurred in the early campaign but declined as elections drew nearer. Similarly, we did not find convincing evidence that less sophisticated voters relied on gender-trait stereotypes to infer leaders' personal qualities. Moreover, to the extent that we did detect signs of stereotyping in the Canadian campaign (where women leaders were more of a novelty than in New Zealand), it was the incumbent prime minister, Kim Campbell, rather than Audrey McLaughlin, the lesser known of the two Canadian women, who was ascribed the stereotypical traits.

Caution is warranted in extrapolating the results from experimental studies to electoral politics, since prescriptive conclusions drawn from the former may be irrelevant to the latter. For example, it is not at all clear that women aspiring to high national office have to "act tough" to offset a supposed disadvantage.[17] In fact, experimental studies may well have overstated the need for women politicians to transcend feminine stereotypes and neglected the possibility that acting tough could backfire. Media coverage already plays up the combativeness of female leaders through the use of metaphors of violence and warfare and the selection of sound bites (Gidengil and Everitt 1999, 2000, 2003a, 2003b). When politicians behave in what is perceived to be an overly aggressive fashion, audiences tend to react negatively (Schrott and Lanoue 1992; Schütz 1998). Perceptions of leadership style in male-dominated settings suggest that negative reactions may be stronger when the leader is a woman (Butler and Geis 1990). There may thus be very real electoral costs for a woman who chooses to "act tough."

Yet, our results suggest some grounds for optimism. First and foremost, voters do not appear to consider leadership a masculine trait. Whether female leaders are perceived to be strong leaders depends on how well their party is doing rather than the mere fact of their being female. To the extent that voters engage in stereotyping, they are more likely to stereotype on the basis of the leader's party label than her sex. The implication is clear: if women aspiring to political leadership in Canada are finding the doors to be less open than they might have hoped, or if they see more obstacles in the passageways than they expected, then the data we have considered show voters are not the source of the blockages.

## Appendix: Question Wording

### 1993 Canadian Election Study

The 1993 Canadian Election Study was funded by the Social Sciences and Humanities Research Council of Canada and conducted under the direction of Richard Johnston, André Blais, Henry Brady, Elisabeth Gidengil, and Neil Nevitte. The fieldwork was carried out by the Institute for Social Research at York University. The campaign survey used a rolling cross-sectional design, whereby the day of interview was a random event. Respondents were interviewed by telephone. The average length of the campaign interview was forty minutes. The sample size outside Quebec was 2,768, with a response rate of 60 percent.

#### *Traits*

*Now, we'd like to know about your impressions of the party leaders. I would like you to tell me how well the following words fit each leader: Does "intelligent" describe [leader's name]: very well, fairly well, not very well, or not at all? Does "arrogant" describe [leader's name]: very well, fairly well, not very well, or not at all? "Trustworthy"? "Can really speak for women"? "Provides strong leadership"? "Compassionate"?* The order of delivery of the leaders was random. Respondents who had previously indicated that they were not at all informed about the leader were not asked about that particular leader. The traits were recoded to run from 0 (not at all) to 1 (very well).

#### *Leader Evaluations*

*Now, I'll ask you to rate each leader on a scale that runs from 0 to 100. Ratings between 0 and 50 mean that you rate that person unfavorably. Ratings between 50 and 100 mean that you rate that person favorably. You may use any number from 0 to 100. How would you rate [leader's name]?* The order of delivery of the leaders was random. Respondents who had previously indicated that they were not at all informed about the leader were not asked about that particular leader. The ratings were recoded to run from 0 to 1. The leader ratings were asked before the leader traits and were separated in the questionnaire by questions on economic conditions, party placements, and issues.

#### *Sex*

A dummy variable, coded 1 for women and 0 for men.

#### *Knowledge*

Interviewer ratings of respondent knowledge on a five-point scale: very high, fairly high, average, fairly low, or very low. This measure was rescaled to run from 0 to 1.

***Education***
A 0 to 1 scale, running from "did not complete high school" to "completed university."

***Television News Exposure***
*How many days in the past week did you watch the news on TV?* Responses were rescaled to run from 0 to 1.

***Gender-Role Attitudes***
*Could you tell me if you strongly agree, somewhat agree, somewhat disagree, or strongly disagree with the following statements: Society would be better off if more women stayed home with their children.* Responses were rescaled to run from 0 (strongly disagree) to 1 (strongly agree).

New Zealand Election Study 1999

***Campaign Period***
The campaign survey is a pre-election telephone survey of approximately thirty-five hundred New Zealanders that began on 18 October and continued daily until election day on 27 November. Using a rolling cross-sectional design, eighty to ninety persons eligible to vote were interviewed each day. The response rate was 58 percent. For more information, see the NZES website.

*Traits*
*Does [compassionate, trustworthy, speaks for women, strong leader, speaks for men, arrogant] describe [Helen Clark, Jenny Shipley]?* 1 = Yes, 0 = No

*Education*
Highest formal education or qualification: 1 = Incomplete primary education/no formal education, 2 = Primary School completed, 3 = Secondary education without diploma, 4 = completed secondary education with diploma, 5 = nondegree professional, trade, or technical tertiary qualification, 6 = university degree.

*Party Identification*
From the question, "Generally speaking, do you usually think of yourself as Labour, National, NZ First, Alliance, Act or some other, or don't you think of yourself in this way?" a series of dummy variables was created including "other party" and "no party."

*Economic Satisfaction*
*What do you think of the state of the economy these days in New Zealand?* 1 = very good, .75 = good, .5 = neither good or bad, .25 = bad, 0 = very bad.

***Post-Election***
The 1999 post-election sample was primarily by mail, with a small telephone supplement. It is made up of three sections, and the first is a "new sample" sampled directly from the electoral rolls (*N* = 1,059, with, at the most conservative estimate, a response rate of 58 percent for the postal component alone, or 64 percent, including the telephone top-up). Further sections are made up of a panel of respondents from the 1990, 1993, and 1990 election studies (*N* = 2,342) and a panel of respondents first sampled in the Campaign Study (*N* = 2,489). For more information, see the NZES website.

*Traits*
*How well does [compassionate, trustworthy, speaks for women, strong leader, arrogant] describe [Helen Clark, Jenny Shipley, Winston Peters, Jim Anderton, Richard Prebble]?* 1 = Very Well, .67 = Well, .33 = Not well, 0 = Not at all.

*Knowledge*
Mean score for the following three true/false items:

*The term of Parliament is four years. Cabinet Ministers must be MPs. The New Zealand Parliament once had an Upper House.* 1 = Correct, 0 = Incorrect or Don't Know.

*TV News Exposure*
Mean score for the following two items: *During the election campaign, how often did you follow political news, discussion and advertising on TV One? On TV3?* 1 = Often, .67 = Sometimes, .33 = Rarely, 0 = Not at all.

*Gender-Role Attitudes*
*Could you tell me if you strongly agree, somewhat agree, somewhat disagree, or strongly disagree with the following statements: Society would be better off if more women stayed home with their children.* Responses were rescaled to run from 0 (strongly disagree) to 1 (strongly agree).

*Party Identification*
From the question, "Generally speaking, do you usually think of yourself as Labour, National, NZ First, Alliance, Act or some other, or don't you think of yourself in this way?" a series of dummy variables was created including "other party" and "no party".

*Economic Satisfaction*
*What do you think of the state of the economy these days in New Zealand?* 1 = very good, .75 = good, .5 = neither good or bad, .25 = bad, 0 = very bad.

*Education*
Highest formal education or qualification: 1 = incomplete primary education/no formal education, 2 = primary school completed, 3 = secondary education without diploma, 4 = completed secondary education with diploma, 5 = non-degree professional, trade, or technical tertiary qualification, 6 = university degree.

*Manual Occupation*
Skilled/Unskilled Manual Occupations = 1; Otherwise = 0.

*Working*
Paid Work Full Time = 1; Otherwise = 0.

***Public Employee***
Work for Government, in Public Sector or for Government Enterprise = 1; Otherwise = 0.

***Union Member***
Respondent is Member of Union = 1; Otherwise = 0.

**Notes**

1 Huddy and Terkildsen (1993a) argue that these gender-trait stereotypes shape the perceived issue competencies of male and female candidates. Other scholars (for example, Sanbonmatsu 2001) prefer to treat perceived issue competencies as a type of gender stereotype in their own right.

2 In experimental studies, female candidates are usually stereotyped as being more liberal and more feminist than their male counterparts (see, for example, Huddy and Terkildsen 1993a).

3 However, Kaid and her colleagues (1984) found that students viewed women candidates not only as more honest and attractive but also as more aggressive, strong, and active.

4 We would like to thank the anonymous reviewer for bringing this point to our attention.

5 For instance, in Thompson and Steckenrider's (1997) quasi-experimental study, the candidate's gender had less of an impact on vote choice than the candidate's party label or position on abortion.

6 Pettigrew (1976) makes a similar point about racial stereotypes.

7 As Sanbonmatsu (2001) notes, gender-belief stereotypes require more political knowledge. Voters cannot use candidates' sex to make inferences about ideological orientations unless they know something about politics. In the United States, for example, voters would need to be aware that women tend to be more liberal and Democratic than men (see Huddy and Terkildsen 1993a). This may explain why Koch (1999, 2002a, 2002b) found gender stereotypes to be most prevalent among well-educated respondents: "Only the politically attentive may have learned theories about gender differences in candidates. These citizens may 'know' that female candidates care more about social issues than their male counterparts" (1999, 95).

8 It should be noted, though, that New Zealand had switched to a mixed-member proportional electoral system in 1996, whereas Canada continues to use a single-member plurality system.

9 We should note that Shipley and Clark were not the only women leading parties in the 1999 New Zealand election. Jeanette Fitzsimmons was co-leader of the Green Party; Fitzsimmons won her Coromandel seat and helped the party cross the 5 percent threshold. Unfortunately, the New Zealand Election Study did not include trait questions about her.

10 Data from the 1993 Canadian Election Study confirm that McLaughlin was much less well known than Campbell. The average self-assessment of knowledge about McLaughlin was 1.31 on a scale that ran from 0 (not at all informed) to 3 (very well informed), compared with 1.71 for Campbell (and 1.75 for Liberal leader Jean Chrétien). McLaughlin was no better known, on average, than Reform Party leader Preston Manning (1.28), despite the fact that Manning had been leading his new party from outside the House of Commons.

11 In a rolling cross-sectional design, the total sample is broken down into sub-samples, one for each day of the campaign (see Johnston and Brady 2002; Romer et al. 2004). Because each daily sub-sample is as similar to the others as random-sampling variation permits, all that distinguishes them (within the range of sampling error) is the date of interview.

12 There are some differences between the two studies. First, due to time constraints, the NZES only asked respondents to provide trait ratings for the two women leaders. However, the NZES post-election survey does contain a parallel set of questions for all five parties that were represented in the previous Parliament. Secondly, the CES used a filter to exclude respondents who said that they knew "nothing at all" about a given party leader. Finally, the CES post-election survey only repeated three of the trait items from the campaign survey (trustworthiness, leadership ability, and arrogance), but it added a fourth trait (aggressiveness).

13 The Canadian campaign and post-election analyses and the New Zealand post-election analyses all use ordinary least squares regression to estimate the models. Since the trait questions in the New Zealand campaign survey simply asked for a yes/no response, the campaign analysis uses logistic regression.

14 Perceived ability to speak for men was not included in the New Zealand post-election trait battery or in the Canadian questionnaires.

15 Respondents in the Canadian Election Study who said they knew "nothing at all" about a given leader were not asked to provide trait ratings. In other words, those voters who might have been most likely to stereotype are excluded from the analyses. Still, the lack of consistent knowledge effects, and the fact that some of the effects were the exact opposite of those predicted, suggests this filter did not seriously compromise our results.

16 As noted earlier, it is possible that gender-trait stereotyping is more prevalent in the United States because party labels matter less and/or because women are less visible in elected office. It is also possible that gender-trait stereotyping is more common for candidates for the US House of Representatives or the Senate than for candidates in a parliamentary system. The typical US legislative candidate, especially if she is a challenger, will not have the public profile of a party leader in a Westminster-style system. Voters may, consequently, be more likely to attribute stereotypical qualities to her.

17 The situation may be different in the United States, especially when it comes to the presidency, given the president's role as commander-in-chief (see Duerst-Lahti and Kelly 1995).

**References**

Alexander, Deborah, and Kristi Anderson. 1993. "Gender as a Factor in the Attribution of Leadership Traits." *Political Research Quarterly* 46, 3: 527-45.

Butler, Doré, and Florence L. Geis. 1990. "Nonverbal Affect Responses to Male and Female Leaders: Implications for Leadership Evaluations." *Journal of Personality and Social Psychology* 58, 1: 48-59.

Carroll, Susan J., and Ronnee Schreiber. 1997. "Media Coverage of Women in the 103rd Congress." In *Women, Media, and Politics,* ed. Pippa Norris, 131-48. Oxford: Oxford University Press.

Conover, Pamela Johnston, and Stanley Feldman. 1986. "The Role of Inference in the Perception of Political Candidates." In *Political Cognition: The 19th Annual Carnegie Symposium on Cognition,* ed. Richard R. Lau and David O. Sears, 127-59. Hillsdale: Lawrence Erlbaum Associates.

Cutler, Fred. 2002. "The Simplest Shortcut of All: Socio-Demographic Characteristics and Electoral Choice." *Journal of Politics* 64, 2: 466-90.

Dolan, Kathleen. 2004. "The Impact of Candidate Sex on Evaluations of Candidates for the U.S. House of Representatives." *Social Science Quarterly* 85, 1: 206-17.

Duerst-Lahti, Georgia, and Rita Mae Kelly. 1995. *Gender Power, Leadership, and Governance.* Ann Arbor: University of Michigan Press.

Eagly, Alice, Mona G. Makhijani, and Bruce G. Klonsky. 1992. "Gender and Evaluation of Leaders: A Meta-Analysis." *Psychological Bulletin* 111, 1: 3-22.

Fiske, Susan T., and Steven L. Neuberg. 1990. "A Continuum of Impression Formation, from Category-Based to Individuating Processes: Influences of Information and Motivation on Attention and Interpretation." In *Advances in Experimental Social Psychology,* Vol. 23, ed. M.P. Zanna, 1-74. New York: Academic Press.

Gidengil, Elisabeth, and Joanna Everitt. 1999. "Metaphors and Misrepresentation: Gendered Mediation in News Coverage of the 1993 Canadian Leaders' Debates." *Press/Politics* 4, 1: 48-65.

–. 2000. "Filtering the Female: Gender Mediation in Television Coverage of the 1993 Canadian Leaders' Debates." *Women and Politics* 21, 4: 105-31.

–. 2003a. "Conventional Coverage/Unconventional Politicians: Gender and Media Coverage of Canadian Leaders' Debates, 1993, 1997, 2000." *Canadian Journal of Political Science* 36, 3: 559-77.

–. 2003b. "Talking Tough: Gender and Reported Speech in Campaign News Coverage." *Political Communication* 20: 209-32.

Harris, Stephen. 2000. "Following the Leaders." In *Left Turn: The New Zealand General Election of 1999,* ed. Jonathan Boston, Stephen Church, Stephen Levine, Elizabeth McLeary, and Nigel S. Roberts, 77-88. Wellington, New Zealand: Victoria University Press.

Hayes, Danny. 2005. "Candidate Qualities through a Partisan Lens: A Theory of Trait Ownership." *American Journal of Political Science* 49, 4: 908-23.

Huddy, Leonie. 1994. "The Political Significance of Voters' Gender Stereotypes." In *Research in Micropolitics: New Directions in Political Psychology,* ed. Michael X. Delli Carpini, Leonie Huddie, and Robert Y. Shapiro, 169-93. Greenwich, CT: JAI Press.

Huddy, Leonie, and Nayda Terkildson. 1993a. "Gender Stereotypes and the Perception of Male and Female Candidates." *American Journal of Political Science* 37, 1: 119-47.

–. 1993b. "The Consequences of Gender Stereotypes for Women Candidates at Different Levels and Types of Office." *Political Research Quarterly* 46, 3: 503-25.

Huddy, Leonie, and Teresa Capelos. 2002. "Gender Stereotyping and Candidate Evaluation: Good News and Bad News for Women Politicians." In *The Social Psychology of Politics,* ed. Victor Ottati, 29-54. New York: Kluwer Academic Press.

Johnston, Richard, and Henry E. Brady. 2002. "The Rolling Cross-Section Design." *Electoral Studies* 21, 2: 283-95.

Kahn, Kim Fridkin. 1992. "Does Being Male Help? An Investigation of the Effects of Candidate Gender and Campaign Coverage on Evaluations of US Senate Candidates." *Journal of Politics* 54, 2: 497-517.

–. 1994. "Does Gender Make a Difference? An Experimental Examination of Sex Stereotypes and Press Patterns in Statewide Campaigns." *American Journal of Political Science* 38, 1: 162-95.

Kaid, Lynda Lee, Sandra L. Myers, Val Pipps, and Jan Hunter. 1984. "Sex Role Perceptions and Televised Political Advertising: Comparing Male and Female Candidates." *Women and Politics* 4 (winter): 41-53.

Kennedy, Mark. 1993. "Pick Me If Choosing between Female Leaders, McLaughlin Urges." *Gazette* (Montreal), 13 September, A6.

Koch, Jeffrey W. 1999. "Candidate Gender and Assessments of Senate Candidates." *Social Science Quarterly* 80, 1: 84-96.

–. 2002a. "Do Citizens Apply Gender Stereotypes to Infer Candidates' Ideological Orientations?" *Journal of Politics* 62, 2: 414-29.

–. 2002b. "Gender Stereotypes and Citizens' Impressions of House Candidates' Ideological Orientations." *American Journal of Political Science* 46, 2: 453-62.

Leeper, Mark Stephen. 1991. "The Impact of Prejudice on Female Candidates: An Experimental Look at Voter Inference." *American Politics Quarterly* 19, 2: 248-61.

Lewis, Kathryn, and Margaret Bierly. 1990. "Towards a Profile of the Female Voter: Sex Differences in Perceived Physical Attractiveness and Competence of Political Candidates." *Sex Roles* 22, 1-2: 1-12.

Matland, Richard E. 1994. "Putting Scandinavian Equality to the Test: An Experimental Evaluation of Gender Stereotyping of Political Candidates in a Sample of Norwegian Voters." *British Journal of Political Science* 24, 2: 273-92.

McDermott, Monika L., 1997. "Voting Cues in Low-Information Elections: Candidate Gender as a Social Information Variable in Contemporary United States Elections." *American Journal of Political Science* 41, 1: 270-83.

Mills, Carol J., and Donald J. Tyrrell. 1983. "Sex-Stereotypic Encoding and Release from Proactive Interference." *Journal of Personality and Social Psychology* 45, 4: 772-81.

Norris, Pippa. 1997a. "Introduction: Women, Media and Politics." In *Women, Media, and Politics,* ed. Pippa Norris, 1-18. Oxford: Oxford University Press.

–. 1997b. "Women Leaders Worldwide: A Splash of Color in the Photo Op." In *Women, Media, and Politics,* ed. Pippa Norris, 149-65. Oxford: Oxford University Press.

Pettigrew, Thomas. 1976. "Black Mayoral Campaigns." In *Urban Governance and Minorities,* ed. H.J. Bryce, 14-29. New York: Praeger.

Powell, Gary N., and D. Anthony Butterfield. 1987. "Is the 'Presidential Image' Reserved for Males? Sex-Role Stereotypes and the 1984 Presidential Election." *Psychological Reports* 61: 491-95.

Rahn, Wendy M. 1993. "The Role of Partisan Stereotypes in Information Processing about Political Candidates." *American Journal of Political Science* 37, 2: 472-96.

Riggle, Ellen D.B., Penny M. Miller, Todd G. Sheilds, and Mitzi M.S. Johnson. 1997. "Gender Stereotypes and Decision Context in the Evaluation of Political Candidates." *Women and Politics* 17, 3: 69-87.

Robinson, Gertrude, and Armande Saint-Jean. 1991. "Women Politicians and Their Media Coverage: A Generational Analysis." In *Women in Canadian Politics: Towards Equity in Representation,* ed. Kathy Megyery, 127-69. Vol. 6, Research Studies for the Royal Commission on Electoral Reform and Party Financing. Toronto: Dundurn Press.

Romer, Daniel, Kate Kenski, Paul Waldman, Christopher Adasiewicz, and Kathleen Hall Jamieson. 2004. *Capturing Campaign Dynamics: The National Annenberg Election Survey.* New York: Oxford University Press.

Rosenwasser, Shirley, and Jana Seale. 1988. "Attitudes towards a Hypothetical Male or Female Presidential Candidate: A Research Note." *Political Psychology* 9, 4: 591-98.

Rosenwasser, Shirley, and Norma Dean. 1989. "Gender Role and Political Office: Effects of Perceived Masculinity/Femininity of Candidate and Political Office." *Psychology of Women Quarterly* 13, 1: 77-85.

Ross, Karen. 1995. "Gender and Party Politics: How the Press Reported the Labour Leadership Campaign." *Media, Culture and Society* 17, 3: 499-509.

Sanbonmatsu, Kira. 2001. "Who Stereotypes? The Determinants of Gender Stereotypes about Political Candidates." Paper presented at the annual meeting of the Midwest Political Science Association, Chicago, 19 April.

–. 2002. "Gender Stereotypes and Vote Choice." *American Journal of Political Science* 46, 1: 20-34.

Sapiro, Virginia. 1981. "If U.S. Senator Baker Were a Woman: An Experimental Study of Candidate Images." *Political Psychology* 3: 61-83.

Schrott, Peter R., and David J. Lanoue. 1992. "How to Win a Televised Debate: Candidate Strategies and Voter-Response in Germany, 1972-87." *British Journal of Political Science* 22, 4: 445-67.

Schütz, Astrid. 1998. "Audience Perceptions of Politicians' Self-Presentation Behaviors Concerning Their Own Abilities." *Journal of Social Psychology* 138, 2: 173-88.

Swan, Suzanne, and Robert S. Wyer Jr. 1997. "Gender Stereotypes and Social Identity: How Being in the Minority Affects Judgements of Self and Others." *Personality and Social Psychology Bulletin* 23, 12: 1265-76.

Thompson, Seth, and Janie Steckenrider. 1997. "The Relative Irrelevance of Candidate Sex." *Women and Politics* 17, 4: 71-92.

Trimble, Linda. 2005. "Who Framed Belinda Stronach? National Newspaper Coverage of the Conservative Party of Canada's 2004 Leadership Race." Paper presented to the 2005 Canadian Political Science Association conference, London, Ontario, 4 June.

Williams, John E., and Deborah L. Best. 1990. *Measuring Sex Stereotypes: A Multination Study.* Newbury Park: Sage.

Wyer, R.S., Jr., and Scrull, T.K., 1986. "Human Cognition in Its Social Context." *Psychological Review* 93, 3: 322-59.

# Part 5
# Remedies and Prescriptions

# 11
# Opening Doors to Women's Participation

*Sylvia Bashevkin*

This chapter reflects on the broader implications of research presented by scholars of women's participation in Canada. What assumptions, whether in received popular or academic wisdom, have been unsettled by the analyses presented in this volume? At the level of remedies and prescriptions, what can be done to enhance both real-world engagement and the study of it? Which research directions appear most promising for scholarship in the field? Do academic studies of the type presented in this volume provide useful lessons for political activism, particularly for Canadians who want to heighten and improve women's public participation? In short, how might research in this area help to open doorways further?

## Unsettling Findings

Both chapters in Part 1 shed critical light on a powerful view that dates back to the late 1970s, when women and politics studies, including work by Vickers (1978, 46), claimed that party organizations constituted a major obstacle to engagement at provincial and federal levels. A logical corollary to this perspective suggested barriers were less significant in non-partisan environments, including local politics and women-only organizations.

Probably the most compelling conclusion that follows from the studies by Andrew and Nadeau in this volume is that limitations on involvement were far from absent in local community and feminist group contexts. In particular, diverse women from immigrant and visible minority backgrounds faced multiple challenges in their efforts to engage in both settings, whether because of limitations in their own time and confidence vis-à-vis mainstream politics (as Andrew's study suggests) or perceptions that women's groups structured anti-racist feminism off the agenda (as Nadeau's chapter argues). Either way, the contributions to Part 1 point towards a conclusion that the doors to participation outside political parties may be open far less wide than is indicated by the existing literature in this area – particularly if the diverse experiences of women are taken into account. Given how little we know about the dynamics of engagement at these levels, closer attention by political scientists to venues such as local politics, community groups, and social movement organizations looms large as an essential part of the future scholarly agenda in this field.

Turning to Part 2, a considerable body of writing dating back to Anderson (1991), Bashevkin (1985), and Brodie (1985) has pressed for remedies to under-representation that include electoral reform in the direction of proportional representation (PR) as well as across-the-board pressure on political parties to nominate more women candidates. One intriguing dimension of Tremblay's chapter is its assertion that significant progress can be made on the numbers of elected women without altering single-member plurality rules. Her account of seat holding in the Quebec National Assembly demonstrates that women legislators could cross the one-third threshold in the absence of PR, if major party leaders were pressed to nominate women in winnable seats. The reality that, since the 1970s, Quebec feminists focused heavily on lobbying the provincial government, and on building close ties with political parties at that level, clearly assisted with this process and contrasted directly with the federal politics emphasis of parliamentary feminism in English Canada.

Obviously, not all provincial parties in Canada shared the relatively centrist positions of the Quebec Liberal and Parti Québécois (PQ) formations during the period studied by Tremblay, nor did all provinces have as egalitarian an attitudinal climate as Quebec in the 1970s and the decades that followed. Moreover, the rise of the Action démocratique du Québec as a right-of-centre populist party towards the end of the period studied by Tremblay could work to undermine the political consensus she identifies, given that women's engagement was far less of a priority for that formation than it was for older parties that hold seats in the National Assembly. Tremblay's chapter, in short, suggests it is possible for women to gain enhanced legislative representation without altering single-member plurality arrangements, particularly if a competitive party environment, parliamentary-focused feminist movement, and constructive movement/party relations are in place as contextual variables.

A powerful counter-argument to this view would posit that in the absence of parallel circumstances in the rest of Canada, women's groups are well advised to continue pressuring for electoral reform. This perspective suggests that keeping alive the claim that the parliamentary representation of diverse demographic groups in Canada matters to the quality of democracy is worthwhile in and of itself. We know, thanks to Tremblay's chapter, that such a goal can be obtained in multiple ways; however, keeping the objective in full public view is obviously essential, regardless of the means pursued to achieve it.

The importance of ideational environments stands out as a theme in Carbert's chapter as well. Given that the dearth of women MPs from rural constituencies transcends regional, party, and chronological divides, this pattern is likely attributable to political context differences between metropolitan centres, on one side, and areas of less dense settlement, on the other. If party activists and voters in rural zones express less sustained demand for women candidates than their urban counterparts, and if sparsely settled areas provide a less visible supply of high-profile women who could serve as MPs, then we can begin to understand the bases for Carbert's findings. Further research on the dynamics of rural-urban differences would help to flesh out this hypothesis, since it would document the origins of what appear to be fairly open doors in Canada's cities versus relatively closed passageways in less densely settled areas. As well, Carbert's study urges both scholars and activists to consider closely the consequences of rural over-representation and urban under-representation in Canadian legislatures. The fact that so few rural seats in the federal House of Commons are held by women cannot be divorced from the reality that, with reference to representation by population, the country has too many rural and too few urban constituencies.

At the level of political activism, data presented in Part 2 encourage greater circumspection or caution vis-à-vis solutions to under-representation. Just as Tremblay implies that people who desire more elected women should not surrender the possibility of creating change within the parameters of single-member plurality systems, her work, Carbert's study, and Goodyear-Grant's chapter can also be interpreted as suggesting that PR alone is unlikely to produce numerical parity – since no formal electoral scheme can by itself act as a substitute for a welcoming attitudinal climate.

Taken together, the Carbert and Goodyear-Grant chapters also shed critical light on assumptions that enhancing educational and occupational opportunities for women would increase the supply of female political candidates, simply because the standard pool of recruits would be larger. Carbert's study shows that rural women in particular may be unwilling to engage in what many view as a hostile political environment, especially for federal representatives from areas beyond the country's metropolitan areas. Similarly, Goodyear-Grant's findings about the consequences of negative media coverage suggest that highly qualified women may voluntarily withdraw themselves from the supply of legislative candidates, even if, as Gidengil et al. propose in Chapter 10, voters in the general public hold relatively open and tolerant views that implicitly constitute a demand for female parliamentarians.

In addition, after reading Carbert's study, women and politics groups in Canada may devote less attention to across-the-board campaigns to ensure that more female candidates are nominated for House of Commons seats. Instead, they may begin to focus in a more selective way on improving prospects in rural areas, and on ensuring that stronger patterns of representation in urban zones are maintained. This latter priority follows from Carbert's data that shows that successors to women MPs in Canadian cities are often not other women. Carbert's findings thus make attempts to exert undifferentiated pressure on parties – whether for formal rules governing candidate nominations or for informal mentoring and recruitment efforts to draw more women – seem far less attractive and promising as a strategy, as compared with targeted campaigns to democratize rural recruitment practices. That being said, Goodyear-Grant's study underlines the valuable contributions that informal efforts do make, including the improvement of confidence in and media profiles of elected women.

Further research in this area can probe many of the promising analytic threads that appear in Part 2. For example, have other provincial or possibly federal parties in Canada successfully increased women's participation in ways that parallel developments in the Quebec Liberal and PQ organizations? Does the rural deficit of female MPs reverberate in some or all of the provinces? Linking back to the studies in Part 1, to what degree have parties recruited diverse women activists from local politics, community groups, and feminist movement organizations, whether for internal party office or for provincial and federal candidacy? How smooth are these transitions from non-partisan to party politics? Returning to the supply-side thesis introduced in Chapter 1, can we gauge the extent to which potential women candidates (including those from rural areas) have refused to get involved in legislative politics, despite the efforts of party recruiters?

The contributions to Part 3 follow directly from questions about movement and party interaction. Byrne's chapter addresses this area with reference to cabinet-level participation in Ontario and recalls Young's (2000) research on the relative compatibility of the New Decmocratic Party (NDP) and feminist movement interests. Yet, Byrne reminds us that NDP provincial governments, which included significant numbers of female ministers with feminist credentials, faced harsh criticism from extra-parliamentary women's movement interests. Her conclusion, that policy changes attributable to Bob Rae's NDP cabinet were less dramatic than the literature would predict and less extensive than movement interests expected, underlines the significance of parliamentary versus extra-parliamentary cleavages – including in the left-of-centre segment of the ideological spectrum.

The question of if and how movements can convert policy claims into policy change also informs party leadership research. Rosemary Brown's 1975 campaign for the top federal NDP post marked a crucial watershed in the efforts of movement activists to stake out space in mainstream party organizations. Yet, Bashevkin in Chapter 7 shows how women who sought to convert their numbers (including at the pinnacle of party elites) into substantive clout in parties had little success outside the less competitive organizations of the centre-left and centre-right. Hard-right parties, even when they operated far from the realm of political competitiveness, seemed unreceptive to female leadership candidates.

The fact that women candidates did better in uncompetitive than competitive formations meant that these leaders were often blamed for the misfortunes of their parties. Everitt and Camp's account offers a compelling reflection on the "loser" treatment of Allison Brewer as a woman, a lesbian, a pro-choice campaigner, and a New Democrat. Not only did her experiences as New Brunswick NDP leader suggest that the conversion from elite numbers to substantive clout on the centre-left of the spectrum was far from automatic; they also reveal the degree to which extra-parliamentary activist experience was used as a negative charge against her in media accounts. Taken together, the Byrne as well as Everitt and Camp chapters present some of the most powerful evidence in the Canadian literature of the representational challenges facing pro-equality women in senior positions on the centre-left part of the spectrum, where their prospects were assumed to be more promising than elsewhere.

Lessons to be drawn from this section relate to parliamentary as well as extra-parliamentary environments and the relations between them. Byrne's chapter suggests movement participants would do well to dampen their expectations of centre-left legislators and governments, dampen their criticisms of them, or both. Parallel with Carbert's contribution, the other two chapters in Part 3 encourage a more selective approach to pressing for increased participation: they point towards the relative success that female candidates have had at winning the leadership of uncompetitive parties and remind us that these victories contain a dangerous underbelly – that is, they reinforce the association of women political leaders with "loser" political fortunes. Electing women as leaders of competitive parties would appear, from this perspective, to be far more promising, although highly challenging as a participatory strategy.

At the level of research opportunities, Part 3 opens up the possibility of multiple comparative studies that could map out more of this interesting terrain. For example, Byrne's chapter leads us to question the impact of women in other NDP provincial governments, notably in British Columbia, Manitoba, and Saskatchewan, where the percentages of women in cabinet may have been lower than in Ontario but where NDP organizations had a longer and more stable history of holding power (see Collier 2008). Were relations between NDP governments and extra-parliamentary women's movements less troubled, as a result, in British Columbia and the Prairie provinces? Compared with their counterpart in Ontario, did NDP governments in BC, Saskatchewan, and Manitoba introduce policy changes that were better received in social movement organizations?

In terms of party leadership, were the actor and stage correlates of women's success as candidates similar at the provincial and territorial levels to Bashevkin's findings for the federal level? How does Canada compare with other Westminster systems, notably Britain, Australia, and New Zealand, when it comes to structural and individual predictors of the election of female leadership candidates? Is there a mirror image story to the one Everitt and Camp present about Allison Brewer, one in which heterosexual women politicians find that some media accounts interrogate their sexuality and turn them, at the level of framing, into lesbians or bisexuals? In this sense, Brewer's experiences may bear some relevance to those of Hillary Rodham Clinton in the United States and Helen Clark in New Zealand.

The popular narrative about steady progress for women in Canadian politics looks especially questionable in light of Goodyear-Grant's contribution to Part 4. Interviews with Canadian MPs show that women parliamentarians were particularly concerned about media portrayals, to the point that their self-consciousness led, in some cases, to self-doubt, discouragement about public life, and mistrust of the larger political setting. Patterns of this type cast doubt on assumptions that contemporary women MPs face no barriers once they reach legislative office, whether they seek to serve as representatives of their local constituencies or as carriers of a larger substantive issue agenda. In fact, Goodyear-Grant's interview transcripts from meetings with MPs offer some of the most poignant testimony currently available on this point; they confirm the reality of doors being far from fully open for women in the Canadian House of Commons.

Gidengil, Everitt, and Banducci's chapter serendipitously concludes this volume on an optimistic note. Consistent with the results of surveys, experimental studies, and actual election returns dating back to the mid-1970s, the comparative Canada-New Zealand project they designed shows that members of the public were reasonably open-minded when they assessed female party leaders (see also Bashevkin 1985, 147-48). The more powerful role of party over gender stereotypes in the surveys analyzed for Chapter 10 offer a hopeful sign that even though media portrayals of female politicians remained bogged down in a discriminatory mindset, voters did not necessarily share or absorb such views.

Political activists may take heart from both Goodyear-Grant's finding that MPs are quite sensitive to their media constructions and Gidengil and her colleagues' evidence that public attitudes towards women leaders appear considerably less biased than the media framings of those same individuals. The challenge for real-world change, as a result, rests beyond the consciousness-raising strategies employed during the past few decades by parties as well as women and politics groups. For example, it no longer appears necessary to teach women in public life (including experienced parliamentary candidates) about how they are framed by the media. Instead, altering the way news organizations report about women politicians jumps out as the heart of the problem. Goodyear-Grant is not entirely sanguine about the possibilities for reform in this area, however. I share her view that it remains to be seen whether distorted media accounts can be challenged effectively by members of the public, by oversight organizations in the sector, and by owners or shareholders.

The untilled fields opened up by both studies in Part 4 are potentially rich and fertile. Goodyear-Grant points to the possibility of employing qualitative interview data to understand politicians' own understandings of their media images. We do not know, for instance, whether the patterns she reports would be confirmed by parallel research in Canada's provinces and territories, or at the local and metropolitan government levels. Comparative research of the type conducted by Gidengil, Everitt, and Banducci would be hard to replicate at the national level, given that multiple women party leaders so rarely compete in a single election. Yet, Canadian legislative elections have, from time to time, featured strong female candidates from multiple parties competing in a single constituency – most often in urban areas. Scholars could conduct constituency-based surveys to learn more about voter perceptions of these candidates, and they might build on Carbert's work to compare, in a more focused way, the attitudes of urban and rural voters, alongside urban and rural party activists.

## Conclusion

If this volume renews scholarly interest in the empirical study of women's participation in Canadian politics, it will have more than fulfilled its purpose. If the studies reported here stimulate new generations of students and faculty to probe the doors and passageways of public engagement, then activists who aim to improve democratic life in this country can draw helpful insights from a reinvigorated research trajectory.

Many significant and difficult questions, beyond those already identified, jump out from these pages. Looming large in the academic agenda for the future is the growing demographic diversity of Canada's urban centres, underlined by the Andrew and Nadeau chapters, and how that diversity may challenge prevailing social movement as well as political institution operations. Will urban and rural areas grow increasingly distinct and politically divergent, whether with reference to women or other traditionally underrepresented groups? Can we expect that the weakening of pan-Canadian feminist mobilization identified in Bashevkin (1998) will diminish demand-based efforts to improve legislative representation and, at the same time, let parties and media organizations off the hook with respect to women's participation and the journalistic portrayal of female elites, respectively? What will happen to the supply of women who are willing to contest public office if, as Carbert and Goodyear-Grant suggest, many refuse to subject themselves to the prevailing invasive treatment of private lives? And finally, can research on participation ignore the reality that, for many decades, citizen engagement in the life of the state as well as civil society has been harshly demeaned? Is it possible to renew scholarly and activist interest in public involvement during a period in which markets so severely overshadow states?

The evident importance of grappling with these questions will hopefully act as a magnet, drawing new eyes and new ideas to academic research and public action.

**References**

Anderson, Doris. 1991. *The Unfinished Revolution: The Status of Women in Twelve Countries.* Toronto: Doubleday.

Bashevkin, Sylvia B. 1985. *Toeing the Lines: Women and Party Politics in English Canada.* Toronto: University of Toronto Press.

–. 1998. *Women on the Defensive: Living through Conservative Times.* Toronto: University of Toronto Press.

Brodie, Janine. 1985. *Women and Politics in Canada.* Toronto: McGraw-Hill Ryerson.

Collier, Cheryl N. 2008. "Neoliberalism and Violence against Women: Can Retrenchment Convergence Explain the Path of Provincial Anti-Violence Policy, 1985-2005?" *Canadian Journal of Political Science* 41, 1 (March): 19-42.

Vickers, Jill McCalla. 1978. "Where Are the Women in Canadian Politics?" *Atlantis* 3, 2: 40-51.

Young, Lisa. 2000. *Feminists and Party Politics.* Vancouver: UBC Press.

# Acknowledgments

This volume has its roots in a one-day conference program at University College, University of Toronto, in May 2006, with the aim of sharing contemporary research in the area of women's political participation. The event would not have taken place without the financial support of the University of Toronto, which made it possible to enlist Sarah Lamble, then a master's student in the Centre of Criminology at UofT, as conference organizer.

Our editor at UBC Press, Emily Andrew, attended the sessions in May 2006 and has offered invaluable advice and assistance ever since. I am particularly grateful to Emily for guiding this study through the scholarly assessment process, and I thank all of the UBC Press reviewers who made the volume measurably better than it would otherwise have been.

The actual preparation of the manuscript moved forward thanks to the research assistance of Lisa Lidor and Alana Catapan and the administrative support of Hilary Browning and Carla Vitoria, for which all the contributors are grateful.

The entire project would have been unthinkable without the enthusiastic cooperation of each chapter author. My warmest appreciation to each and every colleague who contributed to this project, helping to open doors for each other in this field and contributing towards a rethinking of how we can study and improve participation more generally in Canadian politics.

# Contributors

**Caroline Andrew** is a professor in the Faculty of Social Sciences at the University of Ottawa.

**Susan Banducci** is associate professor in the Department of Politics at the University of Exeter.

**Sylvia Bashevkin** is principal of University College and a professor in the Department of Political Science at the University of Toronto.

**Lesley Byrne** is a PhD graduate of the Department of Political Science at the City University of New York.

**Michael Camp** is a lecturer in the Department of Journalism at St. Thomas University.

**Louise Carbert** is an associate professor in the Department of Political Science at Dalhousie University.

**Joanna Everitt** is a professor in the Department of History and Politics at the University of New Brunswick, Saint John.

**Elisabeth Gidengil** is Hiram Mills Professor in the Department of Political Science and director of the Centre for the Study of Democratic Citizenship at McGill University.

**Elizabeth Goodyear-Grant** is an assistant professor in the Department of Political Studies at Queen's University.

**Stephanie Mullen** is a statistical consultant at the Carleton University Data Centre.

**Mary-Jo Nadeau** is a lecturer in the Department of Sociology at Trent University and at Wilfrid Laurier University.

**Manon Tremblay** is a professor of political science at the University of Ottawa.

# Index

*Note:* a = appendix; f = figure; t = table